Resonances of Chindon-ya

Marié Abe

RESONANCES
OF CHINDON-YA

Sounding Space and Sociality

in Contemporary Japan

Wesleyan University Press   Middletown, Connecticut

Wesleyan University Press

Middletown CT 06459

www.wesleyan.edu/wespress

2018 © Marié Abe

All rights reserved

Manufactured in the United States of America

Designed by Mindy Basinger Hill

Typeset in Minion Pro

Library of Congress Cataloging-in-Publication Data

available upon request

Hardcover ISBN: 978-0-8195-7778-8

Paperback ISBN: 978-0-8195-7779-5

Ebook ISBN: 978-0-8195-7780-1

We gratefully acknowledge the support of the
AMS 75 PAYS Endowment of the American Musicological Society,
funded in part by the National Endowment for the Humanities
and the Andrew W. Mellon Foundation

5   4   3   2   1

CONTENTS

ACKNOWLEDGMENTS

For me, both thinking and writing are profoundly social acts. This book would not have been possible without a constellation of mentors, colleagues, friends, and family who have inspired me, challenged me, supported me, and nourished me along the way.

My deepest gratitude goes to the members of Chindon Tsūshinsha in Osaka, and Hayashi Kōjirō in particular, for welcoming me like part of the family and sharing with me their everyday lives—from street routine gigs to traveling on tours and post-gig revelries. I thank Inomata Hajime for his organizational assistance; Kawaguchi Masaaki, Seto Nobuyuki, Kobayashi Shinnosuke, Kariyasaki Ikuko (Pinkie), and Trane DeVore for opening their homes; and members of my Osaka-based band Chichūike for creative inspiration and support. Friendships and musical connections I have developed in Osaka will always connect me to the city as my second Japanese hometown.

In Tokyo, I am indebted to the generosity of Ōkuma Wataru and Kogure Miwazō, who have become close friends and musical colleagues. They have taken me in since the first day I awkwardly approached them, opening opportunities to play music with them around the world—from Hokkaido to Okinawa, from London to Montreal to New York. Ōkuma's deeply intellectual engagement with the world through his craft of improvisation and music continues to astound me.

Numerous other chindon-ya practitioners generously shared with me their time and knowledge for my research: Takada Yōsuke, Yoshino Shigeru, Hananoya Kei, Hotta Yūko, and Ishida Midori. Although I was not able to feature them prominently in this book, their words and insights are present in my analysis. Chindon-inspired musicians Daiku Tetsuhiro, Cho Paggie, Itami Hideko, and Nakagawa Takashi of Soul Flower Mononoke Summit, and Off-note label owner Kamiya Kazuyoshi have all generously accepted me and allowed me to join them and take part in their concerts, radio shows, festivals, meetings, tours, and more. I am very lucky and grateful for their trust, time, and insights. Last but not least, I must acknowledge and honor the legendary veteran chindon-ya practitioners whom I was able to interview or witness performing before they passed away: Kikunoya Shimemaru, Midoriya Susumu, Kozuruya Kōtarō, and Takinoya Hifumi.

My ideas in this book have taken shape through countless conversations, presentations, and workshops where I received productive critique and feedback. I am deeply indebted to my mentors at the University of California, Berkeley, who helped me conceive of the doctoral dissertation from which this book emerged. This book would not have been possible without the patient, rigorous, and compassionate mentorship from a dream team of scholars that I had the fortune of working with: Jocelyne Guilbault, Bonnie Wade, Alan Tansman, and Gillian Hart. Jocelyne's finesse for creatively theorizing music and politics, Bonnie's commitment to historical analysis and attentive reading, Alan's insights into cultural politics of postwar Japan, and Gill's firm commitment to Gramscian reading of Lefebvre's work have left a deep imprint on my thinking. I was also fortunate to develop my materials with Steven Feld's guidance during his Ernest Bloch Visiting Fellowship at UC Berkeley. His scholarship and creative projects continue to inspire me to think more deeply about the trajectory of my work.

I have also been fortunate to have the opportunity to share my work at colloquia in the Departments of Music at Duke University, Columbia University, Harvard University, the University of Pittsburgh, Wesleyan University, Cornell University, Swarthmore College, at the University of Pennsylvania, the University of Toronto, Brown University, Northeastern University, Tufts University, the University of Minnesota, the University of Hawai'i Manoa, and Bard College. Over the course of nine years, I presented segments of this book on many a conference panel, organized at the annual meetings for the Society of Ethnomusicology, the American Anthropological Association, the Association of Asian Studies, the American Comparative Literature Association, and the International Association for Studies of Popular Music. At these university visits and conferences, I received valuable feedback that helped me sharpen my ideas from David Novak, Gavin Steingo, Roger Grant, Ron Kuivila, Matt Sakakeeny, Lila Ellen Gray, Josh Pilzer, Benjamin Tausig, Sumanth Gopinath,

Matt Rahaim, Ian Condry, Anne Allison, Louis Meintjes, Chris Nelson, George Lipsitz, Carolyn Stevens, Nathaniel Smith, Ryan Skinner, Jairo Moreno, Tim Rommen, Carol Muller, Lorraine Plourde, Nate Shockey, Jennifer Milioto Matsue, Hiromu Nagahara, Ric Trimillios, and Tomie Hahn.

I was honored to workshop portions of this book at various symposia: "What Does Democracy Sound Like? Actors, Institutions—Practices, Discourses," at L'École des hautes études en sciences sociales in Paris; "Rethinking Protest Music: The Sounds of Dissent," at Princeton University; "The Sonic Contestations of Nuclear Power Symposium," also at Princeton; "Modes of Multiculturalism in Modern Japan: Marginality and Coexistence," at the East Asian Language and Cultural Studies Japan Foundation Summer Institute at the University of California–Santa Barbara; the "Music, Culture, and Transformation" conference at the Department of Media Studies at MIT; "Placing East Asia: A Graduate Conference on Urbanism and the Production of Space," at the Institute of East Asian Studies, University of California–Berkeley; "Music of Sound," at the University of Chicago; the "Hearing Landscape Critically Symposium," at Oxford University and at Harvard University; and "Sound in Theory, Sound in Practice Conference," at Bard College. I thank wholeheartedly the organizers and fellow presenters at these symposia, whose comments were formative in developing my ideas: Noriko Manabe, Eric Drott, Jessica Schwartz, ann-elise lewallen, Joseph Hankins, Jennifer Robertson, Zeynep Bulup, Daniel Grimley, George Reville, Michael Bourdaghs, Paola Iovene, Katherine Lee, Meredith Schweig, Ian Condry, Lena van der Hoven, Christina Kaps, Maria Sonevytsky, Olga Touloumi, Alex Benson, and Laura Kunreuther.

I thank my colleagues and mentors at Boston University, whose support has made it possible to complete this book: Victor Coelho, Brita Heimarck, Benjamin Juarez, Keith Vincent, Corky White, and Rob Weller. I am particularly fortunate to have an amazing cohort: Michael Birenbaum Quintero has read earlier drafts of many chapters in this book and offered enormously helpful comments and solidarity, and Miki Kaneda nourished both my ideas and health through her intellectual rigor and culinary talent. I also thank the Seeing / Not Seeing seminar fellows at Boston University who offered productive critique on my introductory chapter: Jeff Rubin, Joanna Davidson, Kimberly Arkin, Julie Klinger, Benjamin Siegel, Dana Clancy, Ana Maria Reyes, and Rodrigo Lopes De Barros. Lastly, I thank graduate students in the "Music and the Imagination" seminar for stimulating conversations that informed my inquiry.

Writing can be a challenging process, especially for a nonnative English writer like myself. Mutual support from, and solidarity with, so many fellow writers was indispensable to get through tough moments—whether in the form of writing retreats in cabins or virtual cheerleading squads online. Thank you, Maria Sonevytsky, Shalini Ayyagari, Clara Latham, K-Sue Park, Lily Wong, Annie Claus, Ruth Goldstein, and Kelley Tatro. I'm also grateful for the camaraderie from Matt Rahaim, Nathaniel Smith, and Benjamin Harbert. The writing group Cambridge Cabral was such a treat—thank you, Christine Yano, Julia Thomas, and Hiromu Nagahara for feedback and encouragement on the draft of chapter 5. For critical engagement both in text and conversation, I thank Shūhei Hosokawa, Kim Icreverzi, Paul Roquet, and Anne McKnight.

Stimulating discussions and dialogues at all of these occasions have contributed to the ideas I present in this book. Of course, all errors and mistakes are mine.

Several people deserve special mention for the especially formative roles they played in helping me bring this book to fruition. At Wesleyan University Press, Marla Zubel has been an absolute joy and privilege to work with. Marla's unwavering encouragement and thoughtful feedback made this book possible. I'm grateful to the editor-in-chief Suzanna Tamminen and the series editors Deborah Wong, Jeremy Wallach, and Sherrie Tucker for believing in my work and advocating for my project. Also thanks go to marketing manager Jackie Wilson. I'm very fortunate to have received feedback from David Novak and an anonymous reader, whose critical and generous suggestions and comments have deeply shaped the revision process. Without Sindhu Revuluri's mentorship, I would not be here today; she helped me not only achieve goals, small and large, but also to maintain my integrity, political engagement, and ethical commitment to the world within and beyond academia. Words fail me as I seek to describe and thank the unparalleled generosity of Josh Pilzer, who patiently read all my drafts. His incisive comments and unending encouragement provided a midwifery support for the delivery of this manuscript.

The bulk of my fieldwork was made possible by the Pacific Rim Council Dissertation Fellowship. Hosokawa Shūhei's sponsorship was essential in making this possible. My research was also funded by the Department of Music and Institute of East Asian Studies at UC Berkeley and the School of Music at Boston University. A Boston University Center for the Humanities' Digital Humanities Seminar Fellowship helped me develop this book's companion website. Through the Postdoctoral Fellowship at Harvard University's Reischauer Institute of Japanese Studies, I was able to develop the materials in chapters 3 and 5. At Harvard, I thank Ted Bestor, Ted Gilman, Tomiko Yoda, Kay Shelemay, Robert Goree, Emer O'Dwyer, Yukiko Koga, Katherine Lee, and Corinna Campbell. The Faculty Fellowship at the Newhouse Center for the Humanities at Wellesley College gave me a valuable opportunity to start transforming the dissertation into the book. I benefited from the supportive and brilliant company of Carol Dougherty, Kate Grandjean, Duncan White, Alex Orquiza, Yasmine Ramadan, Carla Kaplan, Eugene Marshall, Kristin Williams, and Beth DeSombre. It was an extraordinary opportunity to be able to host and discuss my work with Pauline Oliveros during my fellowship at Wellesley; may we all continue to listen deeply to the resonance she has left behind for us.

An earlier version of chapter 3 appeared in *Sound, Space, and Sociality in Modern Japan* (Routledge, 2014). An earlier version of chapter 5 appeared in *Ethnomusicology* 60 (2) (2016). I thank Routledge and the Society of Ethnomusicology for granting permission to include the works in this book. All translations are mine, unless otherwise noted. Musical transcriptions in figures P.1 and E.1 are mine. Musical transcription in the appendix is by Kawamura Mitsuji, who has generously given me permission to include it in this book. Cathy Hannabach offered editorial feedback on chapters 2 and 4. At the University Press of New England, I was lucky to work with talented and compassionate production team of Amanda Dupuis and Glenn Novak. Madeleine Fix was fabulous to work with, building the book's companion website. Brian Barone's efficient editorial work, with razor-sharp eyes and masterly typesetting wizardry were absolutely essential in wrapping up the project. I am grateful to Cora Higgins, Madge Walls, Emily Howe, and Jeff Dyer for their help with the last push toward the finish line. Talented Inunko and Chanky have designed the book cover art; I'm so thankful for their friendship.

I am fortunate to have chosen families in the United States who have supported me throughout the years. I'm grateful to the Pasternaks and the Lemeins at Martins Beach, California, who provided serene spaces to have writing retreats at crucial moments. My large chosen Bay Area family—Katie, Dina, Julie, Rebecca, Eliana, Mina, May-li, Federico, the Elephants, and others—has always been there for me, especially during difficult times. The extended family of Debo Band has become my community in Boston; their support and care made it possible for me to keep writing while never giving up musical creativity in my life (special shout-out to Kaethe, Cora, Jonah, Shaw Pong, PJ, Woody, and Danny).

Mountains and skies full of heartfelt gratitude go to Kevin Haas, who closely witnessed the almost six-year span of labor and supported me throughout those years by my side. His love and care nourished me and carried me through each day, together or apart.

Lastly, my sustenance throughout this process has been my parents, Abe Yoshiaki and Michiyo, and my grandmother Mieko. Thank you for your ocean-deep and unconditional trust, love, and support in everything I do, always. *Hontō ni arigatō.*

NOTE ON THE COMPANION WEBSITE

Supplementary audio, visual, and audiovisual materials are available on the accompanying website, http://www.ResonancesOfChindon-ya.com. Relevant materials are organized by chapters to enhance the text. I strongly encourage the readers to consult with the website as you read this book.

NOTE ON LANGUAGE

I use the term *chindon-ya* both in singular to refer to the practice and in plural to refer to a troupe and performers.

All Japanese individuals mentioned in the book are presented following the Japanese convention: family name first, personal name second.

The diacritic ¯ is used to prolong the vowel (ō is pronounced *oh*; ī is pronounced *ee*, and so on).

Japanese terms commonly used in English (such as "kabuki") are not italicized, and well-known place-names (such as Tokyo, Osaka, and Kobe) are written without diacritical markings, unless they appear in a Japanese phrase or as part of a proper name. All other Japanese terms are written with appropriate diacritical markings. In general, Japanese words in the body of the text are italicized only on first use.

Unless otherwise noted, all translations are mine.

Japanese history is conventionally divided into periods based on dynastic names and individual imperial reigns. Where possible, I provide specific dates in Western terms, but the following era names are also used:

> Edo period, 1603–1868
> Meiji period, 1868–1912
> Taishō period, 1912–1925
> Shōwa period, 1926–1989
> Heisei period, 1989 to the present

竹雀 Takesu

FIGURE P.1 *Takesu*. Traditional tune typically played at the beginning of a chindon-ya gig. Transcription by the author.

PROLOGUE

Beginnings

ONE.

On a quiet street in a residential neighborhood of Osaka in 2015, a group of four outlandishly costumed musicians are walking about. The clarinet player, dressed in an orange-brown kimono with bright sash and wearing a stylized period wig and makeup, plays a popular tune from the 1970s, while two others—also wearing vividly colorful kimonos and traditional wigs—rhythmically complement the melody on an assortment of traditional Japanese percussion instruments mounted on wooden frames. The fourth performer zigzags down the street with a deliberate, humorous gait, approaching passersby with a smile and handing out flyers that publicize a big discount at a mom-and-pop butcher shop in the neighborhood. They are *chindon-ya*, a distinctly Japanese roaming advertisement band.

Chindon-ya is often considered at once a musical practice, a commercial activity, and a mere background sound in everyday life. You can hear them from a distance. A third-floor balcony window opens, and a girl with pigtails sticks her head out, trying to determine where the sound is coming from. An old man with disheveled hair emerges out of his house to see chindon-ya, with a slight smile on his face, seeming not to care about the fact that he stepped out in his underwear. Middle-aged women in their aprons and sandals on the street strike up a conversation with one another, speculating on what the musicians might be publicizing that day. Nearby, an older woman on the sidewalk looks on with a bemused, nostalgic gaze, while a few businessmen hastily walk past. Wherever they go, wherever their sounds resound, chindon-ya seem to leave animated sociality behind. My parents' generation remembers chindon-ya as part of the quotidian soundscape of the decade following World War II. Chindon-ya's ostentatious and extraordinary presence was an ordinary part of their everyday life. People of this generation told me stories almost like fairy tales—reminiscent of the Pied Piper of Hamelin—of children who were so enticed that they got lost after following chindon-ya for miles. Something about them was different; somewhat magical, somewhat otherworldly, somewhat "out of place" despite their ubiquitous presence.

Not so with my generation. Growing up in Tokyo as a child in the 1980s, I can't remember chindon-ya being a familiar sound and sight. I do remember, though, that my classmates and I taunted each other in school with a common sung phrase, "*baka, aho, chindon-ya*"—"stupid, fool, chindon-ya." I never even wondered why the name of this sonic commercial practice was considered derogatory. I simply understood that it marked a kind of difference—but what kind?

TWO.

One swelteringly hot summer day in 2004, as I sat in my favorite jazz café in the Shimokitazawa neighborhood of Tokyo, my ears perked up. The owner of the café—grumpy on the surface, but extremely attentive and quietly kind, in classic bartender-like fashion—had played a few albums in a row that couldn't have been more different from one another. Dixieland Jazz, Okinawan folk, Balkan-infused prog rock. But there was a sonic common thread: the sound of chindon-ya percussion. Intrigued, I started to follow the thread, beginning a journey that would last the next decade.

Tracing the sound of chindon-ya took me to an unexpectedly wide range of places and times. In a small nightclub in Tokyo, the band Cicala Mvta blasted out cacophonous and energetic sounds. The clarinet screamed a klezmer-like melody; tuba, drums, and accordion played an intricate, limping odd-meter rhythm reminiscent of music from the Balkans; and an assortment of traditional Japanese percussion invoked the sound of chindon-ya.

In a recording studio on the main island of Okinawa, far south from mainland Japan, traditional folksinger Daiku Tetsuhiro sang an old protest song against US occupation of the island. The song was arranged and backed by a group of musicians from Tokyo—including two women providing rhythmic ornamentation on chindon percussion.

After the 1995 Great Hanshin Earthquake and the 2011 Great East Japan

Earthquake, chindon-ya's sounds echoed across the rubble and makeshift housing projects. With acoustic instruments of various kinds in hand, groups of volunteer musicians walked through the disaster-affected areas, evoking the memories and sounds of chindon-ya to reach out to the survivors of the disasters who were otherwise shut-in in their temporary housing projects.

In front of the prime minister's residence in central Tokyo, chindon percussion's bright metallic gong chime pierced through the roaring drums of the protesters who took to the street each week to contest the restarting of nuclear power plants throughout the country in the aftermath of the 2011 earthquake and the subsequent crisis at the Fukushima nuclear power plant.

Reaching beyond its original advertisement context, chindon-ya's sound seems to resonate with many listeners and contexts. The social power of chindon-ya's sound creates rippling effects, making diffractive patterns in unexpected ways. What is it about this particular practice of chindon-ya, as it appears in such a variety of contexts, that inspires a wide range of musical renderings at these disparate events? What cultural work do these musicians perform by drawing on chindon-ya?

THREE.

Even if you're not Malinowski stranded in the Trobriand Islands, doing fieldwork is often lonely. Being "back home" in a place where I grew up made it all the more alienating somehow. Upon arriving in Osaka to do fieldwork, I spent several nights at an internet café, sleeping in a private cubicle, much in the same manner as the "internet café refugees"—the irregularly employed who live in the café instead of renting apartments.[1] The sense of isolation was so palpable, as if to attest to the fact that loneliness has been diagnosed as the social malady of our time in postindustrial global cities. The *Guardian* writer George Monbiot (2014) has proclaimed ours the Age of Loneliness, marked by the "the ethics of disconnection," in which the principles of individualism and competition that define the neoliberal economic model have undermined the social and moral fabric of our societies (Gershon and Alexy 2011).

Even if you have never been to the infamous "scramble crossroad" in Shibuya, Tokyo, where an average of three thousand people cross the street at each green light (half a million pedestrians per day), you may have experienced the paradoxical feeling of loneliness in a big crowd. The sense of social alienation in a densely populated urban public space is a fairly common experience in global metropolises; among the mass of human bodies, one becomes acutely aware of our solitary being.[2] This crossroad has become an icon of Japan's heightened consumerism propelled by the circulation of global capital and technocultural industry. It is heavily saturated with digitally mediated sounds and sights: gigantic LED screens advertising the release of new movies, TV dramas, and pop music albums alongside temp company ads and property rental companies offering their services; flashing and flickering neon signs publicizing franchised restaurants and bars; and seemingly infinite numbers of speakers blasting commercials onto the streets. These loud and glittery indices of neoliberal capitalism heighten the numbing sense of urban isolation. Enveloped within this sensory excess, most urban walkers remain atomized. It's a miracle that no one bumps into another. Pedestrians perform a kind of socialized urban choreography, carefully navigating the crowded crossroad with hurried and steady footwork, zigzagging through the spaces between others and avoiding physical contact. It seems apt that this crossroad provided a backdrop for the flat affect and isolation of the characters in the film *Lost in Translation*.

One day I walked across this crosswalk. In a particularly vulnerable moment in my life, the pervasive sensory markers of consumerism felt overwhelming, putting into starker relief the sense of isolation I was already experiencing. Suddenly, in the middle of the ocean of people making their way across the streets, I remembered the words of Hayashi Kōjirō, a chindon-ya practitioner I had interviewed in Osaka: "I am playing [music] to people indoors. . . . It's rare to find happy healthy people. . . . You have to play so that the depressed want to come out." At the time of the interview, I thought his comments rather pessimistic; I wondered whether he was projecting his own personal hardships onto the invisible listening public of urban Osaka. But at that moment, halfway through the crosswalk, I suddenly heard the world the same way as Hayashi did. I probably wasn't alone in this crowd feeling the weight of solitude. I understood how chindon-ya practitioners "heard" social relations and disconnections. This shift in perception pulled me out of my own isolation—I suddenly recognized this alienation as a collective social condition. I remember this moment as one of the most profound from my fieldwork. It was when I first realized that chindon-ya's sonic labor is deeply rooted in a particular philosophy of sociality—which I take to mean a dynamic process in which people are inevitably engaged with one another and with their surroundings.[3]

———

Chindon-ya, groups of ostentatiously costumed street musicians who are hired to publicize an employer's business, date back to the mid-1800s. During their heyday in the 1950s, the ubiquitous chindon-ya became closely associated with the everyday soundscape, the notion of *taishū* (the popular masses), and the dynamic sociality that characterized small neighborhood streets. In the 1960s, however, chindon-ya entered a sharp decline. They became the butt of many jokes, evoking nostalgia for some, intrigue or nuisance for others. At best they were treated with indifference. But now, after decades of relative inactivity, chindon-ya is undergoing a resurgence that began in the early 1990s. Despite being labeled as anachronistic and obscure, some chindon-ya troupes today have achieved considerable financial success, while the chindon-ya aesthetic has been taken up by rock, jazz, and experimental musicians, and refashioned into hybridized musical practices. Through the shopping arcades and back-streets of Osaka, in a dance circle at a summer festival in a predominantly Korean neighborhood of Kyoto, on a "Music of Japan" compilation CD distributed internationally, and at the anti-nuclear-power protests in post-3.11 Tokyo—today, chindon-ya's musical sounds echo at the intersections of widely varying locations, historical relations, musical styles, business enterprises, and political aspirations.

This book has emerged from what I have heard in the sounds of chindon-ya at these intersections. As I walked along and performed with practitioners of chindon-ya and its various offshoot musical practices, I heard not only the acoustic resonance of chindon-ya's sounds bouncing around in urban neighborhoods, but also the different types of cultural work performed by these sounds: recalling past memories; inciting various emotional responses; inspiring people to create connections with unexpected events, places, and sounds; and protesting against structural violence of the state. Over nine years of fieldwork, I have become fascinated by the social, historical, political, and affective resonances that chindon-ya produce in the contemporary Japanese urban landscape. Chindon-ya practitioners cultivate particular aural sensibilities as well as performance and social strategies to attend to the affective dynamics of urban sociality. These sensibilities and strategies are their means of making a living; the affective and acoustic production of sociality is the very labor of chindon-ya. As a form of labor whose commercial enterprise is inextricably linked with the production of affect, chindon-ya presents a compelling case through which to examine the relationship between sound, public space, and a sense of public intimacy forged through social relations. By focusing on the affordances of the sound that their labor is intended to produce, I zero in on the understandings of public space as well as the kinds of social connections and disconnections that emerge within the urban spaces in which chindon-ya's sounds echo.

The primary argument of this book is that, contrary to a teleological narrative in which capitalist modernity abstracts lived urban spaces through urban development, privatization, regulation, and gentrification, chindon-ya's sounds proffer a historical continuity in the understanding of streets as always heterogeneous and dynamic space produced through social relations, practices, and imaginaries. Through chindon-ya's attunement to the forces that create the particular site of performance and their flexible improvisatory practices, their sounds make explicit the otherwise intangible sentiments, forces, and relations that are in fact palpable in what constitutes the everyday urban space of streets.

More broadly speaking, at the center of this study of chindon-ya is a simple claim that dynamic interrelations of sound, history, and sociality produce space. The implications of this claim, as it plays out through the affective and acoustic resonances of chindon-ya in urban public spaces across Japan, holds a key to understanding the renewed relevance of chindon-ya—normally considered anachronistic and apolitical—aesthetically, economically, and politically. Sound and space, as Andrew Eisenberg has succinctly put it, are "ontologically and phenomenologically intertwined" (2015, 193). Thinking through this mutually constitutive relation in my work as an ethnomusicologist, I offer a brief reflection on the keywords of space and sound—which have come under scrutiny in the fields of cultural geography and sound studies, respectively.

As the spatial terms—like "terrain," "mapping," and "problem space"—proliferated as free-floating metaphors in cultural theory, cultural geographers Neil Smith and Cindi Katz (1993) have critiqued the underlying assumptions of such spatial metaphors—space as a passive field or container, a Euclidian and Cartesian coordinate system of discrete and mutually exclusive locations (i.e., absolute space). Showing that the emergence of capitalist social relations in Europe established absolute space as the premise of hegemonic social practices since the sixteenth century, they caution us that uncritical appropriation of absolute space as a source domain for metaphors in our discourse naturalizes its constructed absolutism, disguises its complicity in capitalist patriarchy and racist imperialism, and forecloses recognition of multiple qualities, types, properties, and attributes of social space and its relationality.

Likewise, the notion of sound has been problematized in sound studies in recent years. Ethnomusicologists David Novak and Matt Sakakeeny point out that "the generalizability of sound, in its most imprecise uses, can sidestep the effects of institutional histories and the structuring influences of entrenched debates" (2015, 6). Gus Stadler (2015) has also recently taken to task the tendencies within sound studies to assume the universal ear—which, in Anglo-American and European scholarship, is also the white ear. As these critics point out, there is a highly limited focus on Western contexts, and the field of sound studies is desperately in need of global perspective (Novak 2013b and Steingo and Sykes, forthcoming, notwithstanding).

It is in this spirit of taking sound and ethnography seriously in conceptualizing the social production of space that I wrote this book. The analytical and methodological commitment to thinking with and through sound, I believe, is a significant contribution that ethnomusicology can offer to the studies of the politics of public space and spatialized difference.[4] By exploring the acoustic philosophies of the quirky sonic practice of chindon-ya, this book addresses the need in sound studies for more ethnographically grounded work that attends to the cultural and historical specificities of local forms of audition. Calling attention to the interrelation of sound and space, ethnomusicologist Martin Daughtry asserts that "sound coerces bodies into involuntary vibration and co-opts them into participation, through resonance, in the event that is sound itself" (2015, 165). Acoustically conceived, resonance here refers to the capacity of sound to implicate all vibrating bodies and objects within its proximity. While vibration-centered approaches have opened up exciting possibilities for theorizing music and space through embodied socialities (Henriques 2011), what may be left unaccounted for are the indeterminate ways in which sound works on unevenly structured social difference, and how sound articulates the politics of imagination with the politics of the body (Eidsheim 2015 notwithstanding). Highlighting the need to account for both the acoustic and the social, I put forward the trope of *hibiki* (resonance) to attend to the local ontologies of spatiality and local forms of audition, thereby challenging the widely received, so-called Western conceptions of listening and sound that have naturalized the way we think about sound, space, and listening subjects.

This book also contributes to the small but growing body of ethnomusicological monographs on street music and sound in public space (Peterson 2010, Sakakeeny 2013) by advocating for the theoretical productivity of folding sound into the dynamic conceptions of space offered by Lefebvrean thinkers in human geography. One does not need to look too hard to see the significance of music/

FIGURE P.2 Chindon Tsūshinsha on *machimawari*
(street routine). Photo by the author.

sound for Lefebvre in his seminal work *The Production of Space* ([1974] 1991). Although rarely noted, references to sounds and music are peppered through-out his writing.[5] Lefebvre reminds us of the importance of "adopt[ing] a '*listening*' posture" (19);[6] he views music as an embodied practice that effectively opens up the possibility of advancing a unitary theory of space that brings to-gether subjective space, material body, and social life. I am interested in picking up where Lefebvre left off, and in exploring how his understanding of space might intersect with Steven Feld's notion of acoustemology, which attends to "local conditions of acoustic sensation, knowledge, and imagination embodied in the culturally particular sense of place" (1996, 91).[7] In this entanglement of sound, space, and time that I call resonance, I hear rich possibilities for consid-ering sound as integral to the understanding of space as dynamically produced through social relations beyond physical confines.

Ethnographically attending to the historical and cultural particularities of chindon-ya through the analytical lens of resonance has led me to hear the various kinds of work performed by this seemingly innocuous, anachronistic, and apolitical practice. The resonances of chindon-ya challenge the prevalent narrative of Japan as a homogeneous nation by revealing and mobilizing various histories of social marginalization; they complicate the so-called Western narrative of capital by suggesting the simultaneity of different histories of capital in the present moment; they unsettle the liberal conception of the subject by foregrounding a relational understanding of sociality; and they denaturalize the absolutist assumptions of public space that foreclosed political possibilities in the previous modes of street protests in Japan. Much as chindon-ya entice listeners by their sound, so, too, I hope this book will compel readers to think through the many critical resonances of sound-space that encourage us to attune to the multiple histories, the political potentialities, and the relationality of the social worlds in which we live.

INTRODUCTION

Resonances of Chindon-ya

It was only four months after northeastern Japan was hit by the triple disasters of a magnitude 9 earthquake, tsunami, and nuclear crisis at the Fukushima nuclear power plant. I took the bullet train from Osaka with members of Chindon Tsūshinsha, an Osaka-based chindon-ya troupe—practitioners of a uniquely Japanese form of street musical advertisement. Normally they parade through neighborhoods playing musical tunes on their instruments to publicize the local businesses that have hired them to do so. Chindon-ya's employers vary daily and can be anything from a local supermarket to a *pachinko* slot-machine parlor. They may be hired to publicize sales or a special discount on a particular product, such as cell phone plans or even happy hour at a chain bar. The troupe members are paid a flat fee in advance; there is no financial transaction between them and the potential customers on the street. Outlandishly costumed in both colorful traditional kimono and contemporary clownish attire, chindon-ya performers strut through the streets, not to sell products themselves, but to draw customers to an establishment by playing an assortment of instruments. But on this day, they were hired by a wealthy kimono shop owner to visit the disaster-affected towns of Kuji and Yamada-chō in northeast Japan, and to provide entertainment and cheer to the displaced survivors of the disasters living in temporary housing projects.

As soon we arrived at the Hananomaki train station, we were picked up in a van by the host. In the middle of the hours-long drive along the coast toward our first destination, Yamada-chō, we stopped by a small soba noodle restaurant for lunch. Just as we were finishing the meal, we experienced a rather large aftershock—magnitude 4. The ground swayed slowly left to right, the lamps swung, books fell off the shelves, and customers held on to the tables, chairs, and each other. Aftershocks were still a frequent occurrence then, reminding us of the immensity of the devastation and the precarious condition of the present.

Scars left by the tsunami were palpable and visible on the coastal towns as we continued our drive north. Architectural structures were laid bare, houses were abandoned, vehicles were stranded far afield on land, ships washed up on the hill. The sheer destruction left me speechless as I looked out the window of the van; knowing the losses suffered by the displaced and their ongoing struggles, I felt the limits of my empathy. I didn't seem to be the only one in the van shocked and humbled by the sight; gaze fixed on the devastation outside the windows, everyone in the van shared in silence as we imagined the losses, trauma, and frustration of the disaster survivors, while also grappling with the uncertain conditions of the nuclear power plant nearby.

The chindon-ya troupe's performance was received warmly and enthusiastically by the locals—those who survived and became displaced in the nearby towns, from children to the elderly. It wasn't simply a staged entertainment. The troupe walked through the audience, zigzagging between benches and folding chairs, talking, joking, and playing popular tunes from different eras. Inside the makeshift tent on top of a hill near the temporary housing structures, for a short while, a vibrant sociality emerged, as if the audience were encountering chindon-ya in their usual environment—on neighborhood streets, in the shopping arcade. In the post-disaster moment marked by the violent rupture of everyday temporality and spatiality, the extraordinary appearance of the ostentatiously costumed chindon-ya brought a sense of ordinariness.

After the show, I walked up to the chindon-ya members and mentioned how difficult it must have been for the troupe to perform for people who have suffered such unspeakable losses, who are living with uncertainty, with no clear end in sight. I was struck by the answer a member gave me: "This is not so different form our usual routines. This is what we do anyway. This is what we itinerant performers have always done throughout history." The business-minded answer to what I perceived as a profound act of producing social warmth and empathy confused me. It challenged my naïve assumptions around the incommensurability of empathy and money. It was not immediately clear to me how this performance, which took place in the still-precarious moment far from everyday routines in Osaka's neighborhood streets, could have been "not so different." What is it that chindon-ya do that remained constant, when the ordinary sense of everyday temporality and space was so violently altered in the disaster-affected district of Yamada-chō? I became further puzzled as I contemplated how to understand the involvement of some chindon-ya practitioners in the antinuclear protests in Tokyo after the triple disasters. If caring for disaster survivors was not so different from their street routines of advertising for clients, then is some of chindon-ya's involvement in the new politicized contexts of antinuclear rallies also business as usual? This moment captured many of the questions, tensions, and contradictions that animated my research. With these inquiries in mind, this book explores the aesthetic, economic, and political resonances of chindon-ya as a historical form of itinerant performance that gained new relevance as a sonorous form of affective labor—labor that turns social relations into value—in the time of neoliberal precarity and nuclear anxiety in contemporary Japan.

CHINDON-YA AS ACOUSTIC PHILOSOPHERS AND STREET ETHNOGRAPHERS

The chindon-ya practitioners I followed in my fieldwork were themselves both philosophers and ethnographers. Their philosophies of sound, streets, and affect were cultivated through their everyday routines of walking, listening, and sounding throughout the city. In so doing, they engage with locals, listen to their stories, supplement their own knowledge with archival materials, and perform their knowledge publicly through sounding, walking, speaking, and writing things down. Many had astute observations about the rhythms of the city and people's routines, affective dynamics, socioeconomic makeup and acoustics of different neighborhoods, and histories and memories sedimented into the urban landscape. At the end of the day's work, I would often go out drinking with members of Chindon Tsūshinsha. Often we would go to *tachinomi-ya* (standing bars), frequented by working-class men. As our tongues loosened after several cups of *sake* and *shōchū*, conversations would often turn to their observations from the day. They would analyze the social and economic conditions that inflect the everyday lives of the working-class residents they encountered, note how sounds echo differently in different parts of the city or at different times of history, how the weather affected the timbre of their instruments, share existential musings on life and urban solitude, and indulge in speculative historical revisioning of the obsolete form of street performance that they practice.

Much of this book's analytical framework is distilled from these acoustic philosophies and ethnographic insights that chindon-ya practitioners shared with me. Three recurring key terms emerged from our conversations: *hibiki* (resonance), the most central trope, by which I refer to the simultaneously acoustic and affective production of sociality that constitutes chindon-ya's sonic labor; *bachigai* (out-of-place); and *nigiyakasa* (noisiness/liveliness). Taken together, these locally grounded terms serve as a conceptual scaffolding and guide my investigation of chindon-ya's musical labor—or, in the practitioners' words, their "sound business."

Throughout the book, I mobilize the trope of resonance in two different ways. "Hibiki," the local term, is used to analyze the specific work of chindon-ya's soundings that produce sociality, both acoustically and affectively. I will also use the English term "resonance" as an organizing and structuring trope that weaves together the contingent effects of hibiki that I trace across chapters, capturing various work that chindon-ya's sound performs—historical, affective, acoustic, and political.

Related local concepts that recur across chapters are bachigai (out-of-place) and nigiyakasa (noisiness/liveliness)—two principles that undergird the logic of chindon-ya's labor intended to produce resonance. Chindon-ya's out-of-the-ordinary presence is often perceived as out of time, or out of place; "bachigai" refers to this sense of difference—social, temporal, and spatial alterity. The notion of bachigai plays a crucial role in understanding how chindon-ya's hibiki entices listeners and their attentiveness to various forms of socially marginalized difference. "Nigiyakasa" evokes the particularly dynamic and spirited sociality, as well as the raucous sounds of interactions, multiplicity, and economic prosperity that characterize festive gatherings. A simultaneously social, sonic, and embodied trope of liveliness, nigiyakasa is a significant aspect—but not all—of the production of hibiki/resonance. These two principles central to chindon-ya's hibiki/resonance hold a key to understanding how the erstwhile commercial sound of chindon-ya has become politicized in the past two decades (chapters 4 and 5).

Through this lens of hibiki/resonance, I offer my analyses on two different levels. First, within the specific context of contemporary Japan, this book probes the dilemma within which chindon-ya's sonic labor is caught. Chindon-ya is indelibly rooted in capitalist modernity, while also symbolically standing in for those marginalized by the development of capitalism. Today, the yearning for sociality is particularly poignant, as neoliberal arrangements of capitalism have created widespread anxieties around "solitude, job insecurity, familial estrangement, [and] precarious existence" (Allison 2013, 3). Anthropologist Anne Allison lists various social phenomena and buzzwords that signal the dissolution of sociality stemming from the precaritization of life and work in Japan: *hikikomori* (the socially withdrawn); *kodokushi* (lonely death, especially among the elderly and the poor); *muen shakai* (relationless society); and *ikizurasa* (the difficulty of living) (Allison 2013). Within this context, chindon-ya offers an opportunity for social encounters that cut against widespread disconnection. Through the nostalgia evoked by their making accessible historical forms of sociality, or through the distinctly anti-individualistic aesthetic principles that undergird their performances, chindon-ya today valorize the anxiety around socioeconomic precarity by asserting the centrality of the social. This is not a recent phenomenon; chindon-ya has always been complicit with, and dependent upon, the commodification of social relations.[1] But in a time characterized by precarity, their labor finds a particular niche as social relations themselves become inherent to economic production.

Chindon-ya not only feeds on but also reimagines the anxiety around social precarity. Even as chindon-ya continues to participate in the logic of affective labor by valorizing social relations, its sounds inspire kinds of sociality that are not neatly ensnared by this feedback loop of the social and capital. These newly forged socialities perform a range of cultural, social, and political work—from evoking otherworldliness and marginalized difference to transposing chindon-ya's labor to political protests and disaster relief efforts, as I described in the prologue. But if we simply think of chindon-ya's work as a remedy to fight alienation and bring together disconnected individuals, we lose sight of how "the concept of disconnection is put to use in social life in ways that serve to re-inscribe inequalities" (Gershon and Alexy 2011, 802). Put another way, the themes of disconnection that run through narratives of social precarity obscure the uneven relationships and social difference that are produced by—and themselves reproduce—the structural dynamics that have led us to this moment of social precarity in the first place.

Thus, I do not consider chindon-ya's sound as either a mere reflection of, or a panacea for, the insidious effects of neoliberalism in Japan. Instead, by historically situating chindon-ya's labor, I examine the unexpected ways in which their resonances have played with, into, and against the pervasive sense of precarity in contemporary Japan. Chindon-ya's resonance is thus not simply about offering social warmth where there is a thirst for it. Rather, it is to be found in the practitioners' acoustic philosophy of sociality understood through difference and relationality. There is never a guaranteed outcome of the work of resonance: the ways in which chindon-ya's sounds produce and reimagine sociality create ripple effects that are different at each conjuncture.

More broadly then, on the second level, *Resonances of Chindon-ya* offers an analytical approach to attuning to sociality diffractively. I track the ripple effects of chindon-ya's resonances in their dynamic process of interaction, interference, reinforcement, and difference as sound, performers, listeners, and surrounding environment affect and transform each other.[2] In indeterminate and unexpected ways, chindon-ya's sounds provide imaginative resources for both listeners and performers to connect or disconnect with one another in ways that clamor for rethinking of the narratives of social precarity, difference, histories, and public space in contemporary Japan. In this light, instead of romanticizing chindon-ya as a nostalgic antidote to contemporary precarity, or reducing chindon-ya to an opportunistic commercial endeavor that capitalizes on social anxieties and longing for social connection, I probe the imaginative work that performers and listeners put into chindon-ya, and the unexpected ways in which these chindon-ya sounds gain traction at different conjunctures.

SOUNDS AND HISTORIES OF CHINDON-YA

At the heart of chindon-ya is an instrument called the *chindon*. It is a handmade portable drum set consisting of three Japanese percussion instruments: *kane* (a small metallic gong chime, about ten centimeters, or four inches, in diameter), *ōdō* (a two-sided drum, forty centimeters, or about sixteen inches, in diameter), and *shime daiko* (a tension drum that can be tuned by the hemp rope tied around its body). The name "chindon" derives from the onomatopoetic words for the gong (*chin*) and the drums (*don*). "Chindon" can simultaneously refer to the business enterprise, the actual instrument of the chindon drums, and the sounds of the drums.[3] "Ya" refers to business. Throughout this book, I use the term "chindon-ya" both in singular to refer to the practice and in plural to refer to a troupe and performers.

Each chindon musician builds a wooden frame to hold the three instruments together, in order to be able to play while walking. The left hand plays the two drums with a wooden stick, and the right hand plays the gong chime with a bamboo stick fitted with a deer-horn mallet (*shumoku*) at its end. A kane can produce two different pitches: one if it is hit on the edge (*suri*) and another

FIGURE I.1 Typical chindon-ya formation. *From left:* chindon drums (*kane* and *ōdō* on his right, *shime daiko* on his left), *gorosu*, clarinet, and flyer (*bira kurabi*). Photo by the author.

if it is struck in the middle (*hara*) (see appendix). Typically, there is a second drummer in a chindon-ya group, who is often a woman.[4] She plays a large bass drum called the *gorosu*, which derives from the French *gros caisse* (big drum). Gorosu is hung horizontally from the shoulders and played with two different sticks; one is a mallet, and the other is a drumstick.

Along with these two percussionists, one musician (or occasionally more), called *gakushi*, plays a melodic instrument. Most commonly found are the saxophone, clarinet, or trumpet. In chindon-ya groups, emphasis is placed on melody and rhythm—there is a marked absence of bass instruments or harmony.[5] The melodic instrument often plays solo. When there is more than one melodic instrument, they usually play in unison, without harmonizing the primary melodic line. The typical instrumentation has shifted over time. *Shamisen*, the Japanese traditional three-stringed lute found in various traditional and folkloric musical practices, was quite common during chindon-ya's early days. As competing sounds within the urban environment increased with industrialization and the growing popularity of cars, shamisen struggled to be audible, and despite short-lived experimentation with amplifying speakers, shamisen gave way to brass and reed instruments (figure 1.1).

Between tunes, the chindon percussion player—often the leader of the group—usually delivers advertising speeches, while other troupe members walk around and hand out flyers. But chindon-ya rarely, if ever, play jingles specific to their employer or their employer's products. Instead, the repertoire covers a wide range of music: military marches, older Japanese popular songs (*enka*), tunes from traditional comic vaudeville (*yose*), theme songs of children's TV programs, and contemporary J-pop tunes. Although it's rare to find tunes that distinctly and exclusively belong to chindon-ya, certain tunes are considered chindon-ya classics, especially in the Tokyo region: "Takesu" (Sparrow on a bamboo), which is performed at the beginning of the day, and "Shichōme" (Fourth street), the closing tune for the day (figure P.1 and figure E.1, respectively). Both tunes originally came from *geza* (offstage) music played by instrumentalists accompanying theatrical forms such as kabuki and yose, but are also considered chindon-ya standards today.

While musical sounds are a significant aspect of chindon-ya's advertisement practice, speech, small theatrical performance, and gestures are also integral to their work. After luring bystanders and neighbors with their musical sounds, chindon-ya performers communicate with them verbally about what they are publicizing through speeches or informal conversations. Their exaggerated and mellifluous style of delivery and vocabulary is informed by popular theatrical speech, such as that of yose and *shibai* (stage play). In the 1950s, chindon-ya musicians would also often perform choreographed sword fights (*chanbara*) reminiscent of the theatricalized fight scenes between samurai warrior characters once popular in films and itinerant drama theater (*taishū engeki*), though this is no longer common today (figure I.2).[6]

Extravagant, vivid, and creative costumes and makeup are essential as well. Sometimes chindon-ya practitioners dress themselves as historical figures or familiar characters from TV shows, when appropriate for a particular client or product. Typically, while the two percussionists wear traditional Japanese attire, the melodic instrumentalists are often dressed in Western-style clothing. The unwritten chindon code calls for the melodic instrumentalist to wear a hat (Ōkuma 1991, 27).[7] Cross-dressing was more popular in the first couple of decades of the twentieth century; today, there is only one performer who regularly cross-dresses in kimono.[8] Bystanders would not think twice about this vibrant

FIGURE I.2 Chindon-ya Mannen Sha in Nagoya, circa 1970.
Theatrical performance (*middle*) and *shamisen* player with a speaker (*second from right*)
were common features of chindon-ya. Photo courtesy of Hayashi Kōjirō.

hodgepodge of colorful theatrical period costumes combined with more casual, Western-style fashion. But close attention to the material culture of chindon-ya offers us an entry point into the layers of historical, geographical, cultural, and social meanings that chindon-ya has come to embody over the course of its history.

For the past century, the activities and popularity of chindon-ya have waxed and waned in the face of social trends, world events, and new technological developments. While it was not until the 1930s that chindon-ya came to take the form it has today, Ingrid Fritsch locates the roots of chindon-ya in the street performers (*daidōgei*)—particularly the street vendors—of the late Edo period (1603–1868) (2001, 51–52).[9] Sound has long been a medium of self-advertisement for street vendors in Japan, since at least the twelfth century. These street hawkers made themselves known to residents by shouting mellifluously delivered phrases identifying the product being sold, sometimes accompanied by woodblocks, bells, gong chimes, and small membrane drums. The voices and instrumental sounds of itinerant street vendors, from medicine merchants to peddlers selling dried persimmons, tobacco, candies, and New

FIGURE 1.3 Tanbaya (Tōzaiya) Kurimaru of Osaka, forefather of chindon-ya.
Courtesy of Osakajō Tenshukaku.

Year's *sake*, not only announced their presences to those at home but also signaled times of day and seasons (Endō 1958, 78).

The more direct origin of chindon-ya is often traced back to Amekatsu, a townsperson and candy vendor in Osaka who is considered the first to have turned the vendor call itself into his so-called product. As variety theaters, under a ban on posters enacted in 1845, struggled to find new ways of publicizing their performances, Amekatsu came up with the idea of capitalizing on his own voice on the streets, announcing the performances on behalf of the theaters. This entrepreneurial move to use voice and instruments as a proxy advertisement agent spread quickly. Various others in Osaka followed suit in subsequent decades, notably Isakame, Mametomo, and Tanbaya Kurimaru, who for his contributions to the advertising industry has been recognized among the fifty visionaries who "created Japan's advertisement business" (Kōkoku 1996, 17) (figure I.3). Tanbaya Kurimaru became famous in Osaka for using a musical band consisting of entirely Japanese traditional instruments, such as *ōdaiko* (big drum), *shime daiko* (small drum), *kane* (gong chime), *shamisen* (three-string lute-type instrument), *yokobue* (bamboo flute), and *tsuzumi* (tension drum).

While Amekatsu was known for his speech accompanied by bells and woodblocks (*hyōshigi*) only, this idea of a sonic proxy advertisement practice inspired others not only in Osaka but also in Tokyo. In 1886, Tokyo musician Akita Ryūkichi combined the idea with a European-style brass band, expanding the scale and instrumentation significantly from Amekatsu's one-man sonic advertisement performance. The two musical influences—the Japanese traditional instruments and the European-style brass bands—eventually merged over the following decades (see plate 1). At this time, this musical proxy advertisement practice was popularly known as *Hiromeya* in Tokyo, and *Tōzaiya* in Osaka (Horie 1986, 20–25).

Spectacular advertisement bands (*gakutai kōkoku*) flourished as the economy boomed during the period of industrialization between the Sino-Japanese War (1894–1895) and Russo-Japanese War (1904–1905). Symbolizing the forces of modernization and Westernization that followed the end of Japan's seclusion policy (1633–1868), the musical advertisement parades were an awe-inspiring modern spectacle (figure I.4).[10] However, shortly after the Russo-Japanese War, a volatile political climate marked by increasing antiestablishment and antigovernment activities—as well as noise complaints—led to the tightening of regulations on street advertisement practices. By 1910, the Tokyo Police Department had put in place strict limitations on the advertisement bands, allowing

FIGURE I.4 *Gakutai* brass band advertising domestic beer, circa 1910.

them a maximum of ten performers and up to three carriages at a time (Horie 1986, 56). The size of the troupes decreased further as musicians left the advertisement bands for better-paying jobs accompanying silent films. The introduction of new advertisement media (illumination, advertisement towers, balloons, newspaper, show windows, billboards) further contributed to the decline of the musical advertisement business on the streets. The devastating 1923 Tokyo Earthquake and the worldwide depression beginning in the late 1920s further impinged upon the musical advertisement business, forcing many into poverty, so that they could barely afford the day's rent and meals (Horie 1986, 98).[11]

The second peak in the popularity of the musical advertisement business came around the 1930s, when *tōkī* (talkies, movies with sound) came into fashion, costing many musicians their jobs accompanying silent films. As a result, a large number of unemployed movie theater musicians came back into the musical advertisement business. The rise of the film industry also led to unemployment among actors in the itinerant theater, variety hall artists, dancers, and circus performers, who followed musicians in seeking a place in street advertisement groups. Costumes, wigs, makeup, and theatrical routines in the style of taishū engeki (popular itinerant theater) became integral to chindon-ya practice as a result of these newcomers in the 1930s and 1940s.

The term "chindon-ya" is said to have appeared around this time, gradually replacing the names Hiromeya and Tōzaiya (Horie 1986, 112; Kata 1969). The Asia-Pacific War gave Japan's long-stagnant economy a boost, and the urban streets grew busy with chindon-ya troupes. The essayist Takeda Rintarō wrote of the ubiquitous presence of chindon-ya in 1935: "I ran into three Hiromeya troupes while walking within the same neighborhood. They would appear one after another from the alleyways, quite jovial, scattering around the music that blends with the sounds of the wind, resonating melancholically into the sky" (Takeda 1935, 11).

Although female instrumentalists and performers had participated in chindon-ya previously (as early as the first decades of the twentieth century), the demand for female chindon-ya increased as the result of a police ban on cross-dressing in the 1930s. Women performers were so popular that they were paid better than male chindon-ya, especially if they had the musical skill to play instruments. The musicologist Hosokawa Shūhei notes that a "women's school for advertisement personnel," otherwise known as "chindon-ya girls school," was founded in 1933. Over three months, women were given systematic training to cultivate skills in delivering flyers, playing the drums, shamisen, and kane, giving speeches, walking, dancing, and singing popular songs (Hosokawa, n.d. A, 12). To this day, there seems to be a fairly equal gender balance among chindon-ya performers in number, and there is no rigid division of labor by gender, although female troupe leaders are few.

Once World War II began, there was no room for chindon-ya under the harsh wartime conditions. Soon after the war, however, street musical bands for both entertainment and advertisement were high in demand in the open-air black markets (*aozora ichiba*, "blue sky market") that developed across the war-stricken cities. Chindon-ya became very active again in the 1950s, when the informal economies of open-air black markets were officially organized into commercial arcades (*shōtengai*) and markets, where individually owned businesses formed associations. Pachinko slot-machine parlors sprang up rapidly, becoming one of the major employers of chindon-ya troupes, boosting the chindon-ya business.[12] Chindon-ya's extremely localized, in-person style proved to be an effective means of advertisement for these postwar businesses, and chindon-ya enjoyed its third phase of popularity as Japan's economy boomed during the postwar reconstruction era. There were an estimated two thousand to twenty-five hundred chindon-ya performers in Japan at the time (Fritsch 2001, 54), and chindon-ya contests and festivals proliferated across the country, including the Toyama City Chindon *Konkūru* (contest), which started in 1955 and continues today (see plate 8). To highlight how high the demand for chindon-ya was, several chindon-ya practitioners I interviewed similarly recounted how chindon-ya would hire the homeless as banner-holders to supplement the labor shortage.

At around this time, the contemporary association of chindon-ya with notions of the everyday and *taishū*, or "popular mass," emerged. In spite of the rather extraordinary appearance of chindon-ya, its familiarity and ubiquity intimately connected it to the ordinary—temporally, spatially, and socially. Chindon-ya's sound was integral to the sounds of the quotidian, signaling the mundane routines of everyday life. Chindon-ya's sounds also became associated with public space. Words like *roji* (alley), *rojō* (on the street), and *michi* (street) were used recurrently in relation to chindon-ya; chindon-ya's sounds reverberated across public space and became a symbol of neighborhood streets and the sociality therein. Chindon-ya is most commonly popular in historically working-class neighborhoods, known as *shitamachi* (see chapter 2). Socially, particularly after World War II, chindon-ya became synonymous with the notion of taishū or *shomin*: the popular mass, common people.[13] As the postwar reconstruction era created a narrative of a unified nation with a shared goal of economic recovery, chindon-ya's popularity grew together with working-class people, as they aspired for the emergent notion of a homogeneous all-middle-class national public. In popular magazines and newspapers in the 1950s, 1960s, and 1970s, chindon-ya was often characterized as among the *taishū geinō* (popular performing arts), *shomin geinō* (common people's performing arts), *shomin bunka* (common people's culture), or even "popular arts that are most closely connected to the ordinary people" (Tamura 1970). Yet, at the same time, paradoxically, chindon-ya has always been perceived as marginal, as the "other" within the mainstream (see chapter 2).

This third peak in chindon-ya's popularity and activity came to an end in the late 1960s. A 1968 article titled "They Are Disappearing from the Town: Only 500 Chindon-ya Left in the Country" describes how the chindon-ya population in Tokyo went from 800 in 1953 to 150 in 1968, most of whose members were above forty years old (Rōdō Bunka 1968, 6). The economic recession following the 1973 oil shock, the rise of television commercials, and the rise of major corporate-owned supermarkets and businesses led to a sharp decline in chindon-ya. A passage in a magazine from the 1980s describes the fading of the chindon-ya business: "The big waves of rapid economic growth drastically changed the condition of the city. Chindon-ya's march was chased by the flood of cars, and their nostalgic melody was erased by metallic sounds amplified by speakers. Once having paraded through the city so freely, chindon-ya have now become confined to a dot, like a bird that has lost its wings" (Terada 1984, 5).

Despite the bubble economy of the 1980s, the yearlong suppression of street performances that accompanied the mourning period after the death of the emperor Hirohito in 1989 depressed the chindon-ya industry (see chapter 5). Chindon-ya yet again entered an almost two-decade-long hiatus. With little business and very few active practitioners, chindon-ya came to be seen as anachronistic, "uncool," and obsolete.

CHINDON-YA TODAY

With the dramatic decline in number from the twenty-five hundred chindon-ya performers who were active in the 1950s to about thirty chindon-ya troupes existing today (Horie 1986, 192), most people no longer experience chindon-ya as a familiar part of everyday life, but rather as a signifier of a bygone past in novels, comic books, and films.[14] Today's popular perception of chindon-ya largely has its roots in the practice's 1950s heyday, when the sound of chindon-ya was ubiquitous and integral to the quotidian soundscape in urban Japan.

But there has been a resurgence of chindon-ya practice since the early 1990s, albeit a relatively small one. This has taken the form of not only advertisement enterprise, but also new musical performances and recordings. In the past two decades, various musicians have drawn on the older chindon-ya repertoire, instrumentation (particularly the chindon drum set), and performance sites (public space, the street), mixing chindon-ya repertoires and styles with folkloric and popular materials from Japan, Korea, Okinawa, and Eastern Europe, as well as with experimental music, rock, and beyond. To distinguish the older advertisement enterprise from the new contemporary musical practices, I call the latter "chindon-inspired" practices (chapter 4).[15]

The recent increase in attention to chindon-ya was spearheaded almost simultaneously by two figures: Shinoda Masami in Tokyo and Hayashi Kōjirō in Osaka. A saxophone player versed in various styles such as funk, punk, and free jazz, Shinoda joined the veteran chindon-ya troupe Hasegawa Sendensha in 1983. In addition to playing for this and other chindon-ya troupes in Tokyo, Shinoda organized musical groups such as Compostela to play original, experimental music informed by chindon-ya stylings (Ōkuma, Mizuno, and Ikeu-

FIGURE I.5 *Tokyo Chin Don Vol. 1*, album cover.
Courtesy of Teramura Jun, Vivid Sound Corporation.

chi 2008). Until his death in 1992, Shinoda kept chindon-ya as a part-time job
while pursuing his musical career. The release of the double album *Tokyo Chin
Don Vol. 1* (1992), produced by Shinoda, is a hallmark of the recent chindon
resurgence (figure I.5). Until this album, with a few exceptions of recordings
for store advertising or for sound effects, chindon-ya's music had almost never
been documented on record. Shinoda's attempt to capture the sounds of Hasegawa Sendensha was recorded both live and in studio, and aspired to present
chindon-ya "not as nostalgia but as music, as one of the most exciting and
original Japanese musics presently performed" (Hosokawa 1992, 24). Others in
Shinoda's musical circle—many of whom came from free jazz and experimental music backgrounds—later followed suit, working as freelance chindon-ya
melody players for hire by multiple veteran chindon-ya troupes.

Born in Hakata, Hayashi Kōjirō began practicing chindon-ya during his
university days in the late 1970s, becoming an apprentice for one of the last
remaining veteran chindon-ya troupes in Osaka, Aozora Sendensha, in 1981.
Hayashi eventually founded his own chindon-ya in Osaka in 1984, calling it
Chindon Tsūshinsha (Chindon Communications) (see plate 3). This is the

chindon-ya troupe with whom I spent the majority of my time during field-work. They are widely recognized for their great financial success and high level of performance, having won numerous awards at the Toyama City Chindon Contest. The troupe has grown into Japan's largest chindon-ya group, consisting of twenty-six members who earn their livelihood primarily through chindon-ya practice. Hayashi has published three books on chindon-ya, one of which was dramatized as the TV series *Aozora ni Chindon* (Chindon in the blue sky), which aired on NHK (Nihon Hōsoō Kyōkai), the national broadcasting television channel (1994). Now recognized as one of the most prominent faces of the chindon-ya industry, Hayashi frequently contributes essays and articles to newspapers and magazines, and his troupe has also been invited to perform abroad numerous times, from Singapore to Paris, China, and San Diego.

Although it has historically been associated most strongly with urban centers, namely Tokyo and Osaka, you can find chindon-ya troupes across the country today.[16] There are regional differences in the business format and aesthetics among the troupes in various locales. For example, unspoken customary codes about costuming or repertoire choice tend to be followed more closely in Tokyo, where an older generation of chindon-ya still exists and whose members are treated as tradition bearers by younger practitioners. In contrast, in Osaka, where there are not many older-generation chindon-ya practicing today, the contemporary generation of chindon-ya members tend to be less concerned about following such customary codes. Likewise, there is more territorial competition in Tokyo than in Osaka; although rare today, there are tales of chindon-ya getting into fights when encountering each other in the same neighborhood in Tokyo in the 1960s.

My research primarily took place in Osaka, located fifty-five kilometers (34 miles) from the old capital of Kyoto and five hundred kilometers (310 miles) from today's capital Tokyo. The port city of Osaka has historically enjoyed the status of the center of commerce. Considered an underdog city relative to both Tokyo and Kyoto, it is characterized by boisterous energy, uninhibited affect, a caustic sense of humor, and candid, working-class sociality. I chose to focus my research on Hayashi's Chindon Tsūshinsha in Osaka for several reasons. First, Hayashi is considered one of the older and more respected spokespersons of the current chindon-ya industry. Despite stylistic and regional difference and rivalry, chindon-ya troupes across Japan recognize the prominence and contributions of Hayashi's troupe in its scope, size, financial success, and impact on the media. Second, Osaka is a unique ground that has enabled Hayashi

FIGURE I.6 Hayashi Kōjirō (*left*) apprenticing with Aozora Sendensha,
circa 1985. Courtesy of Hayashi Kōjirō.

to pursue his particular approach to historicizing and practicing chindon-ya.
Through his apprenticeship with members of Aozora Sendensha and the archival work he has undertaken since his twenties (figure I.6), Hayashi has both
studied chindon-ya as a historical practice and forged a respectfully irreverent
approach to integrating new elements into his troupe's performances. This has
been possible partly because there are fewer "veteran" chindon-ya in Osaka
whose presence might pose pressure to conform to the previous generation's
expectations. The relative lack of hierarchical dynamics with the older generation or competition in Osaka created desire to pursue genealogical knowledge
of chindon-ya and a degree of bold creativity to reinvent the wheel, propelling forward Chindon Tsūshinsha's distinct aesthetic style and business model.
Nonetheless, as with many popular practices, representations and narratives
of chindon-ya are predominantly Tokyo-centric, if not simply for the fact that
the greatest number of troupes are based in the capital. My primary focus on
Osaka has allowed me to tune in to the distinct regional dynamics and histories that have enabled one of the most economically vibrant and aesthetically

inventive examples in the recent chindon-ya resurgence in Japan. Moreover, as the historical home of chindon-ya's predecessors such as Amekatsu, Isakame, and Tanbaya Kurimaru, Osaka as a central site of my research provides a new perspective on the otherwise Tokyo-centric narrative of most chindon-ya histories and sonic ethnographies of contemporary Japan writ large (Novak 2013b notwithstanding).

What animates contemporary chindon-ya practitioners and chindon-inspired projects is the historical gap between the older generation and themselves. Because chindon-ya went through a period of inactivity during the economic recession of the late 1960s through the late 1980s, the practitioners who lived through the chindon industry's third peak in the 1950s had aged considerably by the time of the recent resurgence. These veteran chindon-ya practitioners were in their seventies and eighties by the time Shinoda and Hayashi, then in their twenties, started to show interest in chindon-ya. The current generation of chindon-ya apprenticed with these veterans, most of whom have passed away over the course of my fieldwork. This generational gap has inspired various musical and discursive projects among contemporary practitioners who research, imagine, reconstruct, and perform not only how chindon-ya once was, but also the ways of seeing, hearing, and walking in the streets in the past. Such a genealogical impulse among the current generation of chindon-ya was evident in the "Chindon Expo" organized by chindon-ya troupes across the country in 2003. Dubbed "The Great Tradition of Tokyo Chindon," the expo highlighted all facets of chindon-ya performance skills—percussion, speech, walking, costuming, and so on—by pairing up veteran and younger performers in a public "open workshop" (see plates 9 and 10). However, the approach was not one of salvage preservationism. Instead, the participants imaginatively situated chindon-ya in relation to various other musical and performance practices, both historical and contemporary, Japanese and non-Japanese. I will discuss further the genealogical performances by contemporary chindon-ya practitioners in chapters 1 and 2.

CHINDON-YA'S AMBIGUITIES

Uniquely Japanese? Transnational Roots

At once a musical practice, a commercial activity, and mere background noise in everyday life, chindon-ya is underpinned by three key areas of tension and ambiguity that render the practice elusive and uncategorizable under the contentious labels of traditional/folk/modern, art/commerce, and noise/music. First, the sounds of chindon-ya—an amalgam of Japanese and European musical elements—highlight the inherent contradictions between the assertion of Japanese uniqueness and Japan's claim to Westernized, modern nationhood. On the one hand, despite the derogatory portrayal of chindon-ya as anachronistic and insignificant, there is simultaneously a discourse of chindon-ya as a distinctly original Japanese music. As early as 1935, the music critic Kanetsune Kiyosuke humorously fantasized about his own version of chindon-ya as a uniquely Japanese music: "I would make a new chindon-ya troupe. With a violin, shamisen, gong chime and drums, and female and male voices, they would stand on the street at dusk, singing beautiful Japanese folk songs. . . . With chindon-ya, there are no restricting traditions, so you can easily do whatever without hesitation. If you do it, it would truly be a great achievement. . . . I would say 'the pioneer of the new Japanese music came from my own chindon-ya!'" (Kanetsune [1935] 1992, 264–65). Many share a similar view today; "roots music" is a term often used to refer to chindon-ya among chindon-inspired practitioners. Osaka-based Chindon Tsūshinsha has been invited to cultural festivals abroad as a representative Japanese performing arts group. And UK-based music producer Paul Fischer included many chindon-related tracks on the *Music of Japan* in the Rough Guide CD series circulated worldwide.

On the other hand, this allegedly uniquely Japanese "roots music" has its roots in places beyond Japan. As evident in the hodgepodge nature of the chindon-ya costume, instrumentation, and repertoire, the material culture of chindon-ya clues us in to the intrinsically transnational character of the practice from its inception. Chindon-ya as it is known today carries traces of both Edo-period Japanese performing arts practices and the imprint of American and European influences, which came to Japan via the military bands introduced to the country at the turn of the century: chindon drum percussion and the percussionist's kimono from Japan, and trumpets, clarinets, and saxophones played by musicians usually dressed in shirts, pants, and a hat from Europe and the United States.

In the liner notes of *Tokyo Chin Don Vol. 1*, Hosokawa argues that chindon-ya's very hybridity of Japanese and Western influences resulted in popular and academic dismissal of chindon music.[17] Hosokawa maintains that

Chindon-ya succeeded at this [compromising between Japanese and Western styles] without getting trapped by nationalism and tradition. That is why nationalists, traditionalists, racial purists . . . have never considered this music significant. Thus, chindon-ya has never been honored by national institutions, universities, or local preservation societies, as has been done for folk music and the folk arts. It was also too close to everyday life to be catalogued by any museum (at least until recently). Chindon-ya's instruments, repertoire and business management style are too "modern" or "commercial" to be labeled a traditional art. (Hosokawa 1992, 74)

Chindon-ya's cultural polyvalence is manifested not only in musical sounds, instrumentation, and costumes, but also in the ambiguities of its popular representation and reception. As the domains of the national, cultural, and ethnic were conflated into one narrative of homogeneity in the latter half of the twentieth century—manifested in the popular discourse known as *nihonjin-ron* (theories of Japaneseness)[18]—performing arts with premodern roots such as noh and kabuki became elevated as the "traditional" cultural practices that represent and authenticate the uniqueness of Japan as a nation.[19] While noh and kabuki constitute the national-cultural imaginary of Japan,[20] "the West" that is audible in the musical sounds of chindon-ya excluded the practice from being considered "traditional"—thus it could not be considered as a repository of the national essence. Chindon-ya, then, sounds out the elusive space where the national discourse of Japaneseness and transcultural multivalence are held in tension. This tension speaks to the broader contradiction within which Japan's modernity is situated: in claiming its own uniqueness as a modern nation state, Japan must negate the West, which is inextricably linked to the notion of the modern in Japan.

Deemed too modern to be traditional but too anachronistic to be modern today, chindon-ya is caught in the Möbius strip of Japan's claim to unique national-cultural homogeneity and its recursive relationship with its constitutive "outside," the West. Anthropologist Marilyn Ivy has identified a logic of this recursive, mutually constitutive relation between Japanese modernity and marginalized cultural practices on the verge of disappearance; she calls this "discourses of the vanishing" (1995). However, while discourses of the vanishing illuminate some of chindon-ya's appeal and its nostalgia today, the rather confusing popular perception of chindon-ya as neither premodern or modern, simultaneously Japanese and yet othered, and both rooted in capitalist modernity and symbolizing precapitalist sociality, begs further analysis. What, then, is that "difference" evoked by and associated with chindon-ya? Is the Westernness mixed up in chindon-ya recognized as non-Japanese difference? If not, what kind of Japanese difference does it embody? I will pursue these questions in chapters 1 and 2.

Soundings: Chindon-ya and the Sound/Noise/Music Debate

The second area of tension in the popular perception of chindon-ya stems from the ambiguity of its sonic presence. Throughout its history, chindon-ya and its precursors have had tenuous relationships with the categories of music, noise, and sound. These comments from contemporary chindon-inspired musicians highlight the tension:

> KIMURA SHINYA: The truth is that nobody listens to chindon-ya as music. There is a lot of noise in the city, and [the sound of chindon-ya] is floating around. I'm not sure if we can call that music.
>
> ŌKUMA WATARU: Certainly, chindon-ya doesn't fit in the concept of music, does it. (Ōkuma 1991, 72–74)

In my fieldwork conversations with chindon-ya practitioners, most of them tended to refer to their practice as producing sound (*oto*) instead of making music (*ongaku*)—which may feed back into an understanding of chindon-ya as "sound business," and the antipathy of practitioners toward the music industry.

Certainly, chindon-ya's premodern roots are entangled with the notion of music, or ongaku, which itself is a product of modernity, popularized by the Meiji government's education policy mandating the teaching of Western music in the public school curriculum from around 1870. The recurrent notion of chindon-ya being simply sound and not music not only speaks to the notion of "music" in Japan as a modern and Western construct itself, but also to how shifting political economies have informed cultural understandings of sound/noise/music, and different ways in which hearing and listening were socialized over the course of history. When large Western brass bands were incorporated into street advertisement performance in the late 1880s, they appealed not because the timbres, rhythms, and genres of the brass bands were already popular—quite the opposite. They were "awfully strange," and their "gigantic sound" surprised people (Hosokawa 1992, 13). During the period of rapid industrialization between 1900 and 1910, when the public landscape and soundscape were rapidly changing, the large-scale band advertisement was considered part of the "noise" of modernization. It was regulated along with other noise-producing technologies in response to mounting complaints about the increasing noises of street traffic.[21] By the 1950s, chindon-ya's ubiquity and embeddedness within sensory experiences of the everyday led to its perception as "mere sound." "It [chindon-ya] was a background sound, or sound effect that was not worthy of listening to. . . . The costumes stood out, but the sound itself was simply there, without anyone noticing it" (Hosokawa, n.d. A, 14). Once considered music, then noise, now chindon-ya is mere sound. Speculating as to why chindon-ya has not received critical attention or documentation, Hosokawa asserts that its proximity to the quotidian has rendered the presence of chindon-ya almost as hard to grasp as "air" (14): "Chindon-ya has been closely tied to everyday life and yet ignored. It was a forgotten music precisely because it was always there, in everyday life. It's been forgotten, not only by foreigners, but also Japanese who take it completely for granted" (Hosokawa 1992, 73).

Neither music nor noise, and never having been canonized, documented, or commodified, chindon-ya was a sound that was hardly *listened to*. It does not necessarily depend on having a conventional audience—it is overheard amid other urban sounds.

Further, the way chindon-ya's acoustic sounds contrast with the increasingly technologically mediated soundscape of urban Japan reveals a certain tension. Cultural critic Shirahara Kenichirō heard chindon-ya's unmediated sounds on the streets as a curious contrast to the sounds of mechanized modernity. In a 1972 piece on a chindon clarinet player, Shirahara comments on the changing soundscape of modern Japan: "Before the mass production and information era, so-called 'sound' had an important place. However, in modern days, such sound . . . has extinguished, and the carcass of civilization that is noise is pervasive" (Shirahara 1972, 132). In his Adornian critique of modern capitalist society whose mechanical sounds are a noisy "carcass," chindon-ya stands out as sound-in-flesh: "Everyone has the impression that chindon-ya means an anachronistic clown. However, somewhere in the circumstantial twist that makes us consider them as such, we discover the odd existence and the natural voice of 'sound'" (1972, 132).

Anthropomorphized as having a "voice," the sound of chindon-ya here is imbued with a sense of humanity. While there is a great sense of nostalgia and romanticization, Shirahara does not hear chindon-ya's sounds as premodern remainders of authenticity. Instead of denying the coevalness of chindon-ya's sonic presence and the noises of industrial modernity, Shirahara points to the curious presence of chindon-ya as something that simply exists as "sound" in the contemporary moment, in public space, evading the music-noise bifurcation.

While the perception of chindon-ya as "not music" but simply part of the soundscape has led to its exclusion from the canonized history of Japanese performing arts, precisely the fact that its sound is so deeply embedded in the everyday soundscape makes chindon-ya a fertile ground for cultural analysis.[22] Like Shirahara, I am interested in the very ambiguity and elusiveness of chindon-ya as a sonic practice that resists the discursive categories of music and noise.[23] Thus, rather than hearing chindon-ya's sounds as an object upon which power relations work to delineate music from noise, à la Jacques Attali ([1977] 1985), I offer an inclusive understanding of chindon-ya's practices as a dynamic process of *sounding*: an always ongoing, embodied and situated practice that brings together discursive and material resources, practices, and relations in order to produce sounds at a specific time and place. Hearing chindon-ya as "sounding" thus offers a way to skirt the contested discourses around chindon-ya in relation to the labels of music, sound, and noise, and instead allows us to understand how social practices and relations involved in sounding are key to understanding the intersection of sound, space, and sociality.

"Sound Business": An Uneasy Position on the Streets

The third area of tension underpinning chindon-ya practice lies in its ineluctable connection with commerce. As the term "sound business" makes clear, chindon-ya is first and foremost considered a business, rather than a musical genre. Performers perceive themselves to be firmly positioned outside the music industry. Chindon-ya troupes are not selling their music per se, but are using musical sounds in the commercial interest of their clients' businesses. Although chindon-ya is commercial, it has kept its distance from mass media, stage, and microphone. Until the aforementioned CD set *Tokyo Chin Don Vol. 1* was released in 1992, chindon-ya sounds had rarely been recorded or broadcast.[24]

Chindon-ya's definition as a sound business puts it in a tenuous position relative to the performing arts. Chindon Tsūshinsha founder Hayashi Kōjirō often noted how chindon-ya was in a double bind in the political economy of the streets: neither selling its own performance nor a product, chindon-ya is seen as inferior by both street performers and vendors (Hayashi 2006, 98). The former sell their performances, the latter sell objects. In contrast, chindon-ya sell their publicity service to their employer, but not to the customers they directly deal with once on the street. Uchino Makoto, a member of Chindon Tsūshinsha now in his late thirties, described how he perceives chindon-ya to be outside the three categories of economic sectors in today's Japanese political economy: the primary sector dealing with raw material, the secondary sector referring to manufacturing, and the tertiary sector involving service and distribution. Although some chindon-ya members consider the practice part of the service industry, Uchino here zeroes in on the ambiguity around what is being sold and to whom. Instead, positioning chindon-ya outside the three demarcated economic sectors altogether, Uchino calls chindon-ya an "unproductive quaternary industry."[25]

This sense of uneasiness around chindon-ya's elusive status relative to other industries, I suggest, comes from the fact that it is a form of what Michael Hardt calls affective labor. Hardt argues that as global capital economies transitioned from industrial modernity to postindustrial "post-modernity" in the mid-1970s, laboring forms shifted toward immaterial labor, which produces immaterial goods, such as a service, knowledge, communication, and affect. Although immaterial labor has always been present in capitalist economies, it has become not only directly productive of capital, but also "the pinnacle of the hierarchy of laboring forms" in the recent turn toward "informatized" economies driven by information and service (Hardt 1999, 90). Affective labor is a component of immaterial labor, grounded in human contact and interaction. Its products are inherently intangible and social, such as "a feeling of ease, well-being, satisfaction, excitement, passion—even a sense of connectedness or community" (96). Insofar as chindon-ya's sound business is not only about communicating information, but is also—and more importantly—about the production of sociality among ordinary people, chindon-ya has always been a form of affective labor.

What makes chindon-ya compelling is that it has been a form of affective labor that has flexibly adapted to, and resiliently persisted through, Japan's different capitalisms in the twentieth and twenty-first centuries. Chindon-ya's forefather Amekatsu's first appearance as a proxy advertisement business coincided with the weakening of the semifeudal economic system and the rise of a vibrant merchant money economy that paved the way toward the capitalist modernity of the twentieth century. Chindon-ya's peaks came at the heights of the industrial economy in the 1910s, 1930s, and 1950s. And the most recent resurgence has happened within the context of the "new" capitalism geared toward service and information, flexible labor, and neoliberal policies.

Far from foreshadowing and benefiting from the increasing emphasis on affective labor in recent decades, however, chindon-ya has remained both socially marginalized and economically precarious. Considering chindon-ya's ambivalence, precarity, and marginality as affective labor against the background of the shifting economic formations in Japan, chapter 3 will dig deeper into how the logic of chindon-ya's labor challenges the perceived tension between social warmth and capitalist economy, while chapters 4 and 5 will explore the potential and limitations of the politicization of chindon-ya's affective labor in the last two decades.

LINES OF INQUIRY

Putting these perspectives together, in this book I explore the intersection of sound, public space, and sociality in contemporary Japanese urban life. Because of its hybridized musical sounds, its commercial nature, and its embeddedness in everyday street life, chindon-ya has evaded preexisting labels and categories such as modern, traditional, noise, sound, music, business, and street performance. It is this ambivalent and polyvalent place chindon-ya occupies in the Japanese popular imaginary that interests me. Chindon-ya, as anachronistic and obsolete as it often is portrayed to be today, caught my attention for the rich historical sedimentations it embodies; its contentious position among other commercial and performance activities in public space; its elusive acoustics relative to the categories of sound, music, and noise; the wide range of emotional responses it elicits from listeners; the historical sensibilities it seems to reactivate; and the diversity of related musical projects it has spawned in various locations and styles. How has chindon-ya become revitalized, engendering wide-ranging cultural and commercial activities among diverse practitioners after decades of relative inactivity? What historical, geographical, and social forces have enabled chindon-ya's sound business to gain traction in contemporary Japan?

Further, chindon-ya's historical embeddedness within everyday life, public space, and the popular masses makes it fertile ground for exploring understandings of public space and sociality in contemporary Japan. As Japan's miraculous economic recovery reached a lull by the early 1990s, spatial and social "ordinariness" in Japanese everyday life started to shift. Open markets and individually owned shops became corporatized; streets became increasingly privatized and regulated, filled with technologically mediated sounds blaring from speakers and shops. How do we understand the significance of such a deliberately nondigital medium in the present moment that is otherwise saturated with so-called virtual and digital media? When neighborhood streets are increasingly regulated and privatized, what kinds of understanding of public space emerge from chindon-ya as its sounds resonate in the midst of these shifting geographies of urban modernity?

Curiously, as chindon-ya—an emblem of the ordinary people—started to regain its popularity in the late 1980s, there was an increasing sense of social fragmentation and crisis of national identity due to the collapse of the economic bubble (Harootunian and Yoda 2006). Together with the neoliberal policies that produced widening social and economic gaps (*kakusa*), the narrative of a homogeneous, classless, unified nation crumbled as Japan went through a long period of economic crisis.[26] Consequently, the country is said to be undergoing a crisis of national identity attributable to the collapse of an economic bubble, the demise of the "all-middle-class nation" in the era of recession, and economic restructuring that resulted in increasing economic inequality and an influx of flexible labor. Within this context of economic precarity and fragmentation of the postwar notion of the popular masses, who constitutes the listening public of chindon-ya? And how has this erstwhile commercial practice become politicized, mobilized in various street protests since the 1990s? What makes chindon-ya viable and sustainable as simultaneously an aesthetic, economic, and political practice today, when the initial conditions in which it developed no longer exist in contemporary Japan?

Extending Steven Feld's call to "imagine auditory culture as historical formations of distinct sensibilities and as sonic geographies of difference" (2003, 223), in this book I examine chindon-ya's sound as audible and embodied history as well as a geography of sociality and public space in Japan through which to explore these questions. I show how chindon-ya's sounds elucidate, valorize, or challenge the normalized understandings of sociality and public space in contemporary Japan, and how the affective resonances of chindon-ya have inspired creative possibilities for reconfiguring these understandings.

HIBIKI / RESONANCE

Central to my analysis is resonance, taken as both an analytical lens that brings together the production of space and sound, and a multifaceted trope that sheds light on the tangible consequences of chindon-ya's practice historically, acoustically, spatially, and politically. Many of the chindon-ya practitioners and chindon-inspired musicians I've encountered in my fieldwork have deeply intellectual, philosophical, and emotional investments in questions of urban geography and sound. Consider, for instance, Hayashi's musings on the acoustic philosophy of chindon-ya, describing how sounding and listening are inextricably linked in chindon-ya's cognitive processes: "Take the drum, for example. You hit it. Then listen to the lingering resonance of your own sound. [These days,] there isn't a habit of listening to the "gong, gong" of the drum after it is hit. Hit the drums in rhythm and you're content. If you can't listen to the resonance, it doesn't work, it's not fun."[27] It is not the moment of sounding or attack, but the consequent decay of sound as it resonates in each location that Hayashi listens to. Effective chindon-ya sound is made through an attentiveness that requires real-time, unmediated listening—something recorded sound cannot imitate. Hayashi attributes the inability to listen to the lingering resonance (*zankyō*) of one's playing, especially among the younger chindon-ya practitioners, to the "Westernization" of listening. For him, attention to resonance is a distinctly Japanese aural sensibility. This somewhat self-Orientalizing discourse of a culturally distinct way of relational listening was persistent in my conversations with chindon-ya practitioners during fieldwork.

Resonance was the central recurring trope I heard in these conversations about the aural sensibilities that inform the deeply social, relational, and affective principles of chindon-ya's commercial work.[28] Over the course of my fieldwork, chindon-ya performers repeatedly emphasized the need to sound their instruments in a way that "resonates with listeners' hearts" (*kokoro ni hibiku*). Drawing on the rich reservoir of meanings of the Japanese word *hibiki* (resonance) in the local discourse, I highlight the processes in which chindon-ya's sound is designed to elicit an affective response from a listener who simply "overhears" chindon-ya in public spaces. Just as in the English translation, the term "resonance" in Japanese evokes a wide variety of meanings: a quality of sound, reverberating, deep, and full; a scientific concept of sympathetic vibration; the ability to evoke images, memories, and emotions; and the sense of space and time produced by lingering sounds. Much like the acoustic phenomenon in which a particular frequency activates a dormant object, which in turn produces sympathetic vibrations, chindon-ya's performance is intended to move listeners through sound, inviting them into unexpected social encounters on the street. To distill the insights of chindon-ya practitioners—who are themselves philosophers of sound, space, and sociality—I postulate hibiki as a simultaneously acoustic and affective work of sounding that articulates latent socialities, the acoustic environment, and sedimented histories. Put another way, hibiki is a dynamic and indeterminate articulation of sound, space, time, and sociality; it is a way to think of these things together.[29] Through the analytical trope of hibiki, I simultaneously probe the materiality of sound and the analytical force of sound (and silence) as a social metaphor.

With its multiple meanings and definitions in various scientific fields as well as literary metaphor, resonance can be a powerful but poetically ambiguous trope. Four theoretical insights have informed my formulation of the analytic of resonance: the production of space (Lefebvre [1974] 1991; Massey 1994); the emphasis on the practice of *sounding*; diffraction (Haraway 1997; Barad 2007, 2014); and the concept of articulation (Hall 1980, 1985). My thinking about hibiki/resonance is deeply influenced by the primary tenets of Henri Lefebvre's conceptualization of space. At the fundamental level of his alternative notion of space is the idea that space is not physically delineated or contained, but rather constituted through interconnections of the social, temporal, and spatial. Lefebvre, and other human geographers who followed him, put forward an understanding of space as a dynamic milieu that is actively produced through multiple social and historical relations, which stretch beyond geographic boundaries (Hart 2004; Hesse 1993; Lefebvre [1974] 1991; Massey 1993, 1994; Smith and Katz 1993).[30] Conceiving space as a "geographical stretching-out of social relations" without physical delineations (Massey 1993, 147) is helpful in understanding the sense of spatiality that emerges from chindon-ya's translocal relations, imaginary evocations, and sounds that permeate physical boundaries. My emphasis on understanding chindon-ya's resonances through soundings, as I discussed above, follows Lefebvre's insistence on analyzing space not as a background or container in which we live, but rather as produced through our social actions and encounters. Sound and social interactions don't happen *in* space, or move *across* space; rather, space *comes into being* through the dynamic interrelations of multiple sounds, social encounters, and histories. I propose a parallel in thinking of space sonically: that space is produced through sonorous practices and encounters, and that sound does not simply happen in space, or across space, but dynamically produces space. By insisting on sound*ing*, I highlight the importance of examining the production of space/sound, instead of "things in space" or "things in sound." Thus conceived, "sounding" is an affectively, politically, and discursively generative practice that produces a conception of space as a socially produced milieu.[31]

If we take the production of space seriously, as Lefebvre urges us to, then "we are dealing with history" ([1974] 1991, 47). Rather than being a dichotomous pair, time and space are inextricably interwoven; historical sedimentations are integral to the dynamic processes by which space is produced (Massey 1993, 152). Thus, I suggest that the power-laden practice of producing space and difference should be examined with attention to the dynamic simultaneity of not only space and time but also sound—in resonance. In the sound-space of resonance, listeners and chindon-ya are physically and imaginatively interrelated. In its temporal capacity, resonance allows practitioners to tune in to the previous relations and histories that have formed the site of performance at a given place and time.

To understand the processes in which sounding practices assemble resources, relations, and histories to produce resonance, I draw on the analytic of "articulation" (Hall 1980, 1985). Articulation is a useful concept for thinking about the production of resonance because it elucidates how various relations and materials have been combined to produce resonance, while resisting a unitary structure to account for its coherence. Ethnomusicologist Jocelyne Guilbault coins the term "audible entanglements" (2005) to call attention to this process, in which musical practices embody and assemble specific constituencies, historical moments, imaginations of longing, belonging, and exclusion. While my understanding of resonance shares the same analytical concern, by referring to the process as hibiki/resonance, I put emphasis on spatiality and cultural specificity.

These articulatory processes do not present a logic that guarantees a certain outcome, but are immanent, indeterminate, and conjunctural. The same soundings can stick with certain people and not others; some soundings may gain traction one time but may not produce the same effects at other times. Once articulated within resonance, chindon-ya and listeners are brought into a new relation with one another, and the social effects of the interaction differ at every encounter. To track these dynamics, I take a cue from the feminist theorist Karen Barad's notion of "diffraction" as "both method of engagement and radically immanent world(ing) where relationality/differentiation are primary dynamics of all material-discursive entanglements" (Kaiser and Thiel 2014, 165). Matter and meanings both emerge and transform each other in diffractive understanding of a physical interaction—like the way a ripple caused by one stone thrown into a pond is transformed by the second, creating new patterns, transforming both. It is an attempt to displace the widely received Western assumptions about matter and meaning; for one to know something, one is inevitably transformed in the process of knowing, being part of the engagement with the matter. The understanding of soundings I gained in my interactions with chindon-ya foregrounds a similar dynamism; agential forces—listeners, performers, cultures, histories, objects, and so on—are processually, relationally, contingently, and asymmetrically produced in resonance. Thus conceived, resonance not only foregrounds the importance of social practice, but also allows for nonhuman agency. Whereas the commonly received phenomenological notion of "place" defines it as an abstract "space" made concrete and meaningful by human subjects (Casey 1996), the notion of articulation "is open to recognizing that nonhumans produce materially consequential sediments that also inform politics" (Moore 2005, 25). As chindon-ya practitioners are constantly producing and listening to resonances in relation not only to each other and listeners, but also as they echo across the acoustic environment of the city streets they walk through, emphasis on physical environment as part of the articulated assemblage that produces resonance is crucial.

The metaphorical polyvalence of the word "hibiki"/"resonance" also allows for analyses of the imaginary and discursive articulatory work made possible by soundings. Hibiki offers a way to discuss imagination; in resonance, listeners and practitioners empathetically embody sensibilities and sentiments that others might be experiencing, or reimagine certain historical moments, both the past and future.[32] This simultaneous consideration of the sociocultural and the acoustic work of resonance troubles, in Veit Erlmann's words, "the binary of the materiality of things and the immateriality of signs that has been at the center of Western thought for much of the modern era" (2015, 181). The power of resonance to incite imagination—of both past and future—is essential in both chindon-ya's street routine and chindon-inspired musicians' hybridizing musical practices. In particular, as part of the trope of resonance, I discuss the significance of affect in chindon-ya practice through what I call "imaginative empathy," an ability to imagine the sentiments of invisible listeners behind walls and to perform accordingly (chapter 3). Just like the acoustic phenomenon of sympathetic vibration, if a sound reaches listeners at the right frequency, certain imaginations, memories, or sentiments are triggered. This imaginative work of hibiki is as tangible and consequential as the practice of sounding itself. Resonance matters because it also conditions what is imaginable.

NOTES ON METHODS

Listening was both a subject and a method of my fieldwork. Chindon-ya practitioners cared greatly about listening, both their own and that of their potential audience who might be overhearing their sound from indoors. So I listened to them listening, and listened to them talk about their philosophies of listening. The methodological challenge in my fieldwork, however, was the fact that access to the listening public of chindon-ya sounds was limited, especially those who overheard chindon-ya's sounds and chose not to interact with them. Reception studies pose methodological challenges in many ethnographies of music, and I chose to compensate for this limitation in a few ways. In conversations with people—not only bystanders and passersby while I was following the chindon-ya troupes, but also friends and strangers more generally—I tried to elicit their impressions and reactions to hearing chindon-ya sounds. I also analyzed journalistic and literary texts in which I could trace responses of writers to chindon-ya sounds. Some of these writers were chindon-ya practitioners themselves, whose experiences of listening to chindon-ya sound played a significant role in their career choice to become chindon-ya.

I also note that, except for a couple of informal occasions where I was invited to jump in or sit in on a tune or two, I did not join chindon-ya on their job. Despite the long-held tradition of participant-observation in ethnographic fieldwork, there were financial and ethical concerns that outweighed the possible insights that might have been gained from performing with the troupe. In Chindon Tsūshinsha, most members are paid per gig. If I were to volunteer to be part of chindon-ya one day, someone in the troupe would lose his or her job for the day. As a nonmember of the troupe, I could not justify taking an income opportunity away from a member, even if I refused compensation for my work. Later in my fieldwork, this decision proved to be favorable in chindon-ya practitioners' eyes. I was told that my decision not to participate was taken as a sign of my understanding of the seemingly simple and often underestimated practice that many assumed "anyone could do." Although at times I doubted my decision not to actively participate in chindon-ya gigs, I considered winning the practitioners' trust by showing my respect for their financial, professional, and aesthetic investments to be a priority, despite the insights I might have gained through participant observation.

Although I did not take part in the street routines, I did stay active as a musician while in Japan, frequently performing with some members of Chindon

Tsūshinsha in their musical groups and collaborating with various musicians who are involved in chindon-inspired projects. This helped to earn a level of trust from chindon-ya practitioners as a gigging musician who shared an understanding of the practical challenges of getting gigs, promoting shows, securing rehearsal spaces, and building audiences. Consequently, even though I did not participate in the daily street routine gigs with Chindon Tsūshinsha, I was invited to join in various chindon-inspired performances—from an opening show for a Chindon Expo in Tokyo, to domestic and international tours (from Hokkaido to London and New York) with the chindon-inspired band Jinta-la-Mvta. These experiences allowed me to gain insights into not only the members' activities in a chindon-ya troupe, but also how the chindon practitioners perceive the relationship between livelihood, musical creativity, different sets of aesthetic values, and their own labor.

In my attempt to constitute an "archive" for my research, instead of identifying a stylistic or formal common denominator, I trace the diffractive effects and possibilities that emerge from chindon-ya's resonances. As such, it was essential that I remained geographically flexible as crucial events, opportunities, and connections presented themselves. Many of the musicians and chindon-ya were extremely mobile. I went along on their tours to festivals, local folk festivals, and concert venues, sometimes as a staff member, and other times as a performer myself. Thus, while I was primarily based in Osaka, I was constantly traveling to other cities, including Tokyo, Sendai, Gifu, Nagoya, Kyoto, Toyama, Hiroshima, Hakodate, Okinawa, London, New York, and Boston.[33] Following the resonances of chindon-ya across places, I trace how chindon-ya and chindon-inspired musicians embody and make audible multiple social relations, political formations, historical sedimentations, and cultural expressions that are geographically and temporally dispersed, but still interrelated.

CHAPTER OUTLINE

The prologue prepared the ground for the core arguments, key analytical moves, and broader disciplinary stakes and aspirations of this book, situating the project in relation to the critical debates within sound studies and cultural geography. Across the next five chapters, four interlocking themes will return and build on each other: (1) historical memories and the pragmatics of genealogical performances; (2) sound and affective labor as performance of enticement in public space; (3) marginality and alliances across social differences that gesture toward multicultural Japan; and (4) the role of sound in political interventions against socioeconomic precarity in neoliberal and post-disaster Japan.

The first two chapters offer historical insights into the logic of chindon-ya's sonic labor by examining contemporary practitioners' genealogical practices—the creative and interpretive historicization of chindon-ya to serve their contemporary interests. Chapter 1 offers a genealogy of chindon-ya as performed by contemporary practitioners, elucidating the entangled histories of Western imperialism and the development of capitalist modernity that informed chindon-ya's history. I examine this genealogy through the trope of "walking" as a creative and imaginative practice by which contemporary chindon-ya practitioners embody different times and temporalities. Through analysis of their genealogical performances, I show how the history of chindon-ya is rooted in the inextricable encounter with the West, and how chindon-ya has been a form of musical labor that has flexibly remained relevant from the moment of its emergence in the proto-capitalist economy of the late nineteenth century to the neoliberal present.

Chapter 2 analyzes chindon-ya's particular forms of advertisement and suggests that it is a sonic performance of enticement. I examine what I call "ethnographic fairy tales" in which chindon-ya are described as magicians of the streets, or likened to the Pied Piper of Hamelin, to unpack this claim. Tracing the premodern history of marginalized, caste-based difference of itinerant performers who are associated with chindon-ya, and the pervasive association of chindon-ya with nostalgia, I suggest that the enticement—the core of chindon-ya's advertisement enterprise—is not simply a longing for an irretrievable past. Rather, it is based on the conception of temporality that lies outside the narrative of capitalist time; the allure emerges from the multiple histories that are made present through the oscillating embodiment of (caste-based) otherness, longing for innocence lost in commercialism, and the notion of the ordinary, which bears a slight xenophobic and nationalist tenor.

Shifting gears, chapter 3 zeroes in on the micropractices of chindon-ya's daily street routines. In this most ethnographically extensive chapter, I investigate how chindon-ya practitioners' performative tactics are informed by what I call "imaginative empathy," chindon-ya's ability to imagine potential listeners' sentiments, and the acoustics of performance sites. By closely listening to chindon-ya's hibiki—the production of acoustic and affective resonances—I show how imaginative empathy highlights the shifting notion of who constitutes chindon-ya's listening public, evincing the politics of exclusion and social precarity within contemporary Japanese society. My analysis contests the widely accepted narrative that equates the development of corporate capitalism with the dissolution of sociality in recessionary Japan by teasing out the tension between chindon-ya practitioners' empathy for listeners and their own pursuit of commercial gain, both of which are at the heart of chindon-ya's sonic advertisement enterprise.

In chapters 4 and 5, I turn attention to contemporary musical offshoots of chindon-ya. Asking how the erstwhile commercial practice of chindon-ya has become newly aestheticized and politicized since the late 1990s, chapter 4 provides a genealogy of some of the key chindon-inspired musicians. By tracing the aesthetic and political aspirations of these musicians, I argue that the class-based social difference and otherness associated with chindon-ya have become articulated with contemporary registers of social difference, thereby raising what Stuart Hall (2000) calls "the multicultural question" in Japan. Building on the previous chapter, chapter 5 focuses on a particular case study of the politicization of chindon-ya, which has become a sonic emblem of recent antinuclear protests in the wake of the earthquake, tsunami, and nuclear disaster in 2011. By juxtaposing the raucous sound of chindon-ya at antinuclear protests and the enforced silence of mourning that followed the triple disasters, I examine what is being silenced in the name of imperial nationalism or disaster-nationalism, and what it means to attempt to repair social fragmentation in these moments of national crisis through chindon-ya's soundings.

The epilogue elaborates the critical import of resonance. The analytic of resonance that permeates this book is a particular way of understanding and sensing sound, space, and sociality that emerged from my walking and listening along with chindon-ya practitioners on the streets in the past decade. The insights gleaned from chindon-ya's soundings have much to offer in thinking more broadly about how a sonic culture produces social space, and how sound's materiality and ephemerality have particular tangible effects on affect and sociality. Resonances, necessarily fleeting and provisional, nonetheless allow us to imagine ourselves in relation to others and the environment differently, and to embody, through our sensory experiences, yet-to-be-imagined political possibilities.

CHAPTER 1

Walking Histories

Chindon-ya walk, on average, about ten kilometers (a little over six miles) a day. Along with ostentatious costuming, musical performance, and sales pitches, walking is one of the main preoccupations of chindon-ya. Despite this obvious centrality of walking to chindon-ya's everyday routine, my attention did not turn to their footwork until well near the end of my fieldwork; for many years, I was listening to their musical sounds, but not to their footsteps.

This changed one day in 2013, when Hayashi Kōjirō, the leader of the Osaka-based chindon-ya troupe Chindon Tsūshinsha, started hosting a monthly chindon-ya workshop called Horyū Shōkogaku Hayashi Juku (Hayashi School of Walking Style and Music of Gong Chime and Drums). According to the flyer, the goal of this school of *horyū*—literally, the style or flow of walking—is the pursuit of "beautiful resonance and lithe body through performance of *kane* [gong chime] and *taiko* [drum]." Catering primarily to aspiring amateur chindon performers, these horyū lessons are hands-on (or, rather, feet-on) workshops where Hayashi demonstrates the philosophies and techniques of walking and performing he feels are essential to chindon-ya practice.

Hayashi asks, "Have you wondered why chindon-ya are always walking around?" Of course, to publicize a client's business—but in reality, Hayashi maintains that there's really no place where chindon-ya are supposed to belong but in the act of walking. Describing the challenge of how chindon-ya must negotiate their physical and sonic presence where they are not meant to be, he maintains that "in short, wherever we go, we are only odd-looking intruders from elsewhere. So there's no space that we can confidently occupy. . . . Originally, the places where chindon-ya are called [to go] are absurdly *bachigai* (wrong place, out of place) for music and performances, such as living spaces in residential areas, financial districts, and downtown areas" (Hayashi 2002, 110–11).

Chindon-ya by definition are constantly carving out a space to perform where there is no preexisting setup or built-in expectations for them. While chindon-ya must blend in well enough to the surroundings sonically and visually in order to be received by the audience, they simultaneously "need to be bachigai. It's meaningless if you become completely transparent."[1] Being in place and out of place at once, he argues, is how you create a place chindon-ya can belong (*ibasho*). It seems fitting, then, that Hayashi decided to hold a workshop on walking—the fundamental act that holds a key for achieving this balance of being simultaneously in place and out of place as chindon-ya strive to maintain their presence on the streets.

The participants of the horyū workshop were to learn the art of carrying oneself spatially and socially, the art of gestural movements, and the art of perceiving one's presence in relation to others and one's surroundings. But the lessons were not simply a type of dance lesson or etiquette school, where one learns appropriate or effective comportment. Rather, Hayashi approached these "art of walking and sounding" lessons as an opportunity to share the many historical insights he has gained over the last three decades of practicing chindon-ya himself. As one of the leading figures of the recent chindon-ya resurgence, which began in the 1980s, Hayashi has been dedicated not only to pursuing chindon-ya as an aesthetic and business practice, but also to historicizing it.

Historicizing chindon-ya is no straightforward task, as there is a dearth of historical documentation and recordings. As with many musical genres, an origin story is almost impossible to pin down. By definition chindon-ya is an elusive subject because of the way multiple practices have informed what we know today as chindon-ya; there is an inherent challenge in capturing wide-ranging, highly localized, and individualized practices that have coalesced under the umbrella of chindon-ya. Furthermore, considered merely a part of everyday urban soundscape and a commercial practice without aesthetic merit, chindon-ya was rarely the subject of institutionalized preservation efforts in the past. But these gaps in historical knowledge were precisely the driving force behind the new generation of chindon-ya performers, led by Hayashi and others in the early 1980s, who sought new creative, economic, and musical opportunities in the once-obsolete practice. In particular, the so-called "blank period" of chindon-ya's history—when the economic slowdown following the "oil shock" of the early 1970s, new electronic and digital advertisement media, and the persistent social stigmatization of chindon-ya kept younger people from joining the business—has inspired the current generation of chindon-ya practitioners to take on careful and long apprenticeships, oral history projects, and archival work.

This resurgence in chindon-ya activities since the 1980s has been a performative and at times intellectual process. It has included following and recording the street routines of the older generation of chindon-ya (then in their eighties and nineties); gathering to host "listening parties" to listen to tapes of old field recordings of the veteran chindon-ya; compiling veterans' oral histories; publishing books and magazine articles on chindon-ya; and even producing a theatrical dramatization of the origin stories of chindon-ya. I call these interpretive historicizations of chindon-ya "genealogical performances," following Foucault's notion of genealogy as "the coupling together of scholarly erudition and local memories, which allows us to constitute a historical knowledge of struggles and to make use of that knowledge in contemporary tactics" (2003, 8). They are creative practices through which contemporary chindon-ya practitioners imaginatively seek to piece together fragmented and localized histories of chindon-ya to serve their varying contemporary interests—which I will unpack throughout this book. In this light, Hayashi's "art of walking" lessons are not only a pedagogical practice but also a genealogical performance: he is distilling, synthesizing, and making present historically specific ways of being in the world through acts of walking, sounding, and listening.

By ethnographically examining the small gestures and everyday practices of contemporary chindon-ya practitioners, with a particular focus on musical sounds and the walking body, this chapter shows how their genealogical performances not only comprise the fundamental techniques of chindon-ya performance, but also are creative practices of assembling and animating historical times. My goal in this chapter is threefold. First, by way of tracing the historical background for chindon-ya's precursors, I introduce the concept of embodied heterophony as a sensory expression of sedimented histories of European and American colonial expansion into Japan, and the entangled relationship between Japan and the "West." Second, by examining the "art of walking" workshops and chindon-ya's movements, I show how the seemingly nonchalant gait of chindon-ya is in fact guided by sonically, aesthetically, and physiologically informed performance tactics grounded in specific senses of historicity and sociality. I highlight two historical forces in these genealogical performances that are central to understanding chindon-ya within the larger social and cultural arcs of Japanese history: histories of European and American imperialism as well as Japan's own colonialist past, and Japan's shifting relationships to the capitalist market economy—from the proto-capitalist market economy of the late Edo period to the industrial economy of the first half of the twentieth century. Third, following anthropologist Jo Vergunst's assertion (2010, 387) that walking "gathers together material and social relations in the street and produces rhythms that the ethnographer can listen to and take part in," I focus on the practice of walking as a way of understanding the historical context in which the chindon-ya resurgence took place.[2] In the only existing scholarly analysis of the chindon-ya resurgence in Japanese, media scholar Watanabe Hiroshi (2013) situates the movement within Japan's participation in the then-emergent "world music boom" in the West in the 1980s, which capitalized on Western desire for the non-Western and the non-mainstream through exploitative commodification of musical sounds from the "rest" of the world.[3] Against a background of increasing internationalization, rising economic power in the global market, and the subsequent popularity of nihonjinron (pop-academic discourse of Japanese uniqueness), Watanabe describes chindon-ya as a representational resource for claiming unique Japaneseness, a nativist effort to assert a Japanese national cultural imaginary through navel-gazing in search of roots, and a reactionary impulse against the West defined by pursuit of the disappearing traces of premodern Japan—what Ivy calls the "discourses of the vanishing" (1995, 155). While this view of chindon-ya's resurgence throws into relief some of the essentializing discourses of Japaneseness that I did hear from time to time in my fieldwork among contemporary chindon-ya, my ethnographic observations revealed more complexity than Watanabe's analysis suggests.

My aim is to augment Watanabe's discursive analysis by understanding chindon-ya as not merely a semiotic resource, but as a constellation of embodied performances that warrant close ethnographic attention—thereby complicating the common view of chindon-ya resurgence as a nativist phenomenon. By historically situating the resurgence of chindon-ya within the cultural movement of rojō kansatsugaku (street observation study) during the 1980s, I posit that chindon-ya's genealogical projects, while partly participating in the discourses of the vanishing, also do the work of what Henri Lefebvre (2004) calls "rhythmanalysis": creatively listening to social relations as integral to physical surroundings, while making various patterns of temporal organization into presences. In doing so, chindon-ya at once capitalize on urban commercialism while refuting commodification through their insistence on walking—being in the body, in every moment, with every step a social and spatial movement.

EMBODIED HETEROPHONY

Chindon-ya's Roots in Military Brass Bands

The first time chindon-ya's footwork came to my attention—although I didn't quite make note of it until much later—was in a conversation with my aunt at the beginning of my fieldwork in 2005. Upon hearing that I was in Japan to do research on chindon-ya, my aunt, who was well known in the family for following chindon-ya as a little girl, reminisced about her childhood memories of chindon-ya in the 1950s. She said: "Chindon-ya would wear long, bright-colored and striped kimonos, and they had this showy walking style where they would kick up one foot a little bit to flare up the bottom of the kimono." With a mischievous smile, she demonstrated the walk—a zigzagging, playful, affected gait with a little bit of humorous hopping gesture accentuating the turns. *Taishū geinō* (popular performance arts) critic Fujii Sōtetsu also provides a similar description of his memory of chindon-ya's movements from the same period: "With a mincing gait, they walked in the shape of the letter S; looking back, that was probably a typical chindon-ya walking pattern" (1977, 173).

This playful footwork, as remembered and reenacted by my aunt, struck me for two reasons. First, compared to what I observed in the field, her demonstration of chindon-ya's movement from decades ago seemed much more exaggerated. Second, this realization allowed me to pay attention to what I took for granted in my observation of chindon-ya's street routines: the free-flowing body movements of chindon-ya practitioners and the lack of synchronicity among them while walking to their own musical accompaniment. This seemed to me rather odd, especially considering that chindon-ya's emergence in the late 1800s coincided with the arrival of European and American military brass bands, which introduced European musical instruments, repertoire, and coordinated movement to Japan as a way of producing new national subjects (*kokumin*). Despite chindon-ya's historical roots in European and American military brass bands, their footwork today shows no trace of the disciplined body movements typically seen in military marches. How did the musical and embodied discipline of military brass bands inform the formation of chindon-ya at its emergence, and how did it transform into the free-flowing, nonsynchronized, playful movements that we see today?

Brass bands were first introduced to Japan by European militaries in the 1850s, just as the Tokugawa shogunate, under European and American pressure to open Japan to trade, was lifting the 220-year-long seclusion policy. As the Japanese central government began to actively incorporate European-style military systems,[4] Satsuma Han (today's Kagoshima prefecture) was the first region in the country to introduce the brass band into its military training program, in 1869.[5] After the overhaul of the shogunate feudal system, the independent feudal domains were unified to build a modern nation under the new Meiji government. In its effort to militarize and unify the nation-under-construction, the government developed military bands (*gungakutai*), which were strategically incorporated into public events like imperial parades and other military displays as a spectacle to inspire awe in the public.[6] Drumming and marching were introduced also as a technology for disciplining, orchestrating, and synchronizing nationalized bodies through sound.

The disciplining of bodies by synchronizing movements to a steady beat was a fundamentally new concept to the Japanese. Until the introduction of European music, marching to a recurrent pulse in a regular meter was absent in Japanese music, from courtly to popular forms.[7] Although there had been forms of parades of samurai warriors in the Edo period, synchronizing one's footsteps with others according to the regular pulse provided by music was an entirely new concept—giving rise to the prevalent discourse of the rhythmically deficient Japanese body, which persists in various racialized tropes to this day.[8] The brass bands disciplined un-metered, unsynchronized bodies through not only military marches but also social dance. As the country was swept up in the national fascination with European "civilization" (*bunmei*) during the Meiji period (1868–1912), brass bands also provided musical accompaniment at dance parties, balls, and sports festivals for aristocrats and politicians (Horie 1986, 39–42; Horiuchi 1936, 10–13). The aristocrats' ardent and awkward attempts to learn to dance—that is, to embody the European concept of synchronizing one's body to others' and to a musical pulse—are humorously depicted by Baron Ōkura Kihachirō: "There were a couple of dancers on the dance floor that stood out. Both were men; one was a huge man like a wrestler, the other was a very thin twig. . . . The big man was the minister of the Army and the small man was the senator of Tokyo. The former in a stoic military uniform, the latter in kimono, they were determinedly trying to do the dance at which they were not so great" (quoted in Horiuchi 1936, 11). The dancing figures of the senator in traditional kimono and the minister of the army in European military uniform appear to satirize Japan's mimetic attempt to modernize and masculinize itself through militaristic efforts. The account exemplifies the awkwardness of this process of embodying a new, European concept of musically synchronized and disciplined national subjectivity at the turn of the century.

While brass bands were initially considered a novelty and a form of cultural capital for the upper class that indexed their alignment with Western civilization, by the time of the Sino-Japanese War (1894–1895) their sonic presence in the cultural landscape became more familiar and accessible in the popular sphere. With growing demand for brass band music at various ceremonies among civilians, bands independent of the military developed around 1886.[9] The war increased both the demand for brass bands and occasions for the general public to be exposed to military songs. Now a commercial enterprise, civilian brass bands (*gakutai*) proliferated in Tokyo and Osaka, performing at silent cinema theaters, sports festivals, send-off ceremonies for soldiers, outdoor social functions, and circuses.[10] Garbed in European military uniforms, gakutai performed European waltzes and marches, Japanese popular tunes, traditional tunes for festivals or variety theaters (*ohayasi*), and military marches—all of which were contemporarily identified as fashionable.

Growing popularity and demand for commercial brass bands led to the downsizing of bands to cater to different needs and budgets, giving way to the smaller, civilian brass bands called *jinta*—a precursor of chindon-ya. A jinta was a small brass band, hired by an advertising agent, that paraded through the streets with banners bearing store or product names, or that performed to entertain audiences at circus shows and festivals (Hosokawa 1989d, 130). What was first a twelve-to-eighteen-person brass band was gradually reduced to five or six members in jinta. The repertoire became smaller as well. For a group constantly in motion about town, it was not necessary to have a large selection of tunes to perform. By 1906, there was even a report of a civilian brass band that could play only one tune.[11] The term "jinta"—allegedly an onomatopoeia for the marching rhythm—came into place around this time to refer to these "downgraded" "pseudo brass bands" formed by civilians for commercial purposes (Horiuchi 1936, 17–18).

Descriptions of jinta around this time took a sharp turn away from the awe-inspiring spectacle of the military bands. In his 1927 retrospective account of jinta, the writer and radio actor Tokugawa Musei wrote of the "magical power of jinta" in its immediate ability to invoke visceral childlike curiosity and adoration, which thrilled him and made him shiver with joy: "The mystery of jinta lies in that self-destructive, tired, nihilistic, decadent manner of playing. There is a rhythm that would make the listener imagine that all of the players are lacking filial devotion, [are] ex-convicts, outlaws, womanizers, and patients of some sexually transmitted disease" (quoted in Horiuchi 1936, 29). The characters evoked by the rhythm of jinta are marginal, subversive, and unethical; however this jinta rhythm actually sounded, one can only imagine that it must have been far from the orderly, orchestrated, synchronized beats of the military brass bands intended to discipline governable nationalized bodies. It is perhaps this transgressive, marginalized sound that emerged in the process in which the military band as a nationalizing "musical weapon" transformed itself into a civilian commercial band as a "musical spectacle" that enticed Tokugawa's mind (Ōkuma 2001, 32).

Jinta as Japanized Brass Band: Embodied Heterophony

Many contemporary chindon-ya practitioners consider this historical moment, when commercial entrepreneurship transformed military brass bands into jinta, a significant point of convergence between jinta and chindon-ya (figure 1.1). During the transitional period in the 1910s, as chindon-ya gradually took the place of jinta, the distinction between the two commercial band practices seemed quite contentious. Commenting on the chindon-ya marching through the town, music critic Horiuchi Keizō wrote, with a sense of lament: "This is no longer the revival of jinta. This is the conquest of chindon-ya" (1936, 26–27). However, rather than endorsing Horiuchi's view that chindon-ya was an inferior derivative of jinta, musicologist Hosokawa Shūhei suggests that we conceive of chindon-ya as a layer of "indigenization" in which the performance style of jinta—which had already been a "Japanized" version of European brass bands—was further inflected by elements of traditional Japanese percussion and local popular performance practices.[12] According to Horiuchi, the Japanizing process in which European brass bands "deteriorated" into jinta was audible in musical sounds: "The quality of the civilian brass bands rapidly declined. Although there wasn't much difference between them and the military bands at the beginning, they ended up being an entirely different entity. Meager bands that perform military songs and popular songs without harmony appeared one

FIGURE 1.1 *Gakutai* band Hinode Ongaku Tai, advertising toothpaste, 1898.
Courtesy of Matsumura Nobuhiko, Lion Corporation.

after another" (1936, 17). This so-called downgrading process, however, was the process by which European music was indigenized. One musical feature in which Horiuchi locates this indigenization process is jinta's lack of harmonies. As military bands became jinta, harmonies and bass instruments were eliminated—the European aesthetic principle of harmony supported by low-register instruments did not exist in Japanese music (1936, 25). This formation has persisted throughout the twentieth century as jinta gave way to chindon-ya.

Referring to the sonic traces of this Japanizing approach to European military music audible in recordings of early twentieth-century jinta performance, Hosokawa coins the term "accidental heterophony" (*gūhatsuteki heterofonī*) (Hosokawa, n.d. B, 6). Whereas a military brass band ordinarily strives for orderliness and consistency in intonation, timbre, rhythm, and volume, jinta players disregarded these principles altogether. For jinta players, "indigenous intonation, sound-form, ornamentation, and elastic sense of rhythm" (6) took aesthetic priority over Western tuning and steady beats. In this light, jinta's musical sounds as well as body movements indexed what Hosokawa calls an "accent" (*namari*), which emerged during the process in which Japanese musicians and people on the streets were socialized to the sounds of European and U.S. colonial expansion in the early twentieth century.[13]

One aspect of this accent was heterophony, a musical texture in which variations of a single melody are simultaneously sounded, not as a pre-composed structure but as an unintended consequence of multiple players performing the same melody with individual variations intact. By calling this sensibility "embodied heterophony," to include not only the musical but also the kinesthetic, I call attention to the sonic sensibility that values relationality and variety among sounds over time, rather than simultaneity or synchronization of sounds at each moment. This is because among the performers, in Hosokawa's words, "there are relations with a certain degree of elasticity, or flexibility" (7).

Despite the danger of reproducing an essentialized discourse of biologically and culturally unique Japaneseness in opposition to the West, the notion of embodied heterophony—a distinctly Japanese embodied sense of musical time— helps us understand how an attunement to sedimented histories informs contemporary chindon-ya practitioners' performances today. As jinta gave way to chindon-ya starting in the late 1910s, certain musical characteristics—an elastic sense of time and pitch, the rejection of bass instruments and harmony, popular tunes from jinta's golden era, and the texture of embodied heterophony, for instance—remained intact in chindon-ya's sounds, and do so even till today. It is these audible, if faint, traces of particular socialities and sensibilities as archived in the memories and gestures of the older generation of chindon-ya practitioners that contemporary chindon-ya practitioners try to rediscover, historicize, and embody in their genealogical performances.

Listening for Colonial Traces

Although—or, perhaps, because—there is no definitive historical narrative that accounts for the connection between jinta and chindon-ya, the imaginary of jinta has inspired various performative interpretations among contemporary chindon-ya.[14] In November 2007, I attended an event that was an illustrative example of a genealogical performance that sought to speculatively perform the historical and aesthetic connections between jinta and chindon-ya. This was a lecture-demonstration event called "Jinta no Yūbe" (an evening of jinta), in Ishinomaki, a small rural town in Sendai prefecture in northern Japan. The event featured Hayashi Kōjirō, the leader of Osaka's Chindon Tsūshinsha, and

Ōsawa Gakutai, the country's oldest (founded in 1926) and only remaining jinta band. Ōsawa Gakutai had been recently "rediscovered" and recorded by the Tokyo-based independent record label Off-note in 2005 in collaboration with Chindon Tsūshinsha. The album attracted attention from both the media and chindon-ya enthusiasts, including the local amateur chindon group in Ishino-maki, Strada Sendensha.

Two years after the record was released, the members of Strada Sendensha organized the Jinta no Yūbe event to provide an opportunity for Ōsawa Gakutai to perform live for a larger audience. Hayashi was invited from Osaka to speak about his view of the relationship between jinta and chindon-ya, and the owner and recording engineer of Off-note also drove from Tokyo to document the performance. When I arrived at the venue, La Strada, right on the Ishinomaki waterfront—where I would return with chindon volunteers after the tsunami devastation of three years later (see chapter 5)—all the seventy-plus audience seats were full, mostly with older local men and women. Shiogama Sendensha, the only professional chindon-ya troupe in the Tōhoku (northeastern) region at that time, also drove all the way to attend the performance. As if to attest to the preservationist impulse that underscored the event, many audience members brought their own video cameras; counting my own, there were six video recorders on tripods, and a local TV crew was also documenting the event for later broadcasting.

The evening's program kicked off with a lecture by Hayashi providing a historical context for jinta and chindon-ya. Showing slides and videos, he demonstrated how he situates chindon-ya in relation to earlier musical practices in Japan, as well as in relation to brass band practices in other parts of the world. After playing a video clip of a New Orleans brass band performing at a jazz funeral, Hayashi excitedly pointed out the similarities between the brass band and chindon-ya in appearance (uniform), movement through space (walking through the streets), and music (instrumentation, timbre). Hayashi went on to describe Sri Lankan and Nepalese wedding bands in relation to jinta and chindon-ya, as he considers them to be similarly "indigenized" versions of the European military brass bands. By illustrating the unlikely continuity between jinta, chindon-ya, and brass bands in other parts of the world, Hayashi not only established a narrative of chindon-ya as the descendant of jinta, but also created an imagined alliance among these musical forms across historical and geographical lines, weaving a colorful narrative out of their multiple historical resonances with European military expansion and colonialism.

FIGURE 1.2 Hayashi Kōjirō (*left*) and five members of Ōsawa Gakutai
at Jinta no Yūbe, Ishinomaki, 2007. Photo by the author.

After Hayashi's surprisingly global contextualization of jinta, the audience
was treated to the eccentric and magnetic live performance by members of
Ōsawa Gakutai, then in their eighties and nineties (figure 1.2). This startled
almost all the audience, including me. The five-piece ensemble consisted of
clarinet, saxophone, trumpet, snare drum, and a bass drum with a cymbal
attached at the top. As if to blast off the salvage-anthropology undertone of
the programming framework that showcased them as a living relic of the past,
they played their repertoire at top-of-their-lungs volume. The performance by
these elderly men, led by the clarinet player Watanabe Kiichi, was simultaneously delightfully exhilarating and disorientingly cacophonous. The melody
instruments defied normative assumptions of tuning in the West, and each
player seemed to be playing in slightly different tempo; they wavered in pitch
and tempo throughout each tune. There was no count-off at the beginning of
tunes—someone would start and the rest would gradually and nonchalantly en-
ter, as if they didn't quite care to synchronize with one another. Ōsawa Gakutai's
unapologetically loud, out-of-tune, timbrally strident, and temporally liberal
performance exemplified accidental heterophony not only in terms of melodic
texture, but also in terms of rhythm and timbre.

Each tune was no more than two minutes, and their performance was interspersed with the leader's humorous banter, most of which I could not understand without asking the locals for clarification, because of his strong northern dialect. The evening closed with Hayashi interviewing the jinta members, who all offered their stories. They recounted how, in their youth, they had been in high demand to play marches at local schools' *undōkai* (sports festivals) or waltzes at circuses. They recollected saving money to purchase musical instruments and practicing after a long day's farmwork—often secretly, to avoid being berated by their family for what was considered a luxurious distraction from honest work in the field.

Genealogical performances of chindon-ya such as this one allow us to hear the privileged moments of emergence in chindon-ya's historical narrative that inherently position Japan in relation to European and American imperialism. Chindon-ya, via jinta, are the sonic remnants of these embodied, accidental heterophonies—the kinesthetic accents, the excesses that evaded the institutionalization and synchronization so widespread in a Westernizing, increasingly militaristic and imperialist early twentieth-century Japan. Interpreted as such, this event in some way reinforces Watanabe Hiroshi's critique of chindon-ya's resurgence as nostalgically essentialist and self-exoticizing. Taking to task both Hayashi and Off-note record label owner Kamiya Kazuyoshi, who recorded this jinta band, Watanabe points out the relativist and globalizing tendencies of the way Japan appropriated world music marketing, playing on the way that chindon-ya is situated as part of the global phenomenon of indigenized military brass bands. He also criticizes the navel-gazing search for an excess of Japaneseness that resisted Westernization—or what Christine Yano calls "internal exoticism" (2002, 15)—which explains the shock value of the unconventional musical aesthetics of Ōsawa Gakutai.[15]

While these nativist undercurrents that Watanabe detects were certainly present, it is too hasty to position chindon-ya's genealogical performances, such as Jinta no Yūbe, squarely in the "anti-Western," "anti-mainstream" category.[16] It is not simply the colonial histories of the West that contemporary genealogical projects and performances of chindon-ya explicate. Japan's militaristic past—its own history as a colonial power—is also made audible. For instance, in an essay titled "Warship March of Burma," Ōkuma Wataru, a clarinet player and writer who started playing with chindon-ya over thirty years ago, illuminates how today's chindon-ya repertoire can provide a point of entry for examining Japan's wartime aggression and militaristic past, as well as its complex and often-hidden historical relations with neighboring countries (2007). It is commonly known, at least among chindon-ya performers and enthusiasts, that many military songs (*gunka*) that were popular during the 1930s and 1940s have become part of the chindon-ya repertoire. In the postwar period, as these military songs were arranged in instrumental versions, the militaristic or nationalistic messages in their lyrics receded into the background in the vast majority of the Japanese listeners' consciousness. However, their familiar melodies remained; for example, it has become almost an unwritten custom among Tokyo-based chindon-ya to play the gunka tune "Gunkan Māchi" (Warship March) in front of pachinko slot-machine parlors. According to several Tokyo chindon-ya practitioners, the previous generation of chindon-ya had dozens of gunka in their repertoire. Now there are fewer than ten gunka songs that they play regularly.

Ōkuma combines his own experience performing with chindon-ya with historiographical research to uncover the residues of Japan's wartime aggression and militaristic past latent within these gunka tunes. In his short essay, Ōkuma recounts the revelatory moment when he recognized a military song played by a Burmese military brass band on a TV news report one night. This came to him as such a shock that he felt "as if history had sucker punched me in the head" (Ōkuma 2007). The Burmese band was playing a tune Ōkuma had learned from a veteran chindon-ya, titled "Gotaiten Māchi" (Imperial Coronation March), a popular military brass band tune he assumed to have been written in 1926 to commemorate the new Shōwa emperor's reign. The song is hardly heard anymore in Japan today; it is almost exclusively confined to the chindon-ya repertoire. This sudden recognition of a familiar chindon-ya tune in the context of the Burmese military was a musical testament to the history of the Japanese involvement with the Burmese military government in the 1940s. In this tune, Ōkuma heard that "Japan's Imperial Army has become deeply embedded within the current 'DNA' of the Burmese military" (2007).

Just as the imperial histories of the West in Japan are audible in an instrumentation rooted in military brass bands, Ōkuma's knowledge of the song through his experiences as a chindon-ya apprentice allowed him to discover the persistent traces of Japan's militaristic past in other Asian countries. In this way, chindon-ya's genealogical projects not only situate chindon-ya aesthetically in a larger historical context, but also reactivate memories and histories of both the imperialist advances of the West and Japan's colonial advances into Asia.

THE ART OF WALKING

Chindon-ya's Embodied Heterophony

I now turn my attention away from the echoes of colonial projects and the distinctly local sensibilities audible in the sounds of chindon-ya, back to the body—and particularly the footwork—of contemporary chindon-ya performers. During the typical chindon-ya street routine, called *machimawari* (literally, "going around the town"), chindon-ya practitioners stroll casually, slowly, and leisurely. The slow pace allows them to visually scan 360 degrees for whoever might be noticing the chindon-ya so that they can deliver flyers to them, or strike up a conversation. At times, they run, backtrack, or look up and wave at people looking down from balconies and windows. They walk at a much slower tempo than almost all other pedestrians on the street, frequently stopping at traffic lights, when someone talks to them, or when members of the troupe get held up in a chat with a passerby and need to catch up. The gestures and footsteps of any one chindon-ya performer are seldom in sync with either the music or the movements of other troupe members. All this seems so informal and unpremeditated—and indeed, many contemporary chindon-ya practitioners rarely discuss their movements or pay close attention to them. Hayashi Kōjirō, for instance, told me that it took him almost three decades of being in the chindon-ya business to realize the significance and potential of walking in chindon-ya.

One of the first chindon-ya workshops I attended was held in a practice room at the workshop of the traditional taiko drum maker Taikomasa, in southern Osaka.[17] There were several participants, some of whom traveled a few hours by train from Nagoya. Most of the regular attendees were amateur chindon-ya performers, who occasionally had performing engagements on a volunteer basis. Some of Hayashi's own troupe members also attended from time to time as models, and told me that they, too, learned a great deal from these lessons, as they were able to observe some of Hayashi's pedagogical approaches that go unarticulated during their street routines.

Not unlike many social dance workshops, much of the lesson time was spent on analyzing and practicing small units of movement in isolation, slowed down and without musical accompaniment. Hayashi would expand on the minute details of gestures: how to shift weight; how to put one foot in front of the other;

which parts of the soles remain in contact with the ground; how to bend the neck when switching directions; how much pressure to apply when holding the mallet; how to use the wrist when hitting the gong chime. Only after the participants understood these individual movements did they try them with musical accompaniment. In one of the first sessions, for example, Hayashi emphasized the different ways of walking required for wearing the kimono and *zōri*, traditional flip-flop-like slippers (figure 1.3). Hayashi spent a good forty-five minutes slowly walking back and forth across the room, telling the participants to be aware of the bend in the knee, to keep each step small, to never lift up the legs too high, to keep the feet in contact with the ground as much as possible. "If you walk the same way you usually do when you're wearing jeans and T-shirts, you will trip. You will kick up dirt and get the bottom of the kimono dirty. You will get tired after a couple of hours. People back in the day walked differently; you want to keep your feet close to the ground and gently slide forward."[18]

Hayashi's attention to the details of footwork is not simply driven by the quest for historical accuracy; playfulness and aesthetic concerns are also his preoccupation. In another lesson, he demonstrated the basic dancing steps for Awa Odori, a folkloric dance from Tokushima prefecture. One foot moves forward, toes first. Knees bent, the weight remains on the other foot. The heels never touch the ground. The impact of the foot on contact with the street is light as a feather. With a light bounce in the knees, the front foot gracefully kicks backward, the heel lightly tapping the back of the thigh, while the dancer's body twists to the side. Every step is accentuated by this playful and graceful gesture to mark the off-beat. Then the other foot goes forward, while the body faces forward again. In Tokushima, Awa Odori dancers repeat this sequence through the city streets for hours on end. I was struck by the similarity between the Awa Odori footwork Hayashi demonstrated and what my aunt demonstrated in her account of chindon-ya's footwork from her childhood—similar flair, playfulness, and accentuation. Hinting at the possibility that such folkloric dances may have informed the earlier generation of chindon-ya's footsteps—a certain claim to authenticity through the folkloric—Hayashi also sheds light on the simultaneously aesthetic and utilitarian advantage of integrating the Awa Odori footwork: "The fact that you don't get tired doing this for several hours at festivals [is remarkable]. Chindon-ya shouldn't get tired either, even when we are walking for hours on end while carrying instruments. One shouldn't be tired, one should have fun, and also [the walk] has to look good in others' eyes."

This aesthetic concern is ultimately also a social one. To ensure the ability to

FIGURE 1.3 Hayashi Kōjirō offering walking workshop (*horyū juku*) at Taikomasa, Osaka, 2013. Photo by the author.

appeal to many passersby, chindon-ya also need to be observant while walking. Hayashi continued, in his typically humorous tone:

You have to be conscious of people's gazes. You want to walk as if you're float-ing, softly wafting from reality. Think of the expert hostesses entertaining clients at a cabaret. All at the same time, she's paying attention to everyone—touching the customer to the right with your butt, to your left with your knee, pour a drink to the customer across the table, poking at the shin of the customer, all while turning around and greeting the customer who just walked in. No one should feel ignored. On the street, too, you need to make them aware that you're watching them, even with your back and with your butt. Express, through your whole body, that you're being seen, and that you're seeing them.[19]

Through this sexualized metaphor of a nightclub hostess's affective labor, Hayashi argues that walking is a way of recognizing, "touching," and making the passersby feel seen. "Nobody should feel ignored"—chindon-ya's movement, for Hayashi, performs the gendered emotional labor of attending to the basic need for recognition among those who happen to be in chindon-ya's proximity. Chindon-ya's aestheticized and historicized walk is a modality of social investigation and embodied communication with those who hear and see them as they move through public space.

One difference between a social dance lesson and a horyū lesson might be that the workshop is *not* about learning standardized steps or gestures that can then be synchronized to music or to the movements of dance partners. Instead of simply instilling a synchronized coordination of gestures and footsteps, Hayashi's walking lesson is meant to help the participants cultivate and embody aesthetic sensibilities and technical efficiencies that enable them to improvise flexibly. This means, among other things, the ability to respond not exclusively to the accompanying sounds but also to the surrounding social environment at large, including fellow troupe members and the passersby on the street. Hayashi emphasized the importance of recognizing how one's body, and way of walking, can and should produce certain types of social encounters and interactions: "Even if you're far from other chindon-ya members, we're connected. As if we were tied with a rubber band. Feeling the gravity between each other. The further we walk apart, the stronger we feel the gravity. The same goes for the customers [bystanders on the street], feeling as if we were connected with rubber bands. We have to pull them toward us, without loosening the rubber band. You have to think a great deal. If you just simply walk closer to them, the rubber band, or the kite string, will slacken. You have to be inventive in a lot of ways."[20]

At least two levels of embodied sociality are at work here. First is that among performers. The farther they drift apart while walking, the greater the pull they should feel toward each other, as if they were connected with long elastic bands. This is not a matter of pre-choreographed movement, or synchronicity: one can walk away from or out of sync with others and still maintain embodied coherence as a troupe. Second, movement and footwork are a non-discursive way of soliciting social interactions with passersby. The way chindon-ya attract the attention of passersby is about elicitation rather than imposition. Simply walking toward a potential customer and delivering a sales pitch is not effective; it will quite likely turn many of them away. Instead, chindon-ya attempt to intrigue, invite, and interact through an embodied negotiation of social dynamics and spaces—what Hayashi calls invisible gravitational forces. Chindon-ya's nonsynchronized, playful, and noncoordinated movements are grounded in particular ways of sensing, eliciting, and producing these invisible gravitational forces of sociality.

The apparent lack of coordination in chindon-ya footwork, whether with a regularly recurring beat or among troupe members, parallels the accidental heterophony that Hosokawa heard in the jinta recordings, or that I heard in Ōsawa Gakutai's performance at Jinta no Yūbe. Taken as a kind of embodied heterophony, chindon-ya's walk is a dynamic assemblage of historicities and socialities that emerges through variants, idiosyncrasies, and particularities. Considered as such, Hayashi's philosophy of walking resonates with Henri Lefebvre's notion of "rhythmanalysis." In his book of the same name (2004), Lefebvre brings to light the interrelation of space, time, and energy. Insisting on the importance of the body, Lefebvre shows the ever-changing, fluid, and multiple senses of time that produce everyday life—a polyrhythmic way of perceiving and embodying time. Both through everyday movements and more codified formalized gestures, Lefebvre's notion of embodied gestures as rhythm brings the sense of time to life. This is not a time that is measured and converted into currency, but time as a lived experience and a social practice that produces social space and "presences"—a dynamic becoming, an ensemble full of meaning, an antithesis of commodifiable and objectifiable "things" (2004, 22–23). Put another way, rhythmanalysis is a way of listening to social relations and physical surroundings together, while making various patterns of temporal organization—biological, cultural, individual, collective, etc.—into presences.[21]

Understood through the lens of rhythmanalysis, walking as practiced by Hayashi's troupe represents a creative investigation into the ways their predecessors listened to sound, used their bodies to respond to music, and performed footwork; it is a kind of embodied historiography, or choreo-historiography. By imagining and practicing historically informed ways of walking, chindon-ya evince historically and culturally specific sensibilities and socialities. But they do so not only as a way of claiming historical authenticity or generating a historically authentic singular narrative. Rather, walking here can be understood as a way of producing presences, which, Lefebvre asserts, resists reproduction and commodification. At once genealogical, utilitarian, aesthetic, and social, walking for Hayashi is an imaginative act that synthesizes differently socialized bodies, across place and time, into the temporally heterogeneous present. Every footstep is a study of the different ways the body has been habituated in different time periods and in different locales—from the early Meiji period when people's bodies were used for walking in traditional kimono, to the footwork of traditional folkloric dance from Tokushima. The embodied heterophony within chindon-ya's footsteps reveals the aliveness of histories within the present moment; even though the ostentatious costuming and heterophonic movement of chindon-ya may appear "out of place" and "out of sync," their footwork in fact gathers historical moments that are irreducibly here and now. Chindon-ya's walking is an ongoing practice—chindon-ya walk, and keep walking into the ephemerality of each moment to produce presences by weaving together embodied and imagined histories and socialities.

Listening While Walking

The sociality produced through walking is informed not only by chindon-ya's footwork, but also their listening. In the negotiation of spatial and social dynamics in chindon-ya's street routines, bodies and sounds are inseparable. Continuing to elaborate the metaphor of gravitational force as an explanation of how walking creates social interactions, Hayashi remarked in his workshop: "You need power if you try to pull the person behind you, right? The question is how to create that invisible gravitation through both movement and sound." Hayashi repeatedly emphasized the importance that "the way of walking doesn't synchronize with the sound [musical accompaniment]." When I asked for clarification, he responded, "You move with lingering resonance after the 'boom' [sound of lightly hitting the chindon drum]. It shouldn't be like *bap, bap* [regular pulse on the drum], as you go one-two-three-four [stepping to the same pulse]. After hitting the drum, you move your feet just so [slowly shuffling, sliding.] The different way of [aural] perception changes your movement."[22] Footwork should not be in sync with the regularly occurring drumbeat at the moment of attack, but should rather move flexibly during the lingering resonance of the decaying sound, echoing through the environment one walks through. In other words, the embodied heterophony—the flexibility and individually varied movements whose coherence emerges through interrelation rather than synchronization—does not stem from the essentialist discourse of the rhythmically deficient Japanese body, but rather from a culturally particular way of listening that informs chindon-ya's movement and footwork. It is this distinct and somewhat nativist discourse of listening and embodied rhythm that the Off-note record label owner Kamiya Kazuyoshi finds to be the defining aesthetic marker of chindon-ya. Quite contrary to the strict rhythm and accompanying marching movement of the body expected in the military march, chindon-ya's music and body movements are malleable, flexible, elastic, and always changing; they are contingent upon the specific site and moment of the performance. Kamiya, while expressing his aesthetic disagreement with some contemporary chindon-inspired musicians for their rigidly executed groove, characterized proper chindon-ya rhythm as a "rhythm that sways with the wind."[23] Although there are many chindon-inspired musicians who invoke chindon-ya in name and in instrumentation in various ways, Kamiya finds that they rarely produce this elastic, malleable sense of time, as if a tree branch were swinging in the air.[24] It is not simply in the instrumentation and timbre, but the embodied aesthetics of listening to the decaying sound instead of the moment of attack that informs chindon-ya's embodied heterophony.

This notion of a culturally distinct mode of listening is one example of Watanabe's idea that chindon-ya's resurgence was a product of the growing desires for anti-Western, anti-mainstream aesthetics and an ethno-nationalist impulse to assert Japanese cultural exceptionalism in the 1980s.[25] To a certain degree, Hayashi's and Kamiya's claims to the unique aural sensibility are complicit within the desires that undergirded the burgeoning world music market and Japanese participation in it: to position oneself outside the assumed superiority of Western aesthetic principles, and to assert the "untouched" and often naturalist discourses of Japanese uniqueness.[26] However, understanding the chindon-ya resurgence as an aesthetic practice on the commodity market of world music recordings and media discourses misses the point. Chindon-ya is first and foremost a livelihood, a form of sonic labor whose goal is the production of social relations, grounded in the embodied practice of sound, listening, and walking. Kamiya's critique of the rigid rhythms of chindon-influenced bands was not exclusively aesthetic; it reflects his conviction that chindon-ya's distinct value lies precisely in the fact that chindon-ya's soundings are not commodities but rather a form of labor.[27] The entrainment that Hayashi consciously studies, imagines, and practices in walking, then, is not simply an homage to perceived cultural or historical difference, but also the work of intense negotiation of individual particularities at every social encounter. It is through this attention to embodied particularities that chindon-ya's choreo-historiography differs from a pursuit of historical authenticity. Rather than simply capturing a collective "essence" of a historical moment or of a nationalized culture, it draws our attention to the kinds of social relations that can be forged and understood through idiosyncrasies and innocuous, and sometimes accidental, deviations. If we take chindon-ya's walking seriously as an embodied, affective labor of producing social relations, then the world music market alone does not suffice as a framework within which to understand the resurgence of chindon-ya and their genealogical performances.

To augment Watanabe's claim, I suggest that chindon-ya's detailed and embodied engagement with their physical surroundings, social dynamics, and details of everyday life on the streets can be considered part of another cultural movement that emerged alongside the chindon-ya resurgence in the 1980s: street observation studies (*rojō kansatsugaku*).[28] Formed in 1986 by a group of public intellectuals, artists, scholars, and writers, street observation studies aimed to critique consumerist culture and technocratic urban development plans by walking through the city in search of physical "properties"—manholes, signs, stairs, architectural ornaments—of little to no economic significance or value. By examining chindon-ya's walks alongside the strolling footsteps of these street observation study artists, who developed new techniques of walking and documenting the city in order to "challenge the 'colonization of the everyday' by bureaucratic rationalism" (Sand 2013, 98), I situate chindon-ya as simultaneously a beneficiary of capitalist urban commercialism and a critique of the very economy, contesting the forces of commodification.

RHYTHMS OF THE CITY:
HISTORICIZING STREET WALKERS

In Japan, walking as a creative social investigation and genealogical project has its roots in *kōgengaku*, or modernology—a kind of do-it-yourself urban sociology movement started by the eccentric sociologist and ethnographer Kon Wajirō (1888–1973).[29] A guerrilla ethnographer who broke away from traditional academic training under the mentorship of the prominent Japanese ethnologist Yanagida Kunio, Kon took to documenting the mundane and embodied particularities of Tokyo's urban dwellers. Modernology was driven by the reconstruction effort that followed the devastating Tokyo Earthquake of 1929. Characterized by detailed attention to innocuous objects, people, gestures, and architecture, modernology was at once a scientific and creative practice that sought to document and understand how the people of Tokyo constructed a new life after the rhythms and spaces of everyday life were drastically disrupted by the earthquake. This movement coincided with the rise of mass culture propelled by the popularization of radio and film. Walking around methodically with a keen eye to the playful creativities of everyday practice, Kon's kōgengaku forged a way to observe, through handwritten notes and sketches, "how mass culture reworked the changing relationship between the human body and the object world" (Silverberg 1992, 34) (figure 1.4).

It is worth noting that Kon Wajirō observed the distinct power of sound to gather people on the streets. Kon illustrated through diagrams how differently people gather around vendors through sight as opposed to sound: while a visually oriented vendor can attract only a small crowd as the spectators obstruct each other's views, a sonically oriented vendor can appeal to audiences 360 degrees all around, forming a large circle of audience (figure 1.5). In this study, Kon notes not only the efficacy of sound to draw passersby into relations, but also the significance of directing attention specifically to those who are "walkers" (*sanposha*) who are aimlessly and simply wandering, instead of consumers and shoppers engaged in the "admirable financial practice" (Kon 1987, 314). In his formulation, consumers are opposed to walkers, who "are attracted by not things that are profitable or unprofitable, but rather something interesting, something curious, something that doesn't amount to anything" (1987, 313). In Kon's analysis of various sensory approaches to engaging people in public space, we detect his political commitment to understanding walking as a practice that is subversively positioned outside "financial or aesthetic practice, life of value—whether internal or external" (1987, 313).

Kon's critical stance against the homogenizing forces of mass culture and the increasing commodification of everyday life was taken up five decades later by the members of the street observation studies collective. In the 1980s, the bubble economy drastically changed urban landscapes through an uncontrolled real estate market, aggressive urban planning, and the subsequent destruction of the Old City. In the midst of this, the artists of the street observation studies movement saw the possibility for creative subversion in the act of walking and documenting what the architect Fujimori Terunobu calls "expressive excess"

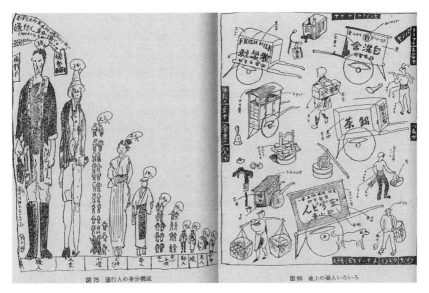

FIGURE 1.4 Modernology sketches by Kon Wajirō (1987).
Left: social survey of foot traffic, listed by occupation, gender, and generation.
Right: various street vendors. Courtesy of Kon Wajirō.

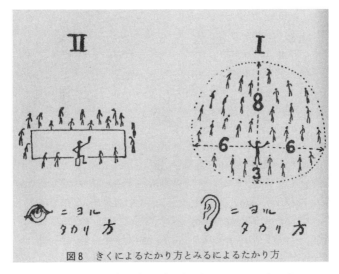

FIGURE 1.5 Modernology sketches by Kon Wajirō (1987).
I: crowd formation with ears. *II:* crowd formation with eyes.
Courtesy of Kon Wajirō.

(1986, 17), or what the historian Jordan Sand refers to as deviant properties (2013, 105). Sand locates the politics of street observation study within physical objects on everyday urban streets that possess a kind of deviant character (*zure*), or "material traces of the past, particularly fragments that failed to conform to present urban patterns and functions," which act as a resilient material symbol of difference amid homogenization (105). While these deviant properties were reminders of individuals' agency in shaping the urban environment, the rojō kansatsu group's practice of walking, archiving, and interpreting these material fragments of the industrial past in the postindustrial present "reaffirmed that the individual consumer could be more than a passive beneficiary (or victim) of capitalism" (105).

At a first glance, the search for deviant properties and traces of the industrial past certainly seems to echo the nativist aesthetic impulses of the world music boom in Japan I described earlier, which took place around the same time in the 1980s. There are key aspects in which the street observation study differs from the world music boom, however. First, it was not a quest for the ethno-nationalist essence of Japaneseness. Its commitment was to finding difference within the homogenizing forces of corporate capitalism that were sweeping the urban landscape. Second, at least in its ideology, street observation study was meant to resist commodification by insisting on the practice of walking and documenting—even though the movement ironically ended up commodifying these "useless" properties as it gained popularity.

Chindon-ya's genealogical performance resonates with many of the commitments and practices of street observation study, as well as the spirit of Kon's modernology. Both modernology of the 1930s and street observation study from the 1980s emerged as a response to the larger historical rhythms that transformed urban Japanese landscapes—the earthquake, war, postwar reconstruction, economic recovery, and the bubble economy. Chindon-ya coincided with, and in some sense participated in, this genealogy of urban walkers in the 1980s who responded to these rhythms of the city, rhythms of socialized bodies, and rhythms of daily lives. Chindon-ya, too, was a historicizing practice that attended to the everyday, the streets, and the sociality therein.

Instead of mapping street observations in diagrams or photos, as street observation study does, chindon-ya's work is a contingent and ongoing act of walking, gathering histories, and eliciting social interactions through improvisation. As anthropologist Jo Vergunst reminds us (2010, 378), the rhythm of walking is a way of paying attention to embodied particularities, multiplicity, and plurality. Chindon-ya's detailed attention to creating subtle and embodied tensions, relations, and situations helps a group attune itself to every individual it encounters on the street.

I return to Lefebvre's notion of rhythmanalysis as I sift through these parallels between street observation studies walkers and chindon-ya, both of whom simultaneously participate within and critique the pervasive consumerist capitalism through their embodied particularities and multiple temporalities. Calling our attention to the ways in which our bodies are entrained to move in accordance with these larger structures that govern our time, space, and bodies, the notion of rhythmanalysis offers a poignant critique of capitalism. Like his critique of normative assumptions of space as Cartesian, absolute, and inert ([1974] 1991), Lefebvre's focus on rhythm contests the standardized, measurable sense of time—what he calls "rational rhythms"—that undergirds the capitalist mode of production by observing, and embodying, multiple lived temporalities. In this light, the footwork of these urban walkers is not an "anti-West" pursuit of aesthetic values inherent to Japan, but rather a simultaneous embodiment of "pre-West" historicities and noncapitalist times, as well as other imagined temporalities.[30]

What is particularly generative about his formulation in *Rhythmanalysis* is that Lefebvre goes beyond a critique of how the capitalist mode of production abstracts social relations, time, and space; instead, Lefebvre offers a way of thinking about time specifically through the body, with all its idiosyncrasies, particularities, and pluralities. A rhythmanalyst "listens to a house, a street, a town, as an audience listens to a symphony . . . [and] integrates these things— this wall, this table, these trees—in a dramatic becoming, in an ensemble full of meaning, transforming them no longer into diverse things, but into presences" (2004, 22–23). Hayashi's aspiration, too, is for his fellow chindon-ya practitioners to cultivate this ability to animate and make various rhythms and histories present through movement and the body, to listen to sounds echoing across the built environment of the city, and to forge relations with strangers on the streets through particular ways of listening and moving.[31] Lefebvre's rhythmanalysis sounds remarkably similar to Hayashi's chindon-ya walking philosophy: "no camera, no image or series of images can show these rhythms. It requires equally attentive eyes and ears, a head and a memory and a heart" (2004, 36).

The embodied aesthetic of chindon-ya, informed by histories of European colonial expansion and inflected by bodies that do not easily conform to the synchronizing beats of Japan's Westernizing and nation-building efforts, lies precisely in the oscillation between two modalities of embodiment: disciplined synchronicity and nonconforming playfulness. Much like the way in which two different resonant frequencies combine to produce a new oscillation, chindon-ya's genealogical performances create a resonance through the oscillation between military influence, which was introduced to discipline the national body, and the embodied heterophony, which arises from bodies that did and do not conform. These seemingly contrasting embodied senses of time are co-present in chindon-ya; in Lefebvre's terms, rational rhythms—calculable, regulatory clock time that trains humans for life under capitalism—and the lived rhythms of the body coexist simultaneously.[32]

Furthermore, within the embodied heterophony of chindon-ya's genealogical performance are the larger historical rhythms of the city, punctuated by the cycles of capital accumulation, urban development, and earthquakes—the rhythm of the city that captured the attention of street observation study. The chindon-ya walking philosophies and practice espoused by Hayashi thus highlight the multiplicity of rhythms and temporalities that constitute the present: simultaneously disciplined and playful, national and individual, rational and "natural," European and indigenously Japanese, collectively synchronized and individually varied, daily routines and cycles of earthquakes, embedded within the urban consumerist culture and yet critical of commodification.

Hayashi's walking workshops are part of the genealogical approach through which his troupe members and workshop participants enact sedimented histories and imaginatively gather historical moments to make them into presences. These presences in turn are renewed every time chindon-ya walk into social encounters during their street routines. In the words of Ingold and Vergunst, "To walk and to feel is to make one's way through a world-in-formation, in a movement that is both rhythmically resonant with the movements of others around us—whose journeys we share or whose paths we cross—and open-ended, having neither a point of origin nor any final destination" (2008, 2). Lessons imparted in Hayashi's walking workshops and chindon-ya's footwork that I observed over the years elucidated the tensions that result from walking—insistence on embodiment, difference, and resistance to repetition and reproduction as a critique of commodification, all precisely to make do as a business that is built on the commodity market, and to maintain their presence

that is otherwise out of place (*bachigai*). Within these contradictions and fric-
tions, and through the heterophony of historical and everyday rhythms that
each footstep creates, we hear the resonances of chindon-ya that engage and
entice listeners.

CHAPTER 2

Performing Enticement

Chindon-ya's performance is not necessarily cheerful and loud. There's
something oddly sentimental, too. Just like the Pied Piper of Hamelin,
it inexplicably attracts children. I have a memory of following behind
chindon-ya as a child. I remember very well the nervousness after arriving
in an unknown town.

Shibusawa Tatsuhiko (1982, 240)

All advertisement is just a variation of a phrase: "follow me."

Amano Yūkichi (1997, 28)

ETHNOGRAPHIC FAIRY TALES

After his gig on a warm spring night in 2007, Cho Paggie, the *zainichi*[1] Korean
singer-songwriter, and I were enjoying midnight snacks and stiff *shōchū* drinks
at a hole-in-the-wall bar in Imazato, a predominantly Korean neighborhood
of Osaka. A tall and broad man in his early fifties, Cho was dressed in a casual
Korean-style shirt, and switched between English and Japanese while talking
with me in his open, well-projected voice. When I asked him how he came to
incorporate chindon sounds in his fourth album, *Garlic Chindon*,[2] Cho nostalgically recounted his childhood memories of chindon-ya in the late 1950s.
He said of chindon-ya: "Street music as advertisement. Chindon-ya was very
popular, and at the same time very discriminated against." I asked why. "I don't
know. . . . When chindon-ya came to my street, I ran to them, and followed. I
had no feeling of discrimination, but my parents said they were contaminated

. . . they're somewhat strange. I recognized that chindon-ya were people from a strange place. . . . [Making an album with chindon-ya meant that] for me too; I wanna be strange." He continued:

> Yeah, it was very common back in the day that a kid would follow chindon-ya and get lost. My sister got lost many times. So my mom sewed a name tag onto my sister's clothing. Just like during the war, when they sewed a tag with a name, address, age, and blood type on children's clothing, so that they could be easily recognized whenever and wherever they died. I didn't follow them [chindon-ya]. I didn't have the courage. My sister was five years younger than me—I was eight or ten, my sister was two or three years old. Now that I look back, they went really far—from Nishinari Ward to Taisho Ward [about 4 kilometers, or 2.5 miles]. My sister would just walk along all the way. One time, chindon-ya even brought her back to our home after she followed them around all day.[3]

When asking people who spent their childhood in the 1950s about what they know about chindon-ya today, I repeatedly heard variations of this story—including a similar one from my mother about her youngest sister, who was notorious for following chindon-ya and getting lost. Now an uncommon sight, the image of children following chindon-ya on the streets evokes a kind of nostalgia, as a sense of longing for times past and the innocence of childhood (figure 2.1). In both Cho's and my mother's stories of their childhood memories of chindon-ya, the naïveté of their younger siblings is revealed by how they easily surrendered to chindon-ya's enticement, following them beyond the familiar boundaries of their own neighborhoods; both Cho and my mother seem to suggest that they themselves lacked the innocence necessary to follow chindon-ya.

The trope of children enchanted by the sounds of a street band dates back further than these narratives (figure 2.2). In 1936, the music writer Horiuchi Keizō wrote a nostalgic homage to jinta—the civilian brass bands that became popular around 1900, now considered a precursor to chindon-ya, as discussed in chapter 1.[4] Lamenting that jinta is no longer a familiar sight on the streets, Horiuchi reminisces about jinta's golden age between the early 1900s and the 1920s, characterizing jinta as a "uniquely Japanese artistic genre" deserving an of obituary of sorts. His description of the jinta players, dressed in various military uniforms and marching through the streets, captures the strong visceral reaction jinta's sounds incited in him as a boy: "The music scattered a terrify-

FIGURE 2.1 Children and chindon-ya, Shōwa Sendensha, Kobe, circa 1952.
Photo by Miyake Yasuo. Courtesy of Misao Fujiwara .

FIGURE 2.2 Early advertisement band in Toyama City, publicizing medicines and
enticing children, circa 1910. Courtesy of Toyama City Baiyaku Shiryōkan.

ing stimulation. The stirring rhythm of the big drum and the snare drum, the bloody scream of the clarinet, the pointed cynical laughter of the cornet, the inebriated silly songs of the baritone [saxophone]—a vivid, throbbing sensation boiled up in me like the blood pouring out of the fingertip cut with a sharp knife. Yet still, the jinta players marched on with calm, even with faint, transcendental smiles. They were Mephistos of the city. They were the magicians of sound" (Horiuchi 1936, 5–6).

As evident in the anecdotes above, descriptions of how the sound of chindon-ya and its precursors affected listeners frequently carry strongly visceral and emotional—even magical—overtones. Allured by chindon-ya's sounds, listeners came out of their apartments, seeking the sounds with their ears and eyes, even trailing them until they were lost. Inexplicable senses of nostalgia, bewilderment, fascination, and enticement are common sentiments associated with these accounts of chindon-ya.

The recurring Pied Piper–like imagery of magical street musicians and enchanted followers, accompanied by nostalgia for both times past and childlike innocence, provides an insight into chindon-ya's renewed appeal as an advertising medium today. The trope of the allured listener can be easily transposed to the market: what more ideal subjects can an advertising enterprise hope for than enticed followers? Chindon-ya's advertisement practice, in other words, can be understood as a performance of enticement, based on spectacle, sounding, listening, and walking.

And there's something more to note in these ethnographic fairy tales of chindon-ya. In accounts of both chindon-ya and jinta, the magically enticing presence of street performers carries a curious undertone: the musicians are somehow considered "contaminated," in Cho's mother's words, or otherworldly, magical, and strange, as in Horiuchi's account.[5] In the same conversation, Cho continued: "Do you know this phrase? [starts singing] 'Stupid, fool, chindon-ya. Your mother has an outie!' [I sing along]. . . . In a sense, chindon-ya is always made fun of. But then, when they come to town, everyone is excited and applauds. I don't really get it. It's a mystery . . . kind of strange. [As a child,] I recognized chindon-ya as people from a strange place. They can't stay long; they shouldn't be common [people]. They should be always strange to us."

The melody that Cho and I sang together is a commonly sung phrase children often use to taunt each other. While, on the one hand, chindon-ya is welcome as a familiar and ubiquitous presence in everyday life, on the other, a clear sense of marginalized difference is evident in the popular perception of chindon-ya. Their "strangeness" indexes something out of the ordinary, both spatially and temporally: they are out of time, and out of place (*bachigai*). This tension between familiarity and strangeness echoes the double-edged sword of innocence: there is a sense of danger—of getting lost—that accompanies the innocent followers enticed by the Pied Piper. Contemporary practitioners are well aware of the perception of chindon-ya as simultaneously strange and familiar, although they have varying opinions as to how this perception of chindon-ya has come to be, and what historical forces have informed the development of the practice. What kind of "strangeness" or "difference" does chindon-ya embody, and how has it come to be marginalized? How do the temporal and spatial parameters of the marginalized difference play into chindon-ya's performance of enticement?

Taking cues from these ethnographic fairy tales, in this chapter I examine the intersection of difference and nostalgia in order to lay bare the logic of enticement in contemporary chindon-ya performances. I do so, in the main, by examining contemporary chindon practitioners' engagement with the past and memories—however incoherent or historically inaccurate they might be. By analyzing what historical relations and moments are privileged in the contemporary chindon-ya practitioners' genealogical performances, this chapter aims both to provide historical background on the social positions, class politics, and modes of sociality that have historically been associated with chindon-ya, and to explore how the shifting discourses of marginalized difference have come to inflect chindon-ya's allure.

Throughout the chapter, I keep listening to the guiding sound of the kane—the metal gong chime that is part of the chindon-ya percussion battery (figure 2.3). The equivalent of the pipe of the Piper of Hamelin, kane is an indexical sound that at once signals chindon-ya's presence, triggers cultural memories, and hails various listening constituents, embodying the ambivalent tension between social difference and social cohesion that has pervaded Japanese history. With the sound of kane in mind, I take three interrelated angles to shed light on the difference and otherness embodied by the contemporary discourse about and performance of chindon-ya. First, situating chindon-ya in relation to the historical forms of marginalized difference produced through the hereditary social status system of the Edo period, I will show how contemporary chindon-ya practitioners develop affective alliances across historical notions of alterity while also being complicit within discourses of social homogeneity. In the second section, I trace the shifting meanings of just who are the taishū (popular masses, or ordinary people)—their listening public—in postwar Japan, showing how working-class solidarity and sociality come to be expressed as a historical difference in contemporary popular discourse.

This in turn has an implication for understanding the prevalent discourse of nostalgia around chindon-ya. In the last section, weaving together the ethnographic observations above with Elizabeth Freeman's (2010) critique of "chrononormativity," a normative designation of time that organizes bodies through capitalist logic, I argue that nostalgia for chindon-ya complicates the assumption of linear progression of time that underlines nostalgia. Instead, chindon-ya's genealogical performances embody the temporal heterogeneity of the present moment, revealing how today's sociality—and social marginalization—are at once produced by the vernacular, precapitalist hereditary hierarchical system and so-called Western narratives of capital. The enticement of chindon-ya, thus, lies in the danger and allure of being cast outside the normative linear narrative of capital, of being suspended in multiple ontologies of temporality—of being led astray not only in place but also in time.

CHINDON-YA, ALTERITY, AND SAMENESS

Autumn Colors, Bustles of the Wild Desert

In the fall of 2008 in an outdoor theater in the Osaka Castle Park, I watched Chindon Tsūshinsha put on a theatrical show titled "Autumn Colors, Bustles of the Wild Desert: A Wild Fantasia on the Origin of Chindon-ya" (Aki no irokusa nobaku no nigiwai: Chindon-ya shigen ni matsuwaru mōsōkyoku). Written and directed by Hayashi, the performance portrayed his multifaceted vision of chindon-ya history. Instead of providing a linear narrative, the performance assembled historical and fictional characters to situate chindon-ya in a constellation of historical figures and street performance arts. Set up on a round stage surrounded by audience seats, the play featured a wide range of itinerant performers and vendors: a folk-religious procession in the Middle Ages (twelfth to sixteenth centuries), an itinerant medicine merchant, a candy hawker in the Edo period, a street vendor selling vegetables and toys, and recyclable can collectors living on the urban streets of Osaka today.

In this theatrical production, the sound of kane figured prominently as a trope that threaded together the time periods and historical characters that Hayashi considers important in tracing genealogies of chindon-ya practice. Made

FIGURE 2.3 *Kane* on a chindon drum set. This one has been
modified by a former owner to enhance its sonority
by creating a hole along the rim. Photo by the author.

of copper, tin, and zinc, kane produces a bright, high-pitched, metallic sound
that rings out and pierces through a distance. The loudness and bright timbre
of kane is hard to ignore; it is often the first sound you hear when chindon-ya is
approaching. Hayashi told me that, in his script, he used kane as a sonic thread
through the various itinerant performers of different historical periods; kane
sonically and symbolically evoked the historical continuity of chindon-ya with
the medieval and feudal past, grounded in the notion of the "popular" or "common people" (*taishū*, or *minshū*) among whom these street characters walked
and interacted.

Through research and imagination, Hayashi wove together hypothetical historical narratives that situated chindon-ya as an extension of the religious and

mercantile practices represented by the street characters—vegetable seller, religious processions, ritual performer offering seasonal blessings—which all shared histories of social marginalization. As I showed in chapter 1, such genealogical performances are both creatively speculative and historiographical. While many contemporary chindon-ya practitioners based in Tokyo tend to treat chindon-ya as an art form to be pursued through assiduous collection of oral histories from the older generation and apprenticeship with them, Hayashi works not only to reproduce a so-called tradition, but also to express his own vision of chindon-ya as a nodal point where various historical forces and social differences have converged. Such a speculative approach to the history of chindon-ya is valued and shared by other younger members of his troupe. Kariyasaki Ikuko, often called by her stage name, Pinkie, is one of them. Speaking of her experience of choosing her career after graduating from university, she said: "When I was trying to figure out which chindon-ya troupe to join, I thought I had no other option but Chindon Tsūshinsha. I liked Tōzaiya [another name for Chindon Tsūshinsha] for both being historically informed, respectful, and daring to do new things at the same time. Because there was a gap of almost thirty years between the previous generation and Hayashi-san's generation, we are no longer just continuing a practice. . . . I think it's important to fill those gaps."[6]

Although Hayashi's troupe is quite distinct in performing genealogical histories of chindon-ya on a stage, he is certainly not alone in his efforts to excavate the histories of marginalization among practitioners of earlier street performance practices. In his 2001 book *Rafu Myūjikku Sengen: Chindon, Punk, Jazz* (Declaration of rough music: Chindon, punk, jazz), Ōkuma Wataru, a Tokyo-based clarinet player active in chindon-ya groups and the bandleader of the chindon-inspired band Cicala Mvta, presents his genealogical investigation of chindon-ya by tracing the histories of various street performance practices in Japan. After having worked in the chindon-ya business for ten years, he says, he learned that "although it appears chaotic and nonsensical, there must be historical memory or culturally genetic work behind chindon-ya." He continues: "Of course, in terms of the name and instrumental structure, chindon-ya is a rather modern art form, originating after the 1920s with regard to form, 1850s at the earliest. However, at the same time, it is certain that chindon carries the elements of various precedents of street performance practices" (Ōkuma 2001, 148).

Ōkuma's list of such street performance practices is extensive and spans over two hundred years: *ameuri* (candy vendors); *sumiyoshi odori* (processional dance with Buddhist roots); *chobokure* (song and dance spread by itinerant beggars in the 1800s); *goze uta* (songs of itinerant blind women); *jinta* (civilian brass band); *gakutai* (street brass band); *enka* (politically satirical songs of the 1880s and 1890s); *naniwa bushi* (popular melodious storytelling in the 1900s); *kamishibai* (traveling storytellers with pictures); and so on. It is out of the scope of this chapter to evaluate the validity of these genres' connections to chindon-ya. Rather, I seek to understand why contemporary chindon-ya practitioners privilege these historical narratives of difference—spatialized, marginalized subjectivities that have been associated with "the street"—in their own renderings of chindon-ya history.

Marginalized Otherness and the Street

Historically, the street represented a means of communication between places, a site of danger, the dialectic between the ordinary and the extraordinary (*hare to ke*). There is a long history of the trope of the street and itinerancy naturalizing and normalizing marginalized social status in Japan, which in turn has been intimately connected with itinerant performers' magico-religious functions. The earliest mention of a street performance seems to be in the *Manyōshū* literature of the eighth century, which mentions *hokaibito*, itinerant performers who offered blessing rituals and other folkloric—and supernatural—performances in exchange for food (Misumi, quoted in Ozawa 1989, 60–61). And kane, integral to Buddhist ritual by the eighth century, was already seen and heard in Buddhist chanting, dancing processions, and street performances. For instance, kane was a featured instrument in the processional *nenbutsu odori* (prayer dance), which stemmed from Buddhist rituals but had become a street entertainment performed by beggars by the late 1700s.

By the tenth to eleventh centuries, these performers were already classed as outcastes, outside the hierarchical status system; performance on the streets often became a means of survival for those who had no other options because of their social status.[7] Street performance, called *tsujigei* by the Edo period (1603–1868), was one of the ways outcastes earned their livelihood, along with begging and other jobs that were considered too vulgar for members of higher classes within the hereditary status system. Outcastes (including Okuni, the woman known as the innovator of kabuki) often worked in the itinerant theater groups that spread kabuki theater throughout country, as well as in various kinds of storytelling, monkey shows, magic, stunts, street noh theater, puppet theater (*jōruri*), seasonal blessing performances (*kadozuke*), and so on. These performance practices often served as opening acts to attract people prior to the sales pitches of medicine vendors (Morita 1974, 72–77).[8]

Their marginalized difference was mapped not only onto the street but also on mobility itself. In a country that has historically placed importance on microgeographies of place and rootedness, itinerancy carries transgressive meanings. As the economic system became centralized and the hierarchical social status system solidified under the Edo shogunate, itinerancy and begging marked street performers as marginalized, and some even racialized, within the hereditary social status system.[9] Considered unproductive labor outside the feudal economic transactions, street performers and their itinerancy cemented the social perception of them as marginalized, inferior, and transgressive; and yet their ritualistic and entertainment services made them an integral part of life cycles, seasonal patterns, and everyday life. Itinerancy thus holds a great degree of ambiguity—the lure and fear of being cast outside the social order; strangeness and familiarity.

Even after the abolition of the strict feudal status system and the "liberation" of outcastes in 1871, the discriminatory attitude of the people toward street performers, and their fascination with them, have persisted. Street performers are often described as poor people who make a living by entertaining the lower classes on the streets (Yokoyama 1941, 45–47) and are at times associated with *buraku* people—a post-Meiji social category created to refer to the descendants of the outcastes. Horiuchi's curiously fantastical commentary on jinta at the beginning of this chapter and Tokugawa Musei's 1927 characterization of jinta players that I discussed in the previous chapter are examples of such a perception of street performers. While descriptions such as "Mephistos of the city . . . magicians of sound" demonstrate Horiuchi's fascination with the alterity represented by jinta, Tokugawa's description of jinta sounds—"self-destructive, tired, nihilistic, decadent"—suggests not only fascination but also contempt. Though affectionately written, his descriptions invoke amoral and castigated characters such as ex-convicts, womanizers, and sex addicts. Horiuchi also comments that, as jinta's popularity declined, the phrase "he's only jinta" became a pejorative tag used by orchestral musicians to express contempt for jinta musicians as a group positioned socially and musically lower than they (Horiuchi 1936, 31). The children's phrase, sung by Cho and me—"stupid, fool, chindon-ya!"— might be explained through this long lineage of articulation between street music performers and social, political, and economic marginalization, which is accompanied by the social perception characterized by the dialectic between disdain and fascination.

Being/Becoming Chindon-ya Today

Chindon-ya's close connection with historically stigmatized populations comes in part through this long history of social bias against street performers; but it also has roots in early chindon-ya practitioners' own demographic backgrounds. For instance, with the condition of anonymity, a couple of chindon-ya practitioners shared with me how they learned some of the older-generation chindon-ya practitioners were from the buraku lineage. While this seems to be more of an exception than the rule, it is no surprise, considering chindon-ya's close connection with itinerant performing arts in the early days of its formation. At various points in the history of chindon-ya narrated in *Chindon-ya Shimatsu Ki* (Chronicle of chindon-ya) (1986), cultural critic Horie Seiji notes that chindon-ya themselves have been connected to underclass, impoverished, discriminated against, or marginalized members of society. Requiring no capital but only the voice and body to start a business, chindon-ya has historically appealed to those in desperate economic circumstances: those freshly bankrupt, unemployed, or cast out from society. Many chindon-ya whom Horie interviewed had either failed in their previous businesses and were forced to live on the street, or were born into extreme poverty (1986, 85). It was also not unusual for poor married couples to start chindon-ya businesses.[10]

From the 1930s through the decades following World War II, with the exception of the wartime years that severely limited commercial and entertainment activities, the destitute rushed to chindon-ya as a means of survival. Those who needed to hide from society for criminal or personal reasons also flocked to the chindon-ya business—examples in Horie's interviews included an alcoholic ex-train driver who lost his job, a tax collector who was fired for corruption, an ex-convict, ex-prostitutes who had lost jobs after the prohibition of prostitution in 1958, a traumatized war veteran, and a transvestite. Located outside the long-term employment system with social security and wearing costumes that hid participants beyond the point of easy recognition, chindon-ya—despite the fact that they parade through public space—provided not only a means of livelihood but also a cover for those who would otherwise face job discrimination or rejection.

Today, chindon-ya business, always vulnerable to the fluctuations of the economy, remains a rather modest means of livelihood, and by no means supports a lavish lifestyle. At Chindon Tsūshinsha, the three founding members—Hayashi, Kawaguchi Masaaki, and Kobayashi Shinnosuke—and a few others who also handle the business are salaried members of the troupe, while the rest of the members are compensated for each gig. Since the business opportunities are never consistent (January and August being the busiest months, for example), some members take additional part-time jobs from time to time, from working for moving companies to night shifts as a security guard. The majority of contemporary practitioners I spoke with during fieldwork do not come from socially stigmatized or economically desperate backgrounds. Chindon Tsūshinsha's founding members, for example, come from middle-class backgrounds. They first met and formed a chindon-ya group at university when they were in their early twenties. Some of the younger members of the troupe also completed their university education before joining chindon-ya as a full-time career. Pinkie, for example, joined an amateur chindon group at a university, and despite some opposition from her family members, she pursued her career in chindon-ya without hesitation. Others joined for various other reasons. Seto Nobuyuki, the clarinet player who leads musical projects and actively gigs and tours across Japan, saw that chindon-ya was the perfect opportunity to learn the instrument when he first picked it up. Without having to buy his own instrument or to rent a rehearsal space to practice, he was able to learn the instrument while being paid on the gig. Hirabayashi Naoko (Nao), now in her twenty-fifth year with the troupe, was a high school student when she first saw a chindon-ya troupe while she was working at a bakery. She was so awe-struck by chindon-ya's presence that she felt compelled to become involved. A few years later, when she saw the troupe being featured on the TV screen, she scribbled down the phone number and immediately called the troupe to join. She didn't have much experience with musical instruments or performance—but she quickly picked up the accordion, chindon drums, and gorosu. For both Pinkie and Nao, the fulfillment of making a living through creating encounters every day has been keeping them in chindon-ya business ever since.

Although they themselves do not necessarily embody the alterity that has been historically associated with chindon-ya, the younger members of the troupe share Hayashi's genealogical curiosity. On Hayashi's recommendation, I attended a weekly lecture series on the historical performing arts and discriminated groups, given by local ethnologist Okiura Kazuteru. When I arrived at the lecture room in the community center in Osaka, I spotted Aki, a dancer and member of Hayashi's troupe in her late twenties at the time. Aki told me that she voluntarily attended this course as she felt understanding chindon-ya in a larger context of itinerant performing arts and the social discriminations that accompanied them would make her a better chindon-ya performer. Sitting next to each other, we took notes on the lectures that touched on the marginalized status of various forms of itinerant performers, ranging from itinerant courtesans (*yūjo*), to historical itinerant bamboo artisans and fisherman (*sanka*) and itinerant entertainers (*yūgeimin*).[11] Like Aki, Uchino Makoto, who transitioned from being in a chindon-ya club in university into a full-time member in the troupe, draws connections between chindon-ya and historically marginalized populations, and imagines a sense of solidarity with them. After giving a disclaimer that he could not speak with authority on the accuracy of historical information, Uchino drew a parallel between chindon-ya and *hyottoko*, a typical mask worn for a comical folkloric performance act. He alleged that hyottoko, known for its asymmetrically placed pursed lips, symbolized the physically deformed, the Other, the marginalized minority. He said he aspired to be like hyottoko: for him, the oppressed, marginalized, and yet beloved "difference" popularized in the hyottoko mask resonated with the histories of marginalization embodied within chindon-ya.[12]

In the popular perception today, chindon-ya is not commonly associated with such archetypes of marginalized itinerant performers. By situating chindon-ya within the same racialized and spatialized feudal-era lineage, in theater productions, classrooms, and the imagination, Chindon Tsūshinsha members are forging what Lawrence Grossberg calls affective alliances (1984, 227): "an organization of concrete material practices and events, cultural forms and social experience which both opens up and structures the space of our affective investments in the world." By reworking sedimented histories of itinerancy and street performers, such affective alliances perform a social critique of the historical continuity of oppression across different social and economic systems in the present. In his insightful analysis of a Japanese blackface doo-wop group from the 1980s, Hosokawa Shūhei (1999) argues that the group's nostalgic use of the 1950s aesthetics of doo-wop can be understood as way for working-class youth to deviate from the musical preferences of elitist and educated students. Such a view of obsolescence as a strategic tool to mark one's class difference provides a productive lens through which to understand chindon-ya's close connection with nostalgia and their genealogical performances. Both in oral histories and genealogical performances, contemporary practitioners align themselves with various modes of difference that have been oppressed by shifting social, political, and economic systems—from the semifeudal hierarchical social status system to capitalist modernity, and, as I will show later, the postindustrial present. In doing so, the chindon-ya practitioners make audible the histories of the production of difference that have always underscored the question of who is considered to be the normative subject within the economic, social, and political arrangement of power at each historical moment. As I mentioned at the beginning of this chapter, the zainichi Korean singer Cho Paggie, whose choice to incorporate chindon-ya in his musical projects came from his desire to identify himself with chindon-ya's "strangeness," is a case in point. As I will explore in the next chapters, these imagined and performed affective alliances with various historically oppressed populations open up new possibilities of social critique and political identification.

Here we arrive at a contradiction, however. While chindon-ya's genealogical performances reveal histories of social oppression and the production of difference, there is a contradictory discourse in which chindon-ya's distinct sounds elicit a collective sense of belonging that elides various kinds of difference. As I will show, the same metallic, high-pitched, and resonant sound of the kane that signaled the hereditary status-based discrimination and the religious and ritual roots of itinerant musicians also carries the sound of essentialized, and at times idealized, nationalist discourse of a socially and culturally homogeneous Japan.

Socialized Listening to Kane and Sameness

Kawaguchi Masaaki, one of the founding members of Chindon Tsūshinsha and primarily a banjo and percussion player, became one of my closest interlocutors. Born and raised in Osaka, he grew up in the 1960s in a household where his mother, Nakahana Genyō, taught as a revered shamisen master of the distinctly local traditional performing art called *jiuta*.[13] While this formed the backbone of his aesthetic sensibility and his familiarity with Japanese folkloric and traditional performance arts, it cultivated within him a certain critical distance from both the Western popular music that he enthusiastically devoured as a teenager—Delta blues, Woody Guthrie—and traditional music, which he rebelled against for its hierarchical and purist tendencies. These experiences, along with childhood memories of chindon-ya and other itinerant vendors and performers coming through the back alleyways of his neighborhood, paved the way for him to jump at the opportunity to join Hayashi's pursuit of chindon-ya when they met in college. Alongside his activity in chindon-ya, he dabbled in touring as an emcee with a strip show—in which his wife performed as an avant-garde actress and dancer—and in an apprenticeship at a traditional taiko maker.[14] As a longtime resident of the city, Kawaguchi is extremely well networked among cultural actors and small business owners. Round glasses and a big smile are his trademarks, and his slight resemblance to Osaka's beloved character Kuidaore Tarō makes him appear familiar and disarming to many. He loves to drink—and much of his philosophizing happens at bars. These drinking sessions doubled as debriefing sessions for his recent chindon-ya gigs, as well as ethnographic tours of the particular neighborhood, introducing me to colorful (and sometimes edgy) local characters. Kawaguchi is generous, but also not afraid to challenge or critique me in our conversations, especially after a few drinks; his frank opinions as a sophisticated philosopher of sound and sociality often compelled me to critically reflect on my own work, as an ethnographer of the ethnographers of the street that is chindon-ya.

Over a drink, Kawaguchi once told me self-effacingly and somewhat jokingly that the sound of chindon-ya was merely zatsuon—noise, or white noise. While the chindon-ya sound is often an unmarked part of an everyday soundscape, at the moment of recognition—when it marshals the attention of listeners— it is instantly heard as chindon-ya. The sonic recognizability of chindon-ya is rooted in the distinct sound of chin—onomatopoeia for the high-pitched and piercing sound of the bronze gong-chime kane, and don—onomatopoeia for the ōdō drum. In particular, the distinct timbre of the kane is a clear sonic signal that shifts the listeners' aural sensitivity from overhearing to listening; its piercing, high-register metallic sound carries through the hubbub of the urban soundscape. Kane is played with a deer-horn mallet (shumoku), creating two distinct sonorities by hitting either the center of the circle or the rim. Kane also marks the beginning of every tune when chindon-ya performs; the chindon drummer provides a percussion introduction called uchikomi by improvising a fast rhythmic patterns on kane together with the other drums, often followed by a few beats on the gorosu (bass drum), which sets a beat and signals the rest of the chindon-ya troupe to join and play the tune.

This sound holds significance for chindon-ya practitioners both aesthetically and socially. Chindon Tsūshinsha members expressed the centrality of the kane in various debates about which kane sounded best, and how the instrument could be made to sound better. Some told me quite insistently that the age of the instrument affects its sound quality,[15] or that one can easily distinguish who is playing just by listening to the sound of the kane. Others claimed that a slightly cracked kane sounds better; and Uchino experimented with putting tape on the rim of the kane to muffle the sound and make the instrument sound sweeter. With so much talk around kane among the practitioners, the timbre of the kane seems to hold a key to understanding how and whom the sound of chindon-ya reaches and entices. How are listeners socialized to recognize the distinct sound of kane? What kinds of meanings and identifications are audible in the sound, and who is hailed by the "hearalding" sound of kane as listeners (Neely 2014)?[16] Or, to put it in Althusser's terms, what kind of listening public does the sound of kane interpellate (1971, 189–94)?

While the Chindon Tsūshinsha members discussed historical connections of the kane with religious and folk practices, as discussed above, popular perception today associates kane with traditional festivals, parades, and popular folk dances such as the summertime communal dance *bon-odori*. A sound that is part of the fabric of festive gatherings and dances, kane is associated by many Japanese listeners with the notion of *nigiyakasa* (noisiness/liveliness), or festivity, prosperity, and sociality (see chapters 3 and 4 for more on *nigiyakasa*). Such collective association of the kane sound with festivals often provokes immediate excitement in listeners, luring them to follow the sound to its source. During fieldwork, I too experienced the enticement of the kane sound coming from a distance. One summer day, the sound of kane came through my apartment window. I found myself leaping through the door, barely taking time to make sure I had my flip-flops on properly, and running downstairs to the street. I didn't know exactly where the sound was coming from or why I was in such a rush to get closer to it. After a couple of turns walking toward the sound, I found Osaka's famous *danjiri* summer festival float, with a kane player standing on it, ringing out the instrument with gusto. On the street were many other neighborhood residents, who must have similarly run out of their houses in everyday clothes and slippers, looking for the source of the kane sound.

This affective response prompted by the sound of the kane has taken on a biological, ethno-nationalist overtone for some. Throughout my fieldwork, multiple bystanders described their reactions to the sound of the kane as "*chi ga sawagu*"—literally, "it makes my blood noisy." The phrase captures well the visceral and affective force of the sound of the kane, which moves the listener toward movement in its pursuit.[17] Kawaguchi described how kane aurally triggers an essentialist notion of Japaneseness: "Maybe an image of this kind of tool evokes the 'Japanese DNA,'" he said, borrowing the words of a university student who used the term to describe her reaction to the sound of chindon-ya.[18] In this narrative, the kane sound hails a Japanese national subject by indexing and inciting a festive (nigiyakasa) and bacchanalian spirit in listeners. In the piercing sound of kane resonating across the street today, we hear the allure of the Pied Piper of Hamelin—but this time, the appeal is in the way the sound of kane interpellates the essentialist notion of national collectivity among listeners, not the dialectic of fascination and contempt embedded within the histories of marginalized difference of the itinerant performers.

At times, members of Chindon Tsūshinsha participated in—or perhaps valorized—this essentialist discourse of Japaneseness by locating it in the timbre of kane. In October 2006, four members of Chindon Tsūshinsha performed with the renowned Bosnian singer Jadranka Stojaković at the Sekihōji temple in Kyoto as part of a curated concert series. Hayashi recounted his conversation with the singer in order to highlight the distinctly Japanese perception of the sound of kane: "She [Stojaković] lives in Tokyo now, and she said that she occasionally runs into chindon-ya publicizing pachinko parlors. And apparently, she just runs away with her hands covering her ears. She never thought she would play together with that. What bothered her most was the kane. The pitch. Can't tell if it's *do* or *re*, but there's a pitch to it. Timpani can be tuned, but you know, [kane cannot be easily tuned]."[19] Here, Hayashi is implicitly asserting that the Japanese have been socialized in such a way that they do not hear the pitched ring of kane—even if it is not "in tune" with the melody—as an irritating sound. In contrast, Stojaković, standing in for the "West" in Hayashi's story, finds it unbearable. This narrative is underpinned by echoes of nihonjinron, the pop-academic ethno-nationalist discourse of Japanese cultural uniqueness grounded in the assumption of class, cultural, racial, and ethnic homogeneity. Kane is here taken as a sonic emblem of a national cultural imaginary, grounded in the historical continuity with the premodern popular pitted against the West. Simultaneously claiming the historical continuity of kane in religious folk practices and its affective power to interpellate a Japanese listenership, these chindon-ya practitioners are evoking the notion of monolithic and nationalized subjectivity, in stark contrast to the marginalized difference that their genealogical performances make audible, as I discussed above.

These contradictory tensions are in fact two sides of the same coin. One might consider the outcaste itinerant performers as what Judith Butler calls a "constitutive outside" in the Edo-period Japanese hierarchical social systems: those considered outside the "human" domain, who are in fact necessary to the self-identification of the "subjects" of the society who establish their dominant social position through the exclusion of Others.[20] The seemingly conflicted narratives of difference and sameness audible within the sound of kane, then, put into relief how street performers have been spatialized Others produced as a necessary byproduct of centralized hierarchy and its shifting modes of subject formation for almost a thousand years.

To a certain extent, the enticement of chindon-ya rests on the mutually constitutive tension between these conflicting narratives of the socially marginalized on one hand and a homogeneous social collectivity on the other. But the listening constituents of chindon-ya, interpellated here as national subjects, are not so monolithic or ahistorical (or transhistorical, rather) as this formulation of social cohesion would have it. As I will show next, the obsolescent sounds of chindon-ya work not only as a way for chindon-ya to mark themselves as sharing something with the historically and socially marginalized, but also as a way to highlight the multiple and fragmented class politics within chindon-ya's allegedly homogeneous listening public: taishū—the ordinary people, the popular masses.

HISTORICIZING TAISHŪ

The term *taishū* was everywhere I went with chindon-ya practitioners: *taishū sakaba* (people's bar), *taishū shokudō* (people's restaurant), *taishū engeki* (popular itinerant theater), *taishū yokujō* (also *sentō*, public bath), etc. Variably translated as "the popular," "the mass," "people," or "populace," the term *taishū*—chindon-ya's listening public—simultaneously indexes a complex and shifting matrix of class, historicity, and commercialism.[21] Close examination of how the term *taishū* and the kinds of attendant socialities have changed in relation to the shifting economic formations over the course of the twentieth century—from the emergence of industrial capitalism in early twentieth-century Japan to postwar corporate capitalism and the post-1990s neoliberal economy—illuminates how the listening public of chindon-ya has always been multiple, contradictory, and historically variable.

Although *taishū* has been used as a translation word for the English words "popular" and "mass" in the universalizing discourses about industrialization, capitalist economy, urbanization, and mass media,[22] its most common usage is tied closely to distinctly Japanese contexts.[23] Its etymology is rooted in the Buddhist notion of *daishū*, which initially referred to those who embraced Buddhism, then later to a body of monks-in-learning who have not yet attained positions and who are thus "ruled" by other powerful monks.[24] The term was adopted by the townspeople of Tokyo, which resulted in the use of *taishū* to mean many people who are ruled, governed, or oppressed.

The history of the advertisement industry in post-Edo Japan indelibly informed the formation of not only chindon-ya but also *taishū bunka* (popular/mass culture) at large. By the early 1900s, industrial capitalism and large-scale consumption society paved the way for the formation of mass popular culture in urban Japan. Advertisement had become an integral part of the development of mass popular culture; store signs (*kanban*) and vendor calls (*monouri no koe, onsei kōkoku*) had already flourished during the Edo period, and were not Western imports.[25] The now-powerful corporate advertisement company Dentsū was established in 1907. Large-scale publicity street processions were a common sight, and the earliest forms of chindon-ya emerged as demands for publicity increased with the mass production of goods (see chapter 1). But it was not until after World War II that both chindon-ya's activities and the notion of taishū gained the currency that they are afforded today.

In the immediate aftermath of the war, locally based populist culture—not yet mass-produced—enjoyed a resurgence for a brief period, as a barter-based primitive capitalist economy thrived, especially in the outdoor black markets (*yamiichi, aozora ichiba*) that popped up in the bombed-out cities of Tokyo and Osaka. This created demands for street entertainment like *kamishibai* (storytelling with pictures) and of course chindon-ya, which made a comeback after a hiatus during the wartime years when entertainment and leisure activities were banned. At the dawn of the rapid economic recovery of the postwar years, the collective sociality of taishū was deeply embedded within what anthropologist David Slater calls nonmarket ties (2009, 105): "geographical alliances or kinship-based loyalties that had once bound Japanese society and served as the foundation for social identity." In discussion with me about what taishū means, Kawaguchi Masaaki asserted that this very brief moment in the early 1950s is the source of the contemporary association of taishū with chindon-ya: "It [chindon-ya] used to be for taishū. . . . After the war, from the bottom of things, the whole nation unified to reconstruct the country. Everyone was poor, and that was taishū. Taishū means everyone's the same. But it's not like that anymore today. People don't say it explicitly, but I think what they call 'gap society' [*kakusa shakai*] today is a contrast to taishū."[26] The strong sentiment I have observed during my fieldwork echoes his view. Taishū that is associated with chindon-ya today is imbued with social warmth, neighborhood- and family-oriented sociality, and working-class solidarity that originates in the 1950s—what the Japanese often call *shōwa 30 nendai*. This dynamic communal sociality is not only temporalized, but also spatialized through the trope of working-class neighborhoods, or *shitamachi* (old downtown).[27] Originally referring to an old merchant quarter, *shitamachi* became a general term for working-class neighborhoods with small, shared alleyways where vibrant communal ties governed everyday life (figure 2.4). Shitamachi has now come to signal at once a locality and a way of life, strongly inflected by working-class identities and socialities (Bestor 1989).

During the high-growth postwar recovery period, especially from the 1960s through the early 1970s, the class associations and sociality implied by the term *taishū* began to shift. This was when the national discourse of class homogeneity became prevalent, as forces of standardization and massive equalization of the growing Japanese middle class resulted in the elimination of difference and privatization.[28] As Jennifer Robertson argues, taishū becomes a transcendent category synonymous with the nation in its superclass, superregional orientations that emerged through the propelling forces of the postwar industrial economy.[29] Taishū, at this time, referred to the popular masses, absorbing and modulating the particular working-class solidarity it had signified in the immediate postwar period into the formation of the middle class. This was also the time that chindon-ya's business reached its peak, publicizing the small to midsize businesses that flourished during the period's rapid economic growth. Twenty-five hundred chindon-ya practitioners were said to be active in the country at this time, and the annual National Chindon Contest in Toyama City reached its largest size, with more than fifty troupes entering the competition.

As corporate capitalism gained a stronger foothold, the national imaginary of collective sociality not only became consolidated into the new class consciousness of the middle-class majority, but also shifted away from kinship-based or community relations to the institutional membership of corporate capitalism. Dubbed "Japan Inc.," the corporate system in Japan replaced familial ties that characterized prewar social cohesion, playing the role of social welfare institution during the high economic growth period of the 1970s and 1980s.[30] Continuing to thrive in this reconstructionist economic boom, chindon-ya came to stand in for the image of the postwar homogenization of consumer culture and sociality defined through the market, despite chindon-ya's deviant past and the social status of the practitioners themselves who contradicted the narrative of class homogeneity.

FIGURE 2.4 Chindon-ya on a lively *shitamachi* street, Debosei,
Kyoto, circa 1970. Courtesy of Hayashi Kōjirō.

In a conversation with me in 2007, Hayashi, whose career in chindon-ya started around this time in the early 1980s, recounted a story that exemplified this shift. Speaking of the large popular diners (taishū shokudō) that flourished in the historical entertainment district of Minami, Osaka, he remarked:

Taishū shokudō was a place where the entire family and followers would gather. Same as Kuidaore [another large and famous taishū restaurant in Osaka]. But the energy of taishū disappeared. In front of Sennichidō restaurant, there was a weird papier-mâché statue of a soft-shell turtle that was a mascot for the restaurant. They used to serve anything from turtle (*suppon*) to ramen and hamburgers and pudding. They [taishū shokudō] used to be everywhere until ten years ago. . . . It was a common custom in the fifties, when today's baby boom generation used to be children, and maybe until the seventies. Now they're gone.[31]

Hayashi reminisced about the taishū shokudō that catered to family outings by appealing to all generations: pudding for the children, soba noodles for the grandmother, and beer for the father. As the collective sociality shifted from kinship ties to market ties, however, the "energy of taishū" dwindled, as Hayashi describes above—and the family-friendly menu lost its currency. This had a tangible consequence for chindon-ya. Kawaguchi mentioned that the choice of repertoire had to change as the supergenerational, superclass, superregional notion of homogeneous taishū disintegrated. He told me: "Back in the day, everyone, from kids to grandmas, knew some songs—like the enka tune 'Naniwa Bushidayo Jinsei Wa' [a hit song in the mid-1980s]. But there is no so-called taishū anymore today, so we change our expressions depending on whom we are playing to. For this person, for that person . . . we didn't have to change [songs] in the eighties."

The aspirational national cultural imaginary of middle-class homogeneity of the 1970s and '80s, however, was never monolithic. The homogeneous, populist register of taishū became fragmented through the development of late capitalism, as consumerist society became further stratified and commodities became diversified via the orchestration of the corporate advertisement industry. Contesting the myth of the all-middle-class homogeneity of the '70s and '80s, anthropologist William Kelly argues that, during the rapid standardization of income and formation of the new middle class, differences were not eliminated, but rather restructured (Kelly 2002). While chindon-ya's ubiquitous presence made it associated with the prevalent discourse of class homogeneity at this time, chindon-ya as a symbol of historical embodiment of working-class solidarity and shitamachi sociality remained relevant, speaking to the persisting, if only restructured, class difference that had not yet been subsumed by the mainstream narrative of all-middle-class-Japan. In short, chindon-ya, thriving during these three decades of postwar economic recovery, doubled as a sound that indexed a coherent monolithic mainstream rooted in corporate capitalism on the one hand, and a disappearing sense of prewar collective sociality grounded in communal and familial ties on the other. Chindon-ya embodied both these faces of taishū. Gradually, as the "all middle class" narrative of contemporary mainstream mass culture rose to prominence and became an unmarked majority, *taishū* became the term to mark the dynamic sociality of the immediate postwar years, evoking a tinge of nostalgia. The term *taishū* by this time was being reconsidered as a replacement for the "seemingly elusive proletariat," harking back to its laboring-class roots (Ivy 1993, 248).

This is when class difference takes on a temporal parameter. The social difference that became restructured, that fell outside the "new middle class" mass of corporate capitalism, was registered as also "the past"—the time when sociality was defined not through institutional ties, but through neighborhood relations, kinship, and micro-interactions of everyday life (*seikatsu*). In other words, *taishū* became a classed term associated with past forms of sociality. Taishū, connoting the popular masses, became defined through its otherness in time. As if to signal this relegation of taishū to the past, the taishū restaurant Sennichidō's popularity declined. Eventually, Sennichidō closed in the early 2000s, along with the other taishū restaurant, Kuidaore—famous for its iconic mechanical doll greeting customers at the entrance door—much to the disappointment of Osaka residents and tourists alike.

Even though these taishū restaurants disappeared, chindon-ya remained— and around the 1980s and into the 1990s, the otherness lurking beneath the concept of taishū took on not only a historical but also an ethnic tone. Hayashi said that one of the factors that changed the reception of chindon-ya and saved it from following the declining path of the taishū restaurant was today's youth:

> Lately, young people travel to Asia and enjoy digesting different cultures. Back in the day, people used to mock Asia, Southeast Asia. An ugly person would be asked whether she came from Cambodia, or told to go back to Vietnam. Or, if you got tanned, people would make fun of you and call you an Indian. This is when taishū was popular. . . . What changed [the anachronistic re-

ception of chindon-ya] was not the ministry of culture and science, but the youngsters who are interested in things "ethnic" [*esunikku*]. So it became easier to do chindon-ya business. Traditional Japanese things are starting to be viewed as something ethnic.[32]

The strangeness of chindon-ya has become not only spatialized and temporalized, but also ethnicized. Struck by Hayashi's comment that there is an ethnic othering of chindon-ya, I asked the same question of Aya, then a twenty-eight-year-old chindon-ya clarinet player who was working with him. She concurred, asserting that she sometimes felt that the gaze from the youth made her feel part of the "ethnic" trend that exoticizes otherness as "cool." Although in the 1950s and '60s Asia was racially coded in Japanese popular discourse—very much a remnant of the wartime colonial discourse—and an object of mockery based on Eurocentric values, now "Asia" is newly exoticized and popularized among the young generation.[33] Historian Jordan Sand, observing a similar trend, shows how the consumer desire for a place or time outside prosperous contemporary Japan gave rise to "neo-Japanesque," an exoticist taste for traditional Japan as non-Japanese perceived it; "Asia syndrome," which was rooted in fascination with Asian popular culture as kitsch; and "ethnic boom," which was an "antimodern, part-European inflected colonial fantasy, and part reaction against American-style consumerism" (Sand 2013, 97).

And chindon-ya, according to Hayashi and other members I spoke with, sometimes are viewed with the same gaze. The parallel Hayashi draws between the ethnicized depictions of Asia and chindon-ya echoes Japan's ambivalent relation to the dichotomous undercurrent of "the West" and "the rest" that was operative in the world music industry around the same time (see chapter 1). This ambivalence created the desire to participate in the exoticizing discourses of the Others ("the rest")—the label *esunikku*, borrowing and transliterating the English term "ethnic"—is a testament to this desire to identify with the West as well as to counter the supremacy of Western music through its self-Orientalizing gaze at its own "authentic" roots.[34] By the 1990s, chindon-ya was no longer the sound of the working-class solidarity of the 1950s or the socioeconomically homogeneous ordinariness of the 1970s and '80s. Especially for the younger generations who grew up after the age of taishū, chindon-ya is heard as Other in the register of not only class and time, but also imaginary and consumable ethnicity.

But this sense of otherness, and strangeness, is precisely what has kept chindon-ya relevant, and what has produced its sense of enticement. Even as late capitalism consigned the notion of taishū to the past through the stratification of consumer culture, and more recently to ethnic otherness, chindon-ya stayed in business—precisely because the articulation of a sense of strangeness and discourses of the past became a desirable commodity. Rapid industrialization and the rise of mass culture in the 1980s propelled popular discourses and consumerist desires based on nostalgia[35]—and as an embodied oscillation of historical modes of difference and sameness, chindon-ya was able to valorize its temporalized class difference *and* its temporalizing genealogical performance to appeal to the increasing senses of nostalgic longing in post-1980 Japan.[36] But instead of understanding this oscillation between familiarity and strangeness as mere ambivalence, I call attention to how sameness and difference are expressed through juxtaposition of multiple historical pasts in chindon-ya's genealogical performances. How, in the present moment, do the evocations of historical sameness and difference in chindon-ya's performances—from the long past of the feudal era to the recent past of the postwar—capture contemporary listeners and passersby? What is the logic of temporality in chindon-ya's nostalgic enticement?

NOSTALGIA, INNOCENCE, AND DIFFERENCE

Nostalgia, according to the anthropologist Kathleen Stewart, is a cultural practice that gains particular significance as social life becomes more diffuse, decentered, and fragmented in late capitalism (1998, 227–28). She reminds us that forms of nostalgia are various[37]—and that it is essential to understand particular nostalgias as historically and geographically situated practices. Many scholars who have examined the cultural logic of nostalgia in 1980s Japan have located its root in the cultural anxiety induced by shifting modes of capitalism: the loss of tradition that accompanied rapid industrialization and the development of capitalist modernity, or the diminishing of economic and social security and national confidence that followed the economic bubble burst of 1989.[38] As I referenced earlier, Ivy (1995) calls attention to the ways nostalgia is rooted in the need for representational survivals of "premodern" Japan by examining simultaneously marginalized and codified cultural-national objects of longing. Other case studies of nostalgia in Japan—from the postwar popular musical genre enka to the Shōwa-era retro fashion boom—have similarly tended to regard nostalgia as a technology for producing the cultural-national imaginary of Japaneseness, accounting for the hegemonic processes of national identity formation in postwar Japan.[39] Nostalgia, in many of these cases, is held in an ambivalent tension that chindon-ya's genealogical performances highlight: marginalized otherness—temporal, social, geographical, and so on—on the one hand, and the national cultural imaginary on the other.[40]

Taking this formulation of nostalgia further, I posit that chindon-ya's discourse regarding kane sounds produces a romanticized nostalgic longing not only for the premodern and pre-Western, but also for a precapitalist economy. In a conversation with me over drinks at an *okonomiyaki* (savory pancake) street vendor, Kawaguchi passionately offered his analysis of the continued demand for chindon-ya:

> I think that people have privatized the act of singing too much. . . . People have been singing without even thinking about it every day, since we were born, where there's nothing to do with economy. While everything tangible and intangible and arts are commodified, chindon-ya is at the very bottom. The act of expression—the most fundamental thing that people possess from time immemorial. Celebrities have made [these acts] into privileges. Maybe we [chindon-ya] are appreciated because we evoke natural acts of dancing, talking, and singing that have existed from a long time ago, before being commodified. Maybe we make them sense "the pastoral." It's innocent, and it gives energy. While everyone is progressing, we [chindon-ya] are just casually floating. That's chindon-ya. Otherwise we won't be getting so many gigs. We have been offered more than a thousand gigs a year these past five to ten years.[41]

Kawaguchi positions himself and chindon-ya as a historical remnant of preindustrial, precapitalist economy, where sound was an uncommodified primal social act. Implicit is a critique of musical experience that has been contracted to professional specialists; there is a longing for a kind of innocence, an aspiration for a re-democratization of music as a practice beyond consumption. By distancing himself from the "progress" of contemporary capitalist society, Kawaguchi's conception of chindon-ya as a sonic evocation of the primal and pastoral merges nostalgia for the premodern with nostalgia for the era before capitalism. The nostalgia for innocence, as seen in the trope of children following chindon-ya on the streets described at the beginning of this chapter, returns here as we extend the trope to the market economy; chindon-ya's allure today in part stems from a desire to recover this romanticized notion of innocence— innocence lost through commodification.

Chindon-ya's performance of enticement rests on this tension—it is a commercial enterprise that caters to nostalgia for the precapitalist past. What is important to note in this complex web of contradictions in chindon-ya is Kawaguchi's comment in the conversation I quoted above: "Otherwise we won't be getting so many gigs." The desire for precapitalist, premodern, pre-Western innocence that chindon-ya's sounds allegedly invoke *brings business*. By referring to "music" and "musicians" as notions embedded within capitalist discourse and by maintaining distance from them, chindon-ya themselves capitalize on the notion of their sounds as "uncommodified." Chindon-ya practitioners' persistent refusal to label themselves as professional musicians, and their self-perception of chindon-ya as sound business rather than music (read: commodified sounds), may be understood as a deliberate move to align their labor as unabstracted, primal, "unproductive"—similar to the itinerant performers during the Edo-period semi-feudal economy. Chindon-ya today, then, strategically valorize modern nostalgia for the innocence lost in capitalist modernity in order to carve out a space in their struggle to stay afloat in the contemporary economy that otherwise deems them obsolete.

The nostalgic demand for older forms of sociality increased further as economic growth came to a screeching halt in 1989, an event that was followed by decades-long economic recession. With the restructuring of Japan's economy toward flexible labor, and especially given the post-1991 recession, contemporary Japan has been characterized by the loss of security through work and the subsequent deterioration of social and affective stability. In contrast to bubble-era "Japan Inc.," after social security through corporate, institutional, and family ties became dismantled by recession and neoliberal restructuring, "sociality today has become more punctuated and unhinged" (Allison 2013, 8). In these narratives, precarity of work, sociality, and life are intimately intertwined with the loss of spatial, temporal, and social stability previously guaranteed through lifelong corporate employment and communal membership in neighborhood associations and kinship groups. In this condition, where the recessionary economy and the dissolution of sociality have become the markers of the era, social intimacy has become an object of desire—so much so that commodifications of social relations like rent-a-family and *enjokōsai* (compensated dating, between teenage girls and older men) make news headlines.

The commodification of sociality is integral to the increasing emphasis on what Hardt and Negri call immaterial labor in the postindustrial economy; as the mode of economic production has changed from industrial (goods) to postindustrial (service and information), sociality has become conflated with economic production (Hardt 1999; Hardt and Negri 2001). And in the current moment when anxiety around social precarity produces yearning for forms of sociality that hark back to a precapitalist past, the uncommodified sociality that chindon-ya offers becomes a desirable commodity.

This longing for uncommodified sociality in an economic system that increasingly commodifies sociality poses a conundrum. And I posit that the allure of chindon-ya comes from their ability to provide a temporary suspension of this dilemma through their multiply temporalized difference. By embodying obsolescence and performing multiple historical pasts—from precapitalist social difference to postwar working-class solidarity and the middle-class homogeneity of the 1970s—the sociality chindon-ya evokes taps into a niche in today's increasingly fragmented market and precarious society. Their performances articulate differently historicized class politics and temporalized social difference, thereby enabling listeners to experience—and believe in—sociality outside of commodification, if only momentarily, and even as chindon-ya do so for their own profit.

Having absorbed and reworked the histories of difference, sameness, and conflictual senses of the term *taishū* spanning centuries, chindon-ya has deftly adapted to the changing desires of consumer culture and the advertisement industry by simultaneously embodying multiple temporalities and socialities. Chindon-ya's nostalgia works through a rhythmic oscillation of overlapping historical memories and forces—between narratives of collective and personal memories; pre-capitalist social hierarchy and capitalist abstraction of labor; essentialist and differential discourses of Japanese sociality; pastoral premodernity and industrial modernity; fascination and contempt; marginalization and homogenization; and innocence and danger. Embodying these tensions, chindon-ya's sensory performances hold past and present at once—as if they are suspending time, like magicians of the streets.

The nostalgia of chindon-ya, then, is not simply about longing for a retrieval of a lost object in the past. Simultaneously articulating different narratives of difference and logics of capital—precapitalist histories of hierarchical social status system on the one hand, and abstraction and exploitation of labor in teleological narratives of capital on the other, for instance—chindon-ya's nostalgia unsettles the very assumption about temporality that makes nostalgia possible in the first place. The perception of time here is not of a singular and linear progression, but rather a coexistence of different types of histories. In her work on queer politics of temporality, Elizabeth Freeman (2010) shows how nostalgic longing is predicated on what she calls chrononormativity, a normative conception of time that organizes individual human bodies toward maximum productivity; the linear development of capitalism leaves behind anxieties and longing for past forms of sociality. Freeman offers an alternative in the "counterpolitics of encounter," which is less about restoring wholeness by retrieving a lost object in the past than about a momentary reorganization of time in which bodies that "meet one another by chance, forging—in the sense of both making and counterfeiting—history differently" (2010, xi). In this reorientation of temporality, subjects "refuse to write the lost object into the present, but try to encounter it already in the present, by encountering the present itself as hybrid" (14). Simultaneously embodying historically ostracized bodies and working within the logic of postindustrial capitalism, chindon-ya's genealogical performances echo Freeman's notion of a counterpolitics of encounter that compels us to reconsider the narrative of nostalgia based on chrononormativity. Instead, just as preindustrial spaces such as small alleyways coexist in an urban space organized by global capital in Tokyo (chapter 1), chindon-ya's performance of enticement shows that the teleological Marxian narrative of capitalism and its attendant forms of social marginalization coexist alongside vernacular, antecedent histories of hierarchy, labor, and production of difference in Japan.[42]

―――

As I have shown through the elusive notion of taishū that is closely associated with chindon-ya, chindon-ya has always been implicated within, and constituted through, the gravitational push and pull between narratives of social cohesion and social marginalization. On the one hand, genealogical projects by contemporary chindon-ya like Hayashi's troupe and Ōkuma reveal histories of oppression in Japan that are closely associated with various street performance practices, making audible the otherwise silenced Others who constitutively underscore the formation of national subjectivity. On the other hand, the discourses of the indexical sound of the kane not only put forward an essentialist postwar discourse of working-class solidarity and the class homogeneity of the following two decades, but also invoke nostalgia for the lost innocence of the premodern, pre-Western, and precapitalist past. Further, the sense of collective sociality invoked through the notion of taishū itself is multiple; it contains a populist sense grounded in everyday interactions in neighborhoods or families as well as in a nationalist discourse rooted in institutional membership—both of which are entangled into the popular perception of chindon-ya. In other words, the listening public as sounded out by chindon-ya has always been simultaneously differential *and* homogeneous—layered through narratives of social difference and cohesion, from the past and present.

The performance of enticement, as evident in the ethnographic fairy tales with which this chapter began, lies within these temporal dynamisms. By assembling and layering multiple and at times conflicting historical narratives, memories, and imaginations—whether historically accurate connections or affectively imagined alliances—chindon-ya's genealogical performances activate and absorb shifting class politics, conflicting desires, and longings. The nostalgia that permeates the ethnographic fairy tales, the desire for times past and for childlike innocence, is not simply a longing for a particular historical period. Rather, it speaks to a modernist anxiety that in turn produces yearning for the premodern and pre-Western, to the contemporary mourning of the innocence lost in the process of commodification, and a yearning for social intimacy in the neoliberal present.

Thus, chindon-ya's continued and renewed relevance is not in spite of anachronism, but because of it; by evoking multiple temporalities that are subjects of longing, chindon-ya reveals the simultaneity of different histories and social difference that coalesce in the present moment. Chindon-ya's multiply historicized *and* historicizing performances remind us that local understandings of difference, time, and value are not only contemporaneous with the Western-derived logic of capitalism, but are also operational within that Western-derived logic of capitalism today precisely because they are outside of it. In this light, what we have been considering nostalgia in chindon-ya's performance of enticement might be better understood as a historical resonance: the assemblages, encounters, and juxtapositions of multiple temporalities and memories. Nostalgia in the case of chindon-ya undercuts the temporal designation that makes capital possible; in their counterpolitics of time, time is constituted dynamically through the simultaneity of different temporalities and socialities that are both within and outside the narratives of capital and labor. At once familiar and yet stigmatized, the magically enticing performance of chindon-ya echoes within these historical resonances, leading listeners astray in place and time. The next chapter will pursue further how chindon-ya practitioners perform enticement by sounding in ways that resonate with not only memories and histories, but also listeners' affect, as well as with the acoustic geography of the city streets through which they walk.

CHAPTER 3

Sounding Imaginative Empathy

Three brightly costumed chindon-ya performers stood in front of a crowd of young and curious domestic tourists in central Osaka. They were in an indoor entertainment theme park called "Paradise Shopping Street" (Gokuraku Shōtengai), which was replete with faux shops reminiscent of an outdoor shopping arcade from the 1920s and 1930s (figure 3.1). The leader of the troupe, Hayashi Kōjirō, began a performance with uchikomi, the rhythmic percussion introduction customary to chindon-ya street routines, as discussed in chapter 2. After the concluding rhythmic gesture on the drums, the clarinet player Kobayashi played a J-pop slow ballad called "Hitomi o Tojite" in his distinctly strident timbre, while Kawaguchi provided harmonic accompaniment on his four-string banjo. Just as the song was ending, Hayashi introduced his group in his well-projected voice with a melodious and eloquent speech: "We are chindon-ya, a ludicrous roadside advertisement business with musical instruments [*narimonoiri kokkei robō kōkokugyō*]. We've been in this from since the Meiji period (1868–1912), allowing Shiseidō, Lion [a well-known personal care and pharmaceutical company], and Asahi Beer to grow into [the large successful companies] they are today. But we have remained as we were: quite modest."[1]

Speaking on behalf of chindon-ya as a whole, Hayashi rather unabashedly and humorously took credit for economic prosperity in Japan. Claiming responsibility for nurturing a few of the largest and most globally successful Japanese corporations, Hayashi situated chindon-ya at the root of the development of Japan's capitalist modernity. However, while boasting of chindon-ya's con-

FIGURE 3.1 Hayashi Kōjirō, Kobayashi Shinnosuke, and Kawaguchi Masaaki of Chindon Tsūshinsha. Ebisuza, Paradise Shopping Street, 2007. Photo by the author.

tribution to the companies that support the nation's economy today, Hayashi also set chindon-ya apart from corporate conglomerates, as if to take the side of the "people," implicitly drawing a social division between the popular masses and corporate capitalism. While Shiseidō, Lion, or Asahi may have expanded over time, Hayashi maintains that chindon-ya groups have stayed the same, still true to their popular roots. Chindon-ya practitioners themselves have often been socially marginalized throughout history, and their sonic and visual presence became synonymous with the working-class majority's everyday life by the 1930s (chapter 2). Combining humorous overconfidence and humility in his rhetoric, Hayashi created an air of familiarity and stoked feelings of affinity between chindon-ya and the audience, assuring the crowd that the chindon-ya are on "their side" of the corporate-proletariat divide. Having thus offered a sense of shared alliance and intimacy, the troupe performed short songs with banjo, accordion, and trumpet to entertain the audience for small tips.

Although this indoor performance is atypical of chindon-ya, Hayashi's self-introduction highlights chindon-ya's dilemma: it is inextricably embedded in capitalist modernity, yet is also often closely associated with those marginalized by corporate capitalism. Furthermore, Hayashi's narrative of chindon-ya's history highlights the shifting conditions of the streets in which their activities take place. As I have discussed in the previous chapters, chindon-ya's ubiquitous presence in the 1950s cemented its association with everyday soundscapes, neighborhood streets, and taishū—the popular masses, or the "people."

Today, however, chindon-ya exists in the midst of city streets saturated with technologically mediated sounds, the results of urban development that has rezoned and paved small alleyways, and an acute sense of widening socioeconomic gaps among the Japanese population that has made the term *taishū* almost obsolete. As neighborhood streets change, and as the homogeneously conceived notion of the popular masses is disintegrating, what do we make of chindon-ya's sustained presence on the streets in Japan today? From listening to chindon-ya's sounds, what kinds of understandings of public space, sociality, and the listening public emerge in the contemporary soundscapes of urban streets in Japan?

In this chapter, I argue that turning an ear to chindon-ya's soundings challenges a widely received narrative that equates the development of a neoliberal capitalist economy with the abstraction of the urban landscape and the dissolution of public intimacy. Such teleological discourse reduces space and sound to merely results or mirrors of economic and political power. Listening to chindon-ya's sounds, however, impels us to understand the significance of what Lefebvre calls "representational spaces": spaces of the lived particularities and contradictions concealed within homogenizing conceptions of abstract space ([1974] 1991). Inherently social and spatial, chindon-ya's soundings elucidate complex social relations that actively produce a dynamic understanding of public space. Through a close ethnographic analysis of chindon-ya's street routines, I examine the notions of public space and the listening public that are heard, seen, sounded, and imagined through chindon-ya's advertisement enterprise in contemporary Japan.

To unfold my claim, I move through the historical, the social, and the sonic. First, I give a historical overview of the spatial aspects of chindon-ya to contextualize the changing geographies of public space and sociality in which chindon-ya has been situated. Next, I explore the social by examining how attention to listeners' sentiments informs chindon-ya's improvisatory musical practices. This aesthetic and ethical sensibility, which I call imaginative empathy, enables chindon-ya to negotiate public space and pursue the twin goal of gaining profit and producing collective intimacy. Lastly, focusing on the sonic, I examine the relationships among sound, space, and sociality, showing how chindon-ya's labor rests upon the production of *hibiki*, or affective and acoustic resonances. Chindon-ya's historical sensibilities, attunement to the acoustic environment, and ethnographic attention to social and spatial dynamics of the streets help produce hibiki, which in turn evinces the unevenness, precarity, and politics of exclusion within the social relations that produce public space.

SHIFTING GEOGRAPHIES OF MODERNITY: STREETS, PUBLIC SPACE, AND SOCIALITY

It [chindon-ya] was not music that controlled space;
the way the music co-existed
with the landscape was refreshing to me.

Ōkuma Wataru (2001, 10)

Paradise Shopping Street, the indoor theme park I described at the beginning of this chapter, was designed as an imitation of a typical Osaka city street in the late Taishō and early Shōwa periods (1920s to 1930s), a time when chindon-ya enjoyed great popularity (see plate 2). Owned by Sega Corporation, one of the largest multinational producers of video game software and hardware, the theme park opened in 2004 in one of Osaka's most popular tourist destinations, Dōtonbori. A bustling shopping and entertainment quarter since the Edo period (1603–1868), Dōtonbori was a host to five theaters for kabuki and jōruri (traditional puppet theater), all of which closed during the economic downturn of the 1990s. Today, many of the individually owned shops have been replaced by larger chain stores and pachinko parlors, which blast music and sales pitches from speakers onto the street. Famous for bright neon signs and large-scale billboards—including the famous Glico runner and the gigantic, mechanized-leg-toting Kani Dōraku crab—Dōtonbori is visually and sonically saturated, teeming with young shoppers and domestic tourists (figure 3.2).

With its long-standing history of popular performing arts and commerce, one might assume that Dōtonbori would provide a natural home for chindon-ya's street routine. However, members of Chindon Tsūshinsha gave me evidence to the contrary. Because of a local shop-association policy, coupled with tight police surveillance of the foot traffic in the area, chindon-ya are not allowed

FIGURE 3.2 Dōtonbori area, Osaka. Photo by Trane DeVore.

on the streets in Dōtonbori. Chindon-ya practitioners instead must perform indoors in a commercially designated site for entertainment. Seizing the business opportunity, Hayashi's troupe gave weekly performances for tourists who would visit the theme park, and also opened a shop in the faux arcade, serving sweet rice ball desserts (*dango*) and tea. Despite the relative popularity of their performances and sweets shop that provided additional income for the troupe, the long-term economic recession impacted the Dōtonbori area, and Paradise Shopping Street went bankrupt in 2008, only four years after its opening.[2]

At a first glance, Dōtonbori's troubles can be read as a story of how the "street," the locale where chindon-ya thrived in the 1930s, became abstracted, commodified, regulated, and eventually eradicated as Japan's economy developed. Indeed, significant shifts in the Japanese urban landscape have taken place since the 1930s, changing the conditions and understandings of the public space in which chindon-ya did their business. While a multitude of such changes warrant detailed analysis, for the purpose of this chapter I will briefly outline the general shifts most relevant to the analysis of chindon-ya's street routines.

Owing to the forces of modernization and capital accumulation that propelled the country's economy, the Japanese urban landscape has shifted drastically in the past several decades. In Osaka and Tokyo, major cities that both suffered major air raids during World War II, postwar city planning and zoning policies transformed small side alleyways and wooden houses into concrete housing complexes and wider paved roads for car traffic. Similarly, open-air black markets were transformed into regulated and enclosed shopping venues. Typical housing for the lower- and middle-class population shifted from *nagaya* (long wooden one-story houses occupied by multiple households, divided by thin walls) to nuclear family apartments beginning around the 1930s. After postwar reconstruction, and during the economic boom of the 1950s and 1960s, *danchi*, or multistory concrete housing complexes, proliferated across cities and suburbia.[3] These physical changes affected the acoustic environment for chindon-ya. As I will discuss later, changes in the layout of cities had tangible consequences for the ways chindon-ya performed, as the permeability of sounds through porous wood decreased and the reflection and reverberation of sounds increased in the new, more concrete landscape.

The shifting geographies of modernity affected not only the acoustic environment for chindon-ya, but also the cultural understanding of public space and the sense of sociality on the streets. While there are several terms in Japanese that correspond to the English word "street," the ones that have historically been closely associated with chindon-ya tend to connote narrow, small pedestrian streets, such as *yokochō* and *roji*, roughly translated as "side alleyways" and "backstreets."[4] These side alleys, often formed by passageways between low-income housing structures such as nagaya, have historically been considered the "place of everyday life" (*seikatsu no ba*) and a discursive site where sociality was produced among the working-class public (figure 3.3).[5]

The disappearance of these neighborhood streets through urban development in the postwar period created narratives of the abstraction of social relations and the alienation of public space. For example, retrospectively commenting on his 1957 photograph of a small alleyway with children at play, the photographer Tanuma Takeyoshi observes, "*Roji* [backstreet] is a story of human sentiments. *Roji* . . . is my favorite place that smells of people's everyday life. However, at the peak of the bubble economy, *roji* was erased, and *nagaya* turned into apartments. There, the everyday life of warmth no longer exists" (1996, 41).

Similar sentiments are shared in contemporary TV programs—including a "walking tour" (*sanpo*) of an old Tokyo neighborhood, during which celebrity

FIGURE 3.3 Chindon-ya on a backstreet, Chindon Shiogama CM Sha, Shiogama, 1957. Courtesy of Sugawara Eiji.

guides wander into a small alleyway in search of the remnants of the old ways of life. Admiring small chairs casually left in the alleyway, the celebrities imagine what kinds of conversations and interactions happen in such small streets: "This feels like the neighbors have good and close relations [*gokinjo zukiai ga yosasō*]." Such comments lament the vanishing sense of dynamic sociality due to urbanization and real estate development—echoing the spirit of the street observation study movement (chapter 1). Privatization of what was once public space and increasingly tight police regulations on performance or commercial activities on the street further cemented the story of capitalist abstraction of public space causing the disintegration of public intimacy.[6]

This sense of social fragmentation deepened further as Japan went through a long period of economic crisis after the collapse of the economic bubble in the early 1990s. Following a series of events that afflicted the national psyche—the Great Hanshin Earthquake, the sarin gas attacks, a widely publicized Okinawa rape case in 1995, among others—sensationalist media coverage of the crisis of public sentiment continued to proliferate.[7] As I detailed in chapter 2, together with the neoliberal policies that widened social economic gaps within the population (*kakusa shakai*) and the shift from industrial to consumer and information industry, the persistent economic recession has brought an end to the lifetime employment system in Japan that supported the prior economic and moral stability. Instead, the Japanese market economy has become increasingly dependent on flexible labor. Today, there are reportedly almost half a million *furītā*—people between the ages of fifteen and thirty-four who lack full-time employment, or who are unemployed or underemployed.[8] The irregularly employed (*hiseiki koyō*) make up about 40 percent of the labor force in Japan today. Sabu Kōsō describes the visibility of furītā on the streets: "Today's young people . . . tend to hang out on the streets instead of shopping in fancy stores. More and more they are beginning to look like what they really are: street kids" (2006, 416). Many of these furītā find themselves on chindon-ya territory, working similar jobs publicizing businesses through the distribution of free tissue flyer-packs and holding advertisement signs.

In some ways, these narratives of spatial and social alienation offer insights into the larger historical shift that Japanese cities have undergone. Chindon-ya's soundings, however, question the teleological narrative that attributes the demise of public space and sociality to the expansion of corporate capitalism. Under this assumption, chindon-ya become simply nostalgia, indexing a disappearing "popular mass" with social warmth, on the verge of vanishing along with the dynamic sociality of side alleys. But, as we have seen in the previous chapters, chindon-ya did not simply become abstracted into the commercial space, or become a remainder of the romanticized notion of social warmth that once existed in small alleys and neighborhoods. Despite being labeled as anachronistic and obscure, some chindon-ya troupes today have achieved financial success, generating up to a million dollars in annual income. After all, the chindon-ya performers I described at the beginning of the chapter continue their usual advertising business on the streets throughout Osaka and beyond, even after the imitation side alleyways of the Paradise Shopping Streets have disappeared. What makes chindon-ya viable and sustainable as both an aesthetic and economic practice today, when the initial conditions in which it developed no longer hold true in contemporary Japan? The key to answering this question, I suggest, lies at the intersection of political economy and economies of affect. As I have shown through historical analyses of chindon-ya's performance of enticement in chapter 2, the forms of sociality chindon-ya attends to have persisted and thrive *within* the current arrangements of capital.

SOUND BUSINESS AND IMAGINATIVE EMPATHY

Chindon-ya's business is first and foremost a work of producing sociality through sound. As I have described earlier, in the words of Kobayashi Shinnosuke, one of the founding members of Chindon Tsūshinsha and an experienced chindon-ya clarinet player, chindon-ya is a "sound business," rather than music business. In this manner, most chindon-ya perceive themselves to be firmly positioned outside the music industry. As advertisement enterprises on behalf of other businesses, troupes are not selling their music per se, but are using music in the commercial interest of their clients' businesses. Chindon-ya's goal is not to sonically produce an immediate correlation between their sounds/voice and a product, service, or brand. Quite unlike jingles, which are designed to trigger an automatic "catchy" association between sounds and products or brands, chindon-ya's enticing sonic performances marshal listeners' attention without directly signaling a particular business or product being advertised.[9]

To conduct this sonic advertisement business soundly, according to Kobayashi, chindon-ya must achieve twin goals: "chindon-ya has two aspects—to bring joy and pleasure to people we've never met before, and to publicize the client's business."[10] I asked Hayashi what the key is to achieving these two goals, and what he considers to be the most important value in chindon-ya. Without hesitation he answered, "Definitely, the ability to imagine. To imagine the state of mind of people. Inside their heart—of people in front of us, of people inside their houses, or perhaps I might somehow intuitively feel them even though they might not even exist."[11]

"Reading the mind" (kokoro o yomitoru), "reading the atmosphere" (kūki o yomu), "imagining the listeners' emotional state": these were recurrent phrases in the conversations I had with chindon-ya practitioners throughout my fieldwork. I was struck by how profoundly these entrepreneurial street performers cared about the sentiments of those their sounds reached—not only passersby on the street, but also shop owners, office workers indoors, and invisible inhabitants behind the walls of residential areas. To be effective in their business meant cultivating the ability to imagine who might be listening, to care about what those listeners' sentiments might be, and to instill joy or spirit in them through music, forging interpersonal connections with and among the audience. In other words, the production of affective interpersonal relationships is at the heart of chindon-ya's musical advertisement enterprise.

I call this practice of caring about and imagining listeners' sentiments imag-

inative empathy. Imaginative empathy informs the social, spatial, and sonic aspects of chindon-ya's performance practice; for chindon-ya practitioners to feel that they have had a successful performance, their playing must create sounds that resound in the listeners' hearts (*kokoro ni hibiku, kokoro ni jīn to kuru*). As musical labor whose commercial enterprise is inextricably linked with the production of affects, chindon-ya presents a compelling case in which to analyze the relation between capital and "social warmth" (Stokes 2002, 146), a sense of collective intimacy forged through social encounters. In the sound business of chindon-ya, this work of affective resonance—sound triggering certain imaginations, memories, or sentiments—is as tangible and consequential as the production of acoustic resonance itself. A closer look at chindon-ya's business practices illustrates how chindon-ya's affective labor challenges the alleged tension between the production of social warmth and pecuniary pursuits; it highlights how their labor regains relevance in the current postindustrial economy, in which social relations and economic production are increasingly collapsing into each other.

MACHIMAWARI: NEGOTIATING URBAN SPACE

Chindon Tsūshinsha's office is in the Tanimachi Rokuchōme neighborhood, one of the oldest areas of Osaka, and one that has retained its historical architecture, monuments, and streetscape. The office is footsteps away from the Karahori Shopping Arcade (Shōtengai), a half-kilometer-long street with a roof over it, lined with individually owned shops, from a tofu store to a fish store to a bar. During my fieldwork, the troupe had two locations one minute's walk from each other: the office space (*jimusho*), where business calls are taken and meetings are held, and the workshop space (*seisakusho*), where instruments, wigs, and costumes are stored.[12] Rehearsals and some other events took place in the workshop space as well; it was the center of the troupe's professional and social activities. On some days, when I follow a street routine gig called *machimawari* ("going around town"), I meet the troupe in the workshop early in the morning, where they put on makeup and costumes before leaving for the destination of the day. They discuss the nature of the gig and their client as they choose their costumes, sometimes taking into consideration the season and what's trending in pop culture. The day before, some members have already designed and printed out a sign for each specific gig: a big sign for the melodic instrumentalist to wear on his or her back, and another smaller sign to hang from the chindon drum set. We usually take the train to the gigs—sitting on the train in full costume with their instruments and signs is already a bit of a publicity act—unless the clients are a long distance away, in which case we take the van. At the end of the day, after several hours of walking and sounding through city streets, we return to the workshop space for post-gig debriefing. As the practitioners take off their costumes and carefully put them away, one of them fills out a report form, while others are relaxing and socializing over snacks and sometimes drinks. Kobayashi calls the report form the "most important document" for Chindon Tsūshinsha; I find these reports to be much like field notes taken by ethnographers. The report form is used to keep records of the client's name, kind of job, location, members, expenses, and impressions and observations, from reactions of the client and customers to the areas they walked through. Any information that might become useful in the future is noted on the form, so that other members who take a similar job can reference it to better prepare their costumes, strategies, and so on.

Chindon Tsūshinsha's work includes a wide range of activities: playing at *matsuri* festivals, New Year's ritual lion dance performances (*shishimai*), entertaining foreign guests at receptions, workshops for schoolchildren, dinner shows, and appearing as extras on TV or film sets. But far and away the most common and central form of business practice remains machimawari, the street routine. Except for starting and ending the day in front of the store of their employers, the routes and their schedules are never predetermined; the itinerary is impromptu. Walking down the streets while playing music and giving out flyers is called *nagashi* (flowing). During nagashi, a troupe member without a musical instrument moves about most actively; he or she approaches passersby and nearby shop owners to hand out flyers (*bira kubari*), striking up small conversations. Occasionally, the troupe stays in one spot for five to twenty minutes, often at the client's storefront or at intersections. This is called *itsuki* (settling). Settling on a street corner, the troupe often delivers speeches about the employer's products or the services that they are advertising. These activities are repeated in different neighborhoods throughout the day, with a short break every hour.

Where to take a break can be much more of a problem than one might expect. On one warm winter day in Tokyo, I was following the troupe Chindon Yoshino. About an hour into the gig, the troupe stopped sounding their instruments to take a break. They walked into the Inari Shrine nearby, which is dedicated to deified fox spirits believed to govern the realms of businesses and scholarship in Shinto religion. I was lagging a couple of minutes behind, and by the time I caught up with the chindon-ya at the shrine, they had already put their instruments on the ground. The gorosu player was paying respects to the deities, throwing coins and praying with palms together in front of her face. Others were drinking tea, sitting down on the stairs (plate 7). "You know, it's hard finding place to take a break. You can't obstruct the foot traffic on the street, you can't just walk into someone's shop or house. Shrines and temples are few of the rare spaces where we can go in and rest comfortably," said Yoshino. I had seen plenty of occasions when chindon-ya took a break at a café or a convenience store; but they would always have to pay, and they would nonetheless stand out a bit. This was part of being bachigai (out of place); their ostentatious appearance and the itinerant presence made it difficult to fit in anywhere enough to rest comfortably. Shrines, which are meant to be open to all visitors, are a children's playground and somewhat of a sanctuary for the itinerant and vagabonds. With the increasing regulation of public space in recent decades that has left less and less room for people to simply linger, rest, or even sleep, the scarcity of such a milieu keeps chindon-ya moving.

While walking, it is no simple task for chindon-ya to navigate the urban streets. One veteran troupe member, Kawaguchi Masaaki, spoke of how seemingly spacious shopping arcade streets are in fact filled with informal and complex territorial lines, leaving very little space available for chindon-ya to walk through (plate 5). The unspoken rule, according to Kawaguchi, is that in front of each shop there is a one-meter radius semicircle that is felt to be the shop's territory. While this may overlap what is legally a public road, overstepping such territorial boundaries would upset the shop owners, hindering the relationships between them and chindon-ya's current employer and those between the chindon-ya and the shops, who might be potential clients in the future. As a result, in a small shopping arcade, chindon-ya troupes almost always walk right in the middle of the path. Whenever possible, they make eye contact with shopkeepers who step out to hear them, and bow while performing and walking, as if to say "sorry for the noise—we'll be done shortly. And if you like us, hire us in the future!"

With all these spatial dynamics to attend to, chindon-ya practitioners constantly scan their surroundings. While walking, they look not only to their immediate surroundings but also into the distance, above and behind: the tenth-floor verandas of a huge apartment complex; the window two floors above street level where people poke their heads out to look down; a storefront thirty meters behind where they have passed, where their sales pitch sparked conversations among passersby (figure 3.4). For example, on a machimawari gig one day, we were stepping into a quiet and narrow residential street in Fuse, Osaka. The chindon-ya practitioners kept playing even though there was no one in sight for as far as my eyes could see. Suddenly, the chindon drummer looked up; there was a young couple on the third-floor balcony of a small apartment complex looking down at the troupe with smiles. He shouted to the couple: "Oh hello all the way up there—it feels like we're playing in a stadium! We are here today to introduce you to the opening of a new bar (*izakaya*) near the station. Please stop by later this evening if you can! Thanks!" The couple waved back as we started walking. These moments always impressed me; even though the troupe seemed to be aimlessly wandering about, and even though there seemed to be no one watching or listening in the immediate vicinity, chindon-ya are acutely aware of the surroundings, noticing listeners and spectators in places where untrained eyes would not catch. It is necessary for chindon-ya members to gauge whom their sounds are reaching, how their presence and sounds may be affecting listeners, and how they might create relations with listeners by walking over to them to talk, or by making eye contact and waving.

In addition to the unspoken social and acoustic dynamics that inform the urban streets, chindon-ya are constantly negotiating official traffic and noise regulations enforced by the police. Since the 1960 implementation of the Road Traffic Law, chindon-ya's activities have become more and more strictly regulated.[13] More recently, commercial associations in many of the vibrant, busy downtown areas in big cities—like those in Dōtonbori, as I described at the beginning of this chapter—have forbidden chindon-ya and other street performance and advertisement activities. In other areas, it is required by law that chindon-ya obtain permission from the local police to march through particular areas if they will potentially obstruct traffic. In reality, however, chindon-ya practitioners do not necessarily always follow this rule, receiving only implicit police approval. The expectations and dynamics between chindon-ya, police, and local merchant associations vary greatly from region to region. In Osaka, in many cases, the police prefer not to enforce any regulations in the interest of saving time and avoiding potential complications; by covertly expecting chindon-ya not to submit applications, the police will not be liable even in the rare instances when chindon-ya cause trouble. In turn, chindon-ya skip the bureaucratic process of submitting the application form and, in exchange, keep their sonic and physical presence modest, particularly around police stations

FIGURE 3.4 Children looking out a window at chindon-ya.
Photo by the author.

and officers on duty. On numerous occasions, I have seen them stop making sound upon encountering police, instead simply walking by while giving a small courtesy bow.[14]

Walking, moving, and listening together with chindon-ya during their machimawari presents a starkly different understanding of public space from the homogeneously conceived notion of absolute space, as those who are anxious about the erosion of Japanese sociality argue has come to dominate the national discourse. Much like Lefebvre's notion of representational space, chindon-ya's spatial negotiations during their street routines elucidate the dynamic and ever-shifting forces that inflect and inform everyday lives on the streets, while their clandestine, informal relationships with law enforcement reveal the porousness and contradictions of allegedly public streets as conceived and controlled by city planners and lawmakers.

HIBIKI: AFFECTIVE AND ACOUSTIC RESONANCES

Physical space is negotiated not only through walking, but also by sound. For example, chindon practitioners suddenly stop their drumming and playing when passing in front of a client's competitors, especially if they have been hired by the other businesses in the past. When they are advertising for a pachinko parlor, they stop and quietly walk past other pachinko parlors in town to avoid inciting unpleasant feelings of competition and annoyance. In quiet residential areas or near hospitals, sometimes the troupe members also stop sounding their instruments out of respect for those inside.

In discussing their performance practices with me, many of the chindon-ya practitioners appear to place high value on a deeply reflexive mode of listening to their own sound at all times. Carefully choosing the repertoire, dynamics, timbre, volume, tempo, etc., they attempt to make their sound resonate with the sentiments of potential listeners, who may be overhearing their sound both indoors and outdoors. This process, in which the performers are constantly improvising to adjust their own soundings to the demographics of each neighborhood, the sensibilities of the (imagined) listeners, and the acoustics of each locality they walk through, is at the heart of chindon-ya's labor that I call hibiki: the production of affective and acoustic resonances. The production of sociality through sound, underscored by a deeply reflexive and relational way of listening and sounding, is central to chindon-ya's affective labor.

Chindon-ya's sounds reflect, deflect, and become amplified or absorbed as they disperse through the surrounding acoustic space and seep through walls and doors to meet the ears of listeners. How these sounds resonate with the physical environment is of prime importance; the acoustics of each space that chindon-ya walk through—a dirty road as opposed to concrete buildings, a residential area as opposed to crowded and loud train stations—affect their performance choices. In order for chindon-ya to lure listeners and to avoid being perceived as a sonic nuisance, Hayashi emphasizes the necessity of carefully listening to one's own sounds and their resonance in the acoustic environment. He noted that he needs to be more sensitive to listening to himself in relation to his surroundings today than he did thirty years ago, as small sounds are amplified when reflected on the concrete surfaces of buildings and pavement, which are more common today than they were in the past. Although sounds do not pass through concrete walls as easily as they used to permeate one-story wooden structures, today, in quiet areas, sounds can still reach some listeners behind concrete walls. Takayoshi, a slender, friendly member of Chindon Tsūshinsha for the past twenty-seven years of so, added how the temperature and weather influence their sound: "It's about whether you can let your sound resonate far through the air. When it's hot and humid, or rainy, the sound of kane feels heavy, for example." This highlights how architecture and the environment—walls, streets, buildings, and the atmosphere—have an active role in the production of hibiki in chindon-ya's sonic performance of enticement.

With imaginative empathy, chindon-ya practitioners listen to the lingering resonance of their sounds (*zankyō*), and the distance and volume with which the sounds travel (see introduction). This careful listening to one's sound is essential, since the degree to which chindon-ya's sounds resonate, or might not resonate, with the potential listeners, indoors and outdoors, has tangible consequences: to gain or lose a potential listener. A multi-instrumentalist who has worked as a flyer person (*bira kubari*), chindon drummer, accordionist, and a gorosu player at Chindon Tsūshinsha for twenty-five years, Nao knows well the difference between effective hibiki that acoustically and affectively resonates with listeners, and an unsuccessful one—and the difficulty of achieving just the right sensibility to make a good hibiki. Having worked as a flyer person when other members of the troupe played the chindon drums, Nao noticed how the sound of chindon drums made a difference in the way townspeople responded.

> Of course, you must be personable, disarming, charming—you have to make an atmosphere to make it easy for passersby to talk to chindon-ya. It's different, depending on a place—a crowded area like Umeda and Namba is hard; the day laborer's neighborhood Nishinari on a payday is relatively easy. You have to think carefully how to select tunes to make a dramatic arc over a twenty-minute period, if you're playing itsuki [staying put in one place]. But at the end of the day, it comes down to the sound on chindon drums. If it's the good sound, people come out in droves. That's when you know. I've experienced it firsthand—when other troupe members play drums and when the drum is resonating nicely, people just come out of the woodwork. And flyers are gone before you know it. But when the chindon drummer isn't doing so well, I have to work like crazy to make up for it, to engage with people on the street.

Nao described to me her ideal sound that she aspires to make as a chindon-ya: "It's not about good technique, but good sound—a sound that's not too loud when you hear it from close by, but that resonates across [*hibiki wataru*] beautifully when you hear it from a distance." The affective and acoustic resonances of hibiki are inextricably linked in chindon-ya's pursuit of the production of sociality on the streets. Chindon-ya constantly negotiate the social and acoustic dynamics that constitute public space, imagining the sentiments of listeners (who may be on the street or at home), listening to the surrounding soundscape, and adjusting their performance practice in real-time to each conjuncture. Deeply grounded in the relational approach to their social, affective, and environmental surroundings, chindon-ya flexibly sound out a site-specific, improvised performance of imaginative empathy in order to produce effective hibiki—and that, after all, is what their clients hire them for.

HIRING CHINDON-YA: *NIGIYAKASA*

Chindon Tsūshinsha do not have a set price for their performances. Potential clients, store owners, and larger advertisement and event organizing companies call their office to negotiate each deal individually. Many factors determine the final cost: the hours, the length of a campaign if it is for more than one day, the size of the troupe, the distance of travel, the type of performance, and the relationship between the troupe and the client. On an average street-routine gig, the troupe charges a flat fee of approximately ¥15,000 to ¥30,000 (approx. USD$130–265) per member, which is usually paid in cash at the end of the day.[15] The pay comes from their clients, not from the potential customers on the street with whom they interact and for whom they are performing. With no direct compensation from their immediate audience, the chindon-ya troupe is free to orient its performance around developing social connections with the listeners outside the confines of a business transaction. The lack of social obligation for the passersby to pay the performers allows chindon-ya to be both closely embedded within the commercial enterprise of advertisement and to be able to develop social warmth with people around them.

What complicates this picture is the practice of *goshūgi*: a type of voluntary audience tipping practice in recognition of good performances. While it is an expected gesture from the audience in *taishū engeki* (popular theater),[16] goshūgi is much more subtle, infrequent, and complex for chindon-ya. For chindon-ya, tipping is not expected, and thus there is no pressure on the audience to tip unless they feel compelled to do so. Goshūgi is often given in small envelopes handed secretly to the chindon-ya practitioners. Since goshūgi is not compensation for their advertising work, the musicians do not consider the tips income, but rather a rewarding sign that they have successfully reached the hearts of the audience and instilled sentiments of joy in them. Thus the money is pooled to fund celebratory occasions instead of being distributed as salary. This form of nonobligatory and affectively motivated money-giving outside the consumerist business-customer relationship again shows the complex ways that money and social warmth complement each other in chindon-ya's business practice. Different modalities of understanding the relationship between money and sociality—the Edo-period custom of money as a social gesture of appreciation, and capitalist modernity's principle of contractual labor—are simultaneously operative.

Interviews with both employers and practitioners show how chindon-ya's economic success is inextricably linked with the production of affective interpersonal relations. The manager of a pachinko parlor right by the JR Sannomiya station, in Kobe, told me of his business's strategic shift from newspaper ads (folding colorful flyers into the evening newspaper) to chindon-ya. While including a colorful flyer in a local paper reaches a wider audience across the city, the manager realized that it would be much more effective to directly target those who pass through the station. For the same cost, the manager preferred to target the local neighborhood in person (*chiiki micchaku gata*), instead of an anonymous wider audience, who may not come near the Sannomiya station on a regular basis. The owner of a hair salon in a lower-income neighborhood in East Osaka explained to me that his primary motive in hiring the troupe for his store's opening was to "enliven the neighborhood." By hiring chindon-ya, he not only gained new customers, but also created new alliances among neighboring shop owners, who all benefited from the chindon-ya's presence and the sense of nigiyakasa (festive liveliness, noisiness) they brought to the neighborhood to stimulate local commerce.

Nigiyakasa is a key term for chindon-ya, especially in Osaka.[17] It is used to describe much of what their business is about: bringing liveliness and sociality on behalf of the establishment they are hired to publicize (figure 3.5). The word originally referred to the harmonious state of being achieved through active gathering of many people; over time, it has taken on additional meanings describing the noisiness that comes with dynamic interactions among a large crowd.[18] Simultaneously referring to the sound and the sociality of large gatherings, *nigiyakasa* describes both the conviviality of social gatherings and the resultant raucous sounds of interactions, multiplicity, and prosperity. Providing nigiyakasa by hiring a chindon-ya troupe thus is a gesture of a business to contribute to the larger community of local residents and commerce. Similarly, a pachinko parlor owner who hired chindon-ya told me that he did so partly to create a friendlier façade for local customers who may otherwise have a negative impression of his establishment, since pachinko is a form of gambling and

FIGURE 3.5 Chindon Tsūshinsha bringing *nigiyakasa* to customers
at a Korean grocery store, 2013. Photo by the author.

is often associated with organized crime. So while chindon-ya's clients' interests are primarily economic, these interests are achieved via the production of social warmth; the clients are equally invested in creating lively relations with surrounding businesses and residents by hiring chindon-ya.

AESTHETICS OF ANTI-INDIVIDUALISM

Chindon-ya practitioners privilege interpersonal communication and social connection over masterly musical performance; it is these facets of the work that give them a sense of reward and success. Seto Nobuyuki, a clarinet player working with the troupe for the past twelve years, told me: "You can get as much done during the break as while walking down the street, because that's when the passersby come over to us to chat." The number of people he gathers for face-to-face conversations is a more tangible sign of accomplishment than the financial return brought to the employer. "It's fine if I don't get around to delivering the sales pitch, and instead just listen to people's life stories and gossip. It's fun to connect with people. That's the best part of being in the chindon-ya business."[19] It is this conviviality that further draws the audience, creating a productive feedback loop where social warmth and pecuniary pursuits are mutually and recursively constitutive.[20]

Sustained through this feedback loop, chindon-ya navigate the various forces that inform and inflect the public space of the streets. Guided by imaginative empathy, they improvise their performances accordingly, determining where to go, how long to stay in one place, where to take a break, what to play, and how to perform. While some choices, such as the size of the troupe, gender balance in the group, and costumes, are made in advance based on the employer's request, most of the performative aspects of their soundings are determined spontaneously—including repertoire, dynamics, timbre, and the duration of a performance. Referring to the importance of improvisatory skills and sensitivity to respond to and reflect setting and atmosphere, Hayashi likened chindon-ya to other performance styles that require such skills, such as jazz and live accompaniment to silent film: "[Is chindon-ya] self-expression? Maybe, but not really. It's more like film music. Adapting to each landscape and atmosphere, we think of what kind of sounds would touch [people's] hearts. Like a jazz improvisation session. You have to walk from *genba* [a place where things happen] to *genba*, and decide [how to perform] based on inspirations you get right there and then. What you play is based on what bubbles up in that spot."[21]

Echoing Hayashi's assertion, Takada Yōsuke in Tokyo also said, matter-of-factly, that chindon-ya is not a form of self-expression (*jiko hyōgen ja nai*); Ōkuma Wataru, sitting next to him, nodded enthusiastically. Deflection of the practitioner's expressive agency was a repeated theme in many conversations I had with chindon-ya practitioners across Japan. The point is not to be heard as an autonomous self; it's not even necessarily to be heard at all, in fact. Hayashi described the ethics of sounding as a chindon-ya by stating that the sales pitch (*kōjō*) must sound in a way that it's okay if it's heard or not heard (*kikoe temo kikoe nakutemo ii oto*). Their cavalier mindset to speak and sound in a way such that it doesn't matter whether they are listened to is at odds with the sense of individual agency central to the notion of a liberal subject. The sounding philosophies behind the production of hibiki, instead, imply an anti-individualistic aesthetics and relational conception of sociality that extends to one's surroundings and climate.

Tokyo-based saxophone player Shinoda Masami captured a similar sentiment, deflecting the aesthetics and ethics of the autonomous liberal subject in his commentary on improvisation in chindon-ya. Shinoda was widely recognized as the spearheading figure of the current resurgence of chindon-ya in

Tokyo, but was also particularly influential among free jazz players and improvisers in Tokyo who have started performing with chindon-ya as freelance melody instrument players (*gakushi*).[22] Although the resulting sounds are vastly different, the sensibilities cultivated through performing as a chindon-ya and as an improviser have a significant overlap. Describing the kind of sounds he strived to produce as a chindon-ya, Shinoda said: "There are many sounds that override noise. I don't want to make such strong aggressive sounds, but rather sounds that can merge with other sounds, sound that can't be overpowered but won't overpower others. It's not something an individual can do, but it can only be possible through collaboration, spatially and temporally. This is the kind of thing that I've thought about while playing with chindon-ya."[23]

Speaking about the listening philosophy he has developed working as a chindon-ya, Shinoda expresses his understanding of chindon-ya's sonic practice as inherently relational—acoustically (creating sounds in relation to other sounds in the environment), socially (through collaboration), spatially, and temporally. For Shinoda, the increasingly oversaturated soundscape of the urban streets of Tokyo does not inherently impede the survival of chindon. Rather, what captivated him, especially as a free improviser, was the challenge of creating sounds that could be simultaneously in place and out of place, without creating hierarchies amid the competing "noise" on the streets. This deeply relational orientation underlines the aesthetic and ethical principles of chindon-ya's approach to their improvisatory practice, whereby resonances are actively produced through sonic, social, temporal, and geographical articulations at every conjuncture.

ON IMPROVISATION

Chindon-ya practitioners' attention to their own acoustic resonance in relation to the physical environment sheds light on two key aspects of their performance of imaginative empathy: listening to one's sounds as if through listeners' ears, and the importance of unmediated sounds (*nama no oto*, live sounds). Hypothesizing that the ears of part-time chindon-ya horn players (*gakushi*) in Tokyo have been socialized differently from those of the full-time chindon practitioners in his troupe in Osaka, Hayashi maintained that "they [Tokyo-based musicians who work part time as chindon-ya] are used to performing on stage, listening to their own sounds through the monitors. But they don't know how they are actually heard by the audience. It becomes the sound engineer's job to create the sound as delivered to the audience. That would feel really uncomfortable and disorienting to us."[24] Hayashi here hints at the relevance of live performance on contemporary streets that are filled with technologically mediated sounds, and highlights the importance of imaginative empathy, grounded in the way chindon-ya practitioners listen to their own sounds as if they were themselves the listening audience.

Such production of multiple resonances that reach listeners effectively requires a constant feedback loop of listening, imagining, and sounding that is engaged simultaneously with the present, past, and the ensuing moment. Here, I take a detour through composer and improviser Pauline Oliveros's conceptualization of improvisation. For her, improvisation consists of four simultaneous and mutually constitutive processes: actively making sound, imagining sound, listening to present sound, and remembering past sound (Oliveros 1974; Von Gunden 1983). I propose a parallelism here: chindon-ya, too, not only actively make sound, but imagine the sound yet to be played, listen to the present sound through both performers' and listeners' ears, and remember sounds and meanings sedimented by the past. In other words, chindon-ya's performance of enticement is deeply rooted in the production of multiple resonances that echo within the acoustic landscape, social space, affect, memories, and bodies of listeners. Sounding in order to create affective resonance is therefore contingent on past, present, and anticipated sounds carefully listened to, and imagined, by practitioners. As Shinoda Masami's quote above highlights, improvisatory performance required of chindon-ya is a relational process in which sound, history, sociality, and geography are imaginatively brought together. For Shinoda and many other contemporary musicians who gravitated toward chindon-ya sounds, improvisation, in Oliveros's sense, offers a key to understanding the appeal and relevance of the allegedly outdated practice today, as well as the unlikely collaborations between chindon-ya and various musical practices (see chapter 4).

When telling me about how spontaneity and sensitivity are required to listen and adjust to particular geographical, historical, and social conjunctures, Hayashi likened his approach to that of a DJ, conductor, or arranger: "[When] playing chindon-ya drums, I have to keep the beat, but that's going to sound boring to the listeners. So I have to think about how to complement the melody instruments. I play drums as a melody instrument, you see? And I'm leading the troupe, too, so I have to be like a conductor. I'm also a DJ . . . because you play so many different kinds of songs. Whatever song you are playing, you need to cook it appropriately [for the occasion]."[25]

Choosing what tune to perform is crucial, as the goal of the chindon-ya performer is to marshal the listeners' attention and to invite them into conversation with the chindon-ya. Chindon-ya practitioners are as much like ethnographers as they are performers in this regard; their intimate knowledge of urban geography, affective dynamics, and the rhythms of people's everyday lives informs their performance choices. For instance, in the Harinakano neighborhood of southern Osaka, where there has been an out-migration of youth to other parts of the city, veteran clarinet player Kobayashi played tunes that would appeal to the elderly who have stayed behind in the neighborhood. Most of the pieces were enka songs, to which some of the passersby mouthed the lyrics.

Kobayashi elaborated extensively on how he determines what tunes to perform and how they should be played. He reminisced about his first days in chindon-ya, when he had only three or four songs that he repeated all day. With experience, however, Kobayashi has not only increased his repertoire (he claims to have fifteen hundred Japanese popular tunes, one hundred Dixieland jazz tunes, and an uncounted number of Western popular tunes under his belt), but also became more sensitive to the variables that determine what tunes he ought to play at a given time and place. The season, time of day, type of business being advertised, listeners' tastes, and whether the troupe is staying put or marching down the street are important factors to consider in tune selection. He described how he chose tunes at a given moment during the street routine: "It's best if the bystanders start to hum along. . . . For those under age fifty, everyone knows 'Nagaragawa Enka' [Enka of Nagara-river]. Under thirty, they know the Doraemon theme song [a popular TV cartoon theme]. There are actually many of those *natsumero* tunes [nostalgic melodies], not today's pop songs and enka songs. You have to think about people of different generations than your own to get this. Hit songs don't necessarily work."[26] Taking this into consideration, Kobayashi chooses the tune that will appeal most widely and effectively to the listeners at a specific time and place—for example, he would play the theme song from the children's animated television program *Anpanman* when walking through a residential area in the late afternoon. By attracting children through their beloved cartoon theme song, chindon-ya are able to appeal to mothers on their bicycles who go to kindergartens to pick their children up, drawing them into conversation (figure 3.6).

Likewise, knowledge of the local population's daily schedule is also an important factor that determines chindon-ya's performance choices. Before the troupe members leave to walk around town, they look at a map to have a rough

FIGURE 3.6 Chindon Tsūshinsha striking up conversations
with passersby, 2009. Photos by the author.

idea of how they might proceed through a neighborhood in order to strategically arrive at certain locations at a specific time. On one occasion, the troupe timed their eight-hour performance so that they would pass by a large electricity company's entrance gate at lunchtime to catch the businessmen taking a break outside. They preferred to walk through residential areas in the early afternoon, when housewives were at home. By the late afternoon, they wandered toward grocery stores to catch housewives shopping for dinner.

At each location, the troupe adjusted the volume of their performance to the surroundings and the reactions of the passersby. When staying put at a busy intersection in a densely populated area, or hired to add festivity at a local summer festival, the chindon drum player would play with enough volume to cut through other competing sounds. They are not afraid to hit the kane and drums loudly; at some festivals, the troupe even doubled the number of drummers. In contrast, when walking through a quiet residential area during the day, the drummer plays much more softly, and uses the kane and larger drum sparingly. With hard concrete buildings reflecting the harsh, high-pitched sounds, they are especially sensitive to those who may be napping, or needing peace and quiet at home. Hayashi elaborated on the drummer's sensitivity to volume: "In quiet residential areas, you can hear small sounds. So if you play loudly, people won't come out [of their home]. You have to play with sensitivity and delicacy. Otherwise you'll be annoying them." Listeners indoors in these residential areas with acoustically reflective architectural surfaces seem to respond most to the spaciousness between the melody and the faintly audible but distinct sound of kane—with just enough drumming to imply the rhythmic framework of each tune.

CULTIVATED IMPERFECTION

While choosing an appropriate tune that will appeal to the targeted generation is a crucial skill in sounding imaginative empathy, chindon-ya practitioners' focus is never on developing a vast repertoire, or acquiring mastery in performance skill. In fact, a virtuosic performance is consciously avoided. On numerous occasions, members of Chindon Tsūshinsha have shared with me their trick of intentionally making mistakes. Impressing the audience with an awe-inspiring performance is counterproductive; it would reproduce the conventional audience-performer framework within which an audience passively observes and is often expected to pay performers.

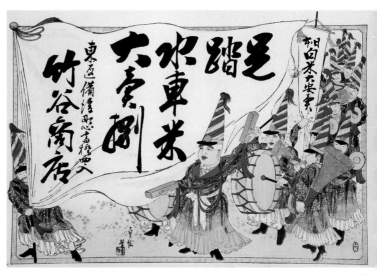

PLATE 3 The whole troupe
Chindon Tsūshinsha, 2015. Photo
courtesy of Hayashi Kōjirō.

PLATE 4 Three founders
of Chindon Tsūshinsha:
(*from left,*) Kobayashi
Shinnosuke, Kawaguchi
Yoshiaki, Hayashi Kōjirō.
Unless otherwise specified, all
photos in the plate section were
taken by the author.

PLATE 5 Chindon Tsūshinsha,
walking in the middle of
shōtengai (shopping arcade).

PLATE 6 Chindon Tsūshinsha
in Kamagasaki, 2017.

PLATE 7 Chindon Yoshino,
taking a break at Inari Shrine,
Shinmaruko, Kawasaki, 2010.
Yoshino, the leader and the
only cross-dressing chindon-ya
in Tokyo, is at bottom left.

PLATE 8 Annual Toyama City Chindon Conkūru (contest), 2007. *From left:* Kawachiya Ryūtarō (Nagasaki), Takinoya Hifumi (Tokyo), Takada Yōsuke (Tokyo), and Midoriya Susumu (Tokyo).

PLATE 9 Adachi Tomoshige (*left*) and Kozuruya Kōtarō (*right*), demonstrating the art of costume construction. Chindon Hakurankai (Chindon Expo), 2007.

PLATE 10 Chindon Hakurankai (Chindon Expo) in Ueno, Tokyo, 2007.

PLATE 11 Takada Sendensha
at Menuma Summer
Festival, 2008.

PLATE 12 Tōhoku Chindon
Summit: Chindon-ya from
across Japan gathering in disaster-affected Ishinomaki City to
cheer up the locals, 2013.

Chindon-ya also try to avoid being perceived as a representative of their client, instead maintaining a somewhat neutral presence as "hired guns" that just happen to be publicizing a particular store one day. They maintain autonomy from the sphere of business in a way that reflects the line Hayashi drew between large corporations and chindon-ya in the speech I quoted at the beginning of this chapter. Hayashi explained this delicate endeavor of establishing neutrality with humor, intentional mistakes, and cultivated imperfection:

> We are irresponsible. If we identify ourselves completely with the client, the potential customers will drift away. So we have to be somewhat random and neutral. If you follow the manual, then the audience will not even be interested in having conversations with us. So we would sometimes deliberately mispronounce the name of the shop, or pretend to not know exactly where the shop is when somebody asks us where it is. Instead we ask the local people to tell us where exactly it is. That kind of irresponsibility invites the agency of the audience; they are interested in engaging with us.[27]

By deliberately sounding amateurish, or by mispronouncing the names of local businesses and schools, chindon-ya performers are hoping to make themselves more approachable. The cultivated imperfection of their performance in turn invites audience interaction. Passersby laugh at the mistakes; some even come up to correct them. Many choose to stay and listen instead of hurriedly walking away to avoid the expectation of payment after the performance. The lack of financial transaction between chindon-ya and potential customers, and the intentionally humorous and "irresponsible" performance style, thus minimize the distance between chindon-ya and audience, inviting listeners to engage in social relations in which they did not expect to participate.[28]

Kobayashi also told me that while choosing a tune to appeal to a particular generation can be an effective tool for reaching the audience, he does not always prioritize song selection. Rather, Kobayashi sometimes chooses songs for his own enjoyment, even if they are tunes that not all passersby will recognize. For example, I once heard him play tunes by ABBA, the Bee Gees, and Earth, Wind & Fire within the same hour. His rendition of "September" by Earth, Wind & Fire caught me off guard; I couldn't be sure if I was hearing what I thought I was hearing. The unique instrumentation of the clarinet, bass drum, and chindon drums without any harmony or bass line made the tune not immediately recognizable. It took me listening through the chorus of "Stayin' Alive" to realize what tune Kobayashi was playing—the tune was obscured by the strident and nasal timbre of the instrument and particular inflections of the melody. Kobayashi once told me that chindon-ya's clarinet must imitate the "horizontal breathing" technique for vocal production, rather than the "vertical breathing" technique that characterizes Western conservatory training. Kobayashi sang in *bel canto* to illustrate the latter; then he argued that the former cuts through the urban hubbub much better, just like the street vendor calls—now imitating a fish store clerk selling the catch of the day. These different vocal timbres, he said, translate to the clarinet. Furthermore, chindon-ya's melody instrumentalists often make generous use of *kaeshi* (scooping up to a pitch from below) at the beginning of each phrase—a small vocal gesture widely found in Japanese popular musical genres. Through these distinct timbral and ornamental approaches to his instrument, Kobayashi made the clarinet sound like a Japanese enka voice even when performing the U.S. pop hits.

During the break, I asked him whether he had indeed played the tunes I thought he had. Kobayashi smiled and said: "Well, I thought I'd play a game to see if you'd recognize those tunes. Good ear!" This was a striking moment—not only was he playing for his own enjoyment, but he also gestured toward me, the ethnographer who constantly followed him around. I considered this a testament to his skill in the art of deepening relations with listeners, both imagined and abstract audiences and specific individual listeners on site. Kobayashi was able to do this without risking the loss of the audience, because, in his words, "it actually doesn't really matter all that much what you play; it's more important to make *good sound*. As long as the sound blends well with the sound of the chindon drums and the kane."[29]

At another instance, Kawaguchi echoed Kobayashi: "You don't have to put on a good performance, but you have to make good sound." Rather than the excellence of a musical performance or the choice of a tune, chindon-ya's performance of imaginative empathy pivots around the production of *good sound*. What, then, is a "good sound" that produces effective resonances for chindon-ya's advertisement enterprise? Why do chindon-ya's sounds, in particular, have such an immediate and enticing effect on listeners? And how, exactly, is good sound heard by listeners?

HIRED TO BE OVERHEARD

Hayashi Kōjirō and Shinoda Masami, two influential figures who spearheaded the chindon resurgence in the late 1980s and early 1990s, respectively, have their own stories about how they became enticed by chindon-ya's sounds—so enticed, in fact, that they eventually became chindon-ya themselves. Shinoda described his first experience of chindon-ya, which came in 1983, on his afternoon walk through a small neighborhood in Tokyo: "Inexplicably awe-inspiring sound was being carried my way—it wasn't music, it wasn't anything soft and simple like that. Elderly people dressed up in flamboyant military band uniforms were making unidentifiable, flaccid music. . . . Although flaccid, everyone's vibration was in total sync, and I felt something so powerful I couldn't speak. It was something that never existed in the music that I had heard of or passed through before" (Okuma 2001, 104–5). Hayashi recounted a similar experience and the strong and inexplicable emotional reaction he felt during his first encounter with chindon-ya's sounds. One day when he was a university student, he was at home feeling somewhat depressed about his own musical abilities: "Then, the sounds of the raw trumpet came through the window—sound that I'd never heard before. The melody bounced off the walls of my small apartment room as if they were mirrors, animating my heart. I couldn't help opening the window and leaned out of the second-floor window. Then I saw the chindon-ya disappearing into a small alley right beneath me" (Hayashi 2006, 9). Chindon-ya's sounds seeped through Hayashi's apartment window and walls, transforming his living space and making him curious to find their source, only to disappear. In Hayashi's account, the ephemerality of this sound and its directional nature triggered a strong and immediate affective response—one so strong that Hayashi wanted to make similar sounds himself. Importantly, it was not a particular repertoire or virtuosic skill that made a lasting impression on either of these listeners. Rather, they highlight the importance of the irresistible and arresting effects of sound. In both narratives, there is a moment of recognition, a moment in which their ways of listening shift.

Several important features of the way the two men describe sounds leap out of their accounts. First, they were surprised by unexpected sounds; they were not attentively listening, but nonetheless the sounds *came* their way without being anticipated. Second, they did not see the practitioners at first; they heard the sounds at a distance. Third, the intrigue came from knowing that there were actual live performers producing this sound. The unexpected, spatialized, disembodied, live sounds of chindon-ya made both Shinoda and Hayashi impulsively look out the window to find out where the sound came from.

Commonplace Japanese words used to describe the practice of "listening" help to explain much about local modes of audition around chindon-ya's sounds. When chindon's sounds are described in conversations, people use the verb *kikoeru*—a special inflection of the verb *kiku*, to hear or to listen. Although one usually uses the standard form of the verb *kiku* to describe listening with intention, such as to an iPod or a concert performance, it is extremely rare, if not awkward, to use the same verb for chindon-ya sounds. Instead, one uses the conjugation *kikoeru*—to be / can be heard. The subject of the sentence here is no longer the listener but the sounds; in this grammatical structure, to a certain extent, sound takes on an agentive quality. The direct translation would be "chindon-ya sounds can be heard."[30]

In addition, once it is inflected passively, a sense of spatiality emerges in the connotation of the verb. While *kiku* is simply "listening," *kikoeru* carries a sense of "overhearing"; without the intentional, focused activity of listening, sounds are carried over space to reach one's ears. Nao used another verb to confirm this point, saying that chindon-ya need to make sound that can be let past through their ears—*kikinagaseru*, literally "let-flow-listening." The sound is evanescent and flowing, meant to be sensed by the ears of the listeners but without discerning attention. Using her neighbor-auntie who developed neurosis as an example, Nao described the kind of listening an ideal sound would elicit. The neurosis made her neighbor-auntie extremely sensitive to sounds, and she could not stand the sounds of TV or radio, and almost all music. For Nao, good chindon-ya must make a sound that would gently pick up even this neighbor-auntie's oversensitive ears (*mimi sobadateru yōna oto*), as she overhears chindon-ya amid the sounds of everyday life. One does not listen to chindon-ya sounds; one *overhears* them. This means that to perform so as to entice listeners involves sounding in ways that promote peripheral, spatialized listening. One does not need to intentionally listen to be touched by the sounds of imaginative empathy.

HIBIKI AND PUBLIC INTIMACIES

The notion of sound "touching" a listener—a physical metaphor for the effect of sound on one's affect—shows how sound can be a significant dimension through which a sense of intimacy can be produced.[31] R. Murray Schafer explains (2003, 11): "Hearing is a way of touching at a distance and the intimacy of the first sense is fused with sociability whenever people gather together to hear something special." This attention to sound's ability to reach across physical boundaries and elicit embodied sociality across distance underscores chindon-ya's sound business "to be overheard."

This becomes particularly relevant when listeners at a distance can be touched by chindon-ya sounds *without seeing* the chindon-ya performing. The separation of sounds and visible sound source can have a powerful affective effect on the listener. The primal hide-and-seek initiated by sounds without visible sound sources has been theorized by Michel Chion as *acousmêtre* (1994, 1999).[32] Originally coined by Pierre Schaeffer in the 1950s, the term "acousmatic" refers to sounds that are heard without their cause or source being seen. With development of telephone, radio, TV, recording, and film technologies (where one might hear sounds in the sound track that do not match what is on screen), the disconnection between what you hear and what you see—what Shafer calls schizophonia—has become a common modern sensory phenomenon (Shafer 1977). Although this notion was coined to describe technological mediation, it nonetheless helps highlight this sonic particularity of chindon-ya, as chindon-ya's sounds are often heard at a distance and often indoors, from a place where listeners do not see the performers. Film editor and theorist Walter Murch argues that this gap between what one hears and what one sees can produce "mass intimacy," highlighting sound's ability to speak to a large number of people in a such a way that each viewer feels the filmmakers are speaking to him or her alone. Murch explicates how sounds can achieve this effect:

> This metaphoric use of sound [without its literal source visible on the screen] is one of the most flexible and productive means of opening up a conceptual gap into which the imagination of the audience will reflexively rush, eager (even if unconsciously so) to complete circles that are only suggested, to answer questions that are only half-posed. What each person perceives on screen, then, will have entangled within it fragments of their own personal history, creating that paradoxical state of mass intimacy where—though the audience is being addressed as a whole—each individual feels the film is addressing things known only to him or her. (2004, 1)

As the earlier quote from Hayashi demonstrates, the analogy he draws between chindon-ya practices and live film scoring might not be a coincidence, especially in light of the fact that Hayashi reveres the older generation of chindon-ya practitioners who had the experience of playing in silent cinema theaters. Elaborating on how he imagines the sentiments of the listeners while performing, he evokes an effect of mass intimacy much like Murch's:

> What moved me when I was playing the trumpet with an experienced older chindon drum player was how they arranged a dark, morbid song into an energetic tune with their drumming. . . . It [the performance] needs to be sad, but we also need to bring it in a positive direction. That wins sympathy . . . people with a dark shadow need to be pulled toward the sound, but they want to be cheered up. It's just like taishū engeki [popular itinerant theater]. Often their stories are about tragic heroes. It's sad, but there's something powerful behind them. But if there's a happy ending, the audience won't be satisfied. They'll feel like, "Oh, it's just me who's unhappy and miserable." I think that's the secret of taishū entertainment. We have to bring the audience to the state that's much more tragic than they are, then pull them out of it.[33]

Chindon-ya's sounds, addressing listeners at large in public space, resonate with individual listeners who overhear in ways that they imaginatively make relevant in their personal stories. During a machimawari gig in a residential area, I saw a woman in her sixties who came out of her apartment wearing an apron and sandals. Seeing me following the troupe from over twenty meters behind with a video camera, she walked over to ask me what the chindon-ya troupe was advertising that day. After I told her that there was a new Korean barbecue restaurant opening near the train station, she said: "Ah. I felt so melancholic listening to their sounds. Funny how they sound so cheery, but it reminds me of my childhood friend who just passed away. She and I used to go see chindon-ya on the streets all the time when we were little." Another woman, on her way home with burdensome grocery bags, responded to her, speaking of her own childhood memories of chindon-ya. The two women, who didn't seem to know each other previously, began to chat. I followed the chindon-ya, and the women were still deep in conversation when I looked over my shoulder a few blocks down the street. Chindon-ya's soundings not only elicit individualized mass intimacy, as Murch suggests, but also facilitate social relations among those who would not otherwise interact.

Unlike cinema, however, chindon-ya's sounds are live, and not recorded for reproduction; the acousmatic allure does not come from schizophonia, or the technologically mediated splitting of sound from its original source. The audience can overcome the schism between the sound and its source by tracing sounds to their sources. Even when one hears chindon-ya only from afar, or behind the walls, there is a shared knowledge that chindon-ya practitioners are performing live—therefore guaranteed social encounters—where the sound is coming from. The chindon-ya sounds arouse curiosity in listeners and invite them to close this gap, thereby drawing them into unexpected social interactions with the troupe members or others who similarly have been lured by chindon-ya's soundings.

What makes chindon-ya's soundings more complex, and potentially more enticing, is that the sound sources are constantly in motion, thus making the search for the sounding source more of a challenge, if not a mystery. The bulk of my fieldwork was taken up by this auditory hide-and-seek; unless I left together with the chindon-ya troupe in the morning to the site of their work for the day, I could only show up in the relative vicinity, then listen for the chindon-ya sound in order to chase after the moving target with my ears until I caught up with the practitioners. Marked by unpredictability, chindon-ya sounds echo against alleyways and buildings, are muffled by layers of walls, merge with other sounds present in daily life, sounding at the threshold of possible perceptibility at times. It is the promise of sociality offered by the alluring acousmatic sound-in-motion of chindon-ya that motivates and entices listeners to seek the sound source. Catering to the listeners in particular places, chindon-ya practitioners sound out imaginative empathy to create a sense of collective intimacy that resonates across both the individual listener's personal history and the public urban streetscape. Sounding and listening, both among the chindon-ya practitioners and listeners, are entangled in hibiki—this process of acoustic and affective production of sociality. Resembling what Kathleen Stewart calls ordinary affect—"public feelings that begin and end in broad circulation, but they're also the stuff that seemingly intimate lives are made of" (2007, 2)—chindon-ya's resonances work both ways: chindon-ya practitioners address listeners at large through their sounds, imagining the listeners' sentiments; in turn, the listeners hear in ways that are distinct to each of them, imbuing the sound with their own personal stories, imaginations, and memories.

CHINDON-YA'S PRECARIOUS LISTENING PUBLICS

As shown above via Murch and Chion, chindon-ya's sound can provoke powerful questions about public intimacies, as its acoustic properties reach individuals across physical boundaries, and its affective qualities elicit kinds of attachments that enable individuals to forge unexpected social relations.[34] Referring to the variety of contacts among people made possible by live musical performance, and the spatial proximity it helps create, Jocelyne Guilbault offers an analysis of public intimacies in Trinidadian *soca* music (2010, 17).[35] I extend her analysis of musical sounds and public intimacies to think through the contacts and proximity that emerge through chindon-ya's soundings as they stretch out across and beyond immediate geographical environments and into the potentialities latent in the affective and imagined resonances of hibiki. I ask: What kind of listening public emerges from the fine textures of the collective intimacy forged by chindon-ya's soundings and attendant forms of listening? When the sense of postwar working-class solidarity embedded within the notion of taishū has become obsolete in the neoliberal present, who constitutes chindon-ya's listening public (*chōshū*) today?

While there are always many who hurriedly pass by chindon-ya and choose not to listen—this happened frequently in busy urban areas, especially near train stations—certain patterns emerge among those who overhear, listen, and respond to chindon-ya's sound during my fieldwork. A few elderly folks clap along or hum along to the tunes chindon-ya play, while children run up and start excitedly talking to the troupe, tugging at their instruments or the costumes. Some—many young women, but also some middle-aged men—take pictures or videos of the troupe with their cell phones or SLR cameras, sometimes requesting to pose together with the chindon-ya. Some bicyclists dismount and stop, asking the troupe what they are publicizing. Many walkers turn around to look and listen from some distance away, while chatting with others who did the same. In residential areas, and especially during warm months when windows are kept open, many people stick their heads out their windows, while others step out of their houses in their casual outfit, sometimes even in their pajamas or underwear. Although one might expect that some would step out to complain, this is very rare; I witnessed no incidents of complaint during the two years I followed chindon-ya almost daily, and when I ask chindon-ya both in Osaka and Tokyo, they answer that complaints are rare exceptions rather than a frequent occurrence.[36]

Among those who stop mid-walk on the streets or come out of their apartments, more often than not overhearers who engage with the sound of chindon-ya have smiles on their faces. The elderly would almost always say, "Ah, chindon-ya! They're still around!" Another frequently heard phrase among these listeners was "*genki o moratta*" (they gave me good spirit, or they lifted me up). Nao recounted to me a story that made her feel that she had done her job:

on a street routine, she noticed a grandmother waving at her a good distance behind where they had passed. When she trotted back to her, she noticed that the grandmother was crying, saying, "Thank you for coming, I've been sick and homebound for so many days, but I heard your sound and it made me want to step out. I was wondering what was up. Thank you." If a chindon-ya could have one interaction like this—meaningful conversations, affective engagement that showed that their hibiki did touch a listener—then they would feel their job was successful that day.

This is no simple cheerleading task on the part of chindon-ya, according to Hayashi. He offered a lengthy comment, elaborating on the way he perceives sounds, space, listeners, their sentiments, and his role in reaching out to them:

> After all, I am playing to people [who are] at home. It took me twenty years to realize that: [I need] to make them want to come outside. [To do that I have] to understand who is at home during the day on a weekday. [I have to] look at the atmosphere of the town, and [their] income. Happy healthy people are out at work. Those who are home are the sick, housewives, unemployed, physically disadvantaged, the elderly, grandchildren. It's rare to find a happy full-time housewife. [Housework is] heavy work, and the husband is busy and rarely home. They are doing laundry sadly. So we take them outside and make them feel like something good could happen. It's almost . . . like visiting hospital rooms to cheer them up. It's like a mental hospital of the town. It's rare to find happy people around here. . . . We have to make sound that would make the depressed want to come out.[37]

Chindon-ya practitioners' empathetic sounds reach across physical boundaries in hopes that their resonances might invite those inside to come out of their rooms, onto the veranda or into the street to forge new social relations with chindon-ya, among themselves, and with local commerce. Streets, often assumed to be an abstract space of social anonymity, become a site of social warmth when home is considered a place of isolation.

In this elaboration on how imaginative empathy inflects chindon-ya's sounding practice, Hayashi highlights chindon-ya's ethnographic sensitivity to geographically delineated difference produced in the registers of gender (housewives and their domestic labor), class (the unemployed), physical ability, and age. On the streets, where chindon-ya's sonic practice is oriented toward any and all who might overhear their sound, chindon-ya cannot assume that everyone is readily available to be part of the boisterous, prosperous, and lively sociality of nigiyakasa. In fact, Hayashi's observation above demonstrates how few people are predisposed to that affect of liveliness and prosperity. And chindon-ya are less invested in capturing the attention of those who are already participating in the lively sociality. Rather, their imaginative empathy is put to work in engaging those who are otherwise staying indoors, who would have been alienated from economic and social entanglement with others. Moments that chindon-ya practitioners prized as rewarding, shared in talks with me, involved intimate and personal conversations, such as with a lonely child whose parents were absent from home; an elderly person whose spouse had passed away recently; or a middle-aged man who had lost his job and family after being laid off. It is such people, whose lives have been marked by the insidious effects of precarity, that chindon-ya make particular efforts to reach through soundings of hibiki.

Imaginative empathy allows chindon-ya to attune to not only those who are excluded from the productive forces of the economy, but also those who are bounded within the physical confines of walls and segregated neighborhoods. When speaking of places where chindon-ya are particularly welcome, or where it is easy for them to do work (*shigoto ga yariyasui*), other Chindon Tsūshinsha members mentioned that the neighborhoods where they are well received tend to be lower-income neighborhoods in Osaka, such as zainichi Korean neighborhoods in Ikuno Ward, or the day laborers' district of Kamagasaki. Particularly in Osaka, these spatialized differences are often produced along ethnic and class lines.[38] In producing hibiki, therefore, chindon-ya are attuned to social differences that are often drowned in noises, hidden behind walls, or marginalized from the labor force. Put another way, the acoustic and affective permeability of chindon-ya's resonances allows us to listen to the politics of exclusion in contemporary Japanese urban life.

Many of the Chindon Tsūshinsha members note the strength of empathetic relations their hibiki makes during their street routines in these neighborhoods—segregated through class, ethnicity, or historical occupational discrimination—as well the sense of reward that comes with fostering such relations. One area where they feel exceptionally appreciated is Kamagasaki, otherwise known as Nishinari or Airin district.[39] Kamagasaki is the largest *yoseba* (a gathering place for day laborers) in Japan. It has an estimated transient population of thirty thousand—living either in temporary hostels intended for day laborers (*doya*) or on the street—in a fifty-acre area, and is notorious for its roughness, high crime rate, and history of violent protests and riots. For the past couple of years, two pachinko parlors in this area, owned by the same company, have been hiring Chindon Tsūshinsha twice a month as a strategic move to directly engage the locals; and the members have many a colorful story of reactions, interactions, and encounters with the men who live there.

When walking through Kamagasaki with chindon-ya, one immediately notices ubiquitous things unique to this area: "no public urination" signs, temporary lockers (to store belongings between nights in a hostel room or on the street), Laundromats, older men on crutches or in wheelchairs, minivans with a sign seeking labor for the day (usually around U.S.$80 per person) in the front windshield, and a lot of standing bars offering karaoke—a beloved pastime. Japan's oldest red-light district, Tobita, is blocks away from the pachinko parlor, and occasionally sparklingly polished white expensive cars with tinted windows—often carrying members of organized crime, who run the informal economy in the area—pass through. Signs for food and doya hostels show exceptionally low prices; the daily rate for a room is as low as ¥500 (four dollars), a small lunch box for ¥80 (70 cents), and beer for ¥180 ($1.50). With the decline of the industrial economy, the demand for manual labor has significantly decreased in the past decades, which has led Kamagasaki to become a neighborhood of mostly unemployed retirement-age day laborers living on welfare and/or a pension. With the local men's labor not only abstracted but also rendered obsolete by the postindustrial economy and their aged, exhausted bodies, Kamagasaki has become alienated both geographically and socially.

On one gig for the pachinko store, we arrived in Kamagasaki one morning around 9:30 (see plate 6). Street cleaning vehicles were whirling by, and some of the day laborers were picking up trash with tongs as part of a clean-up crew hired by the city, while others had already begun their drinking, walking with cans of beer in their hands. As usual, the pachinko store gave chindon-ya paper tokens for a free beverage to distribute to the locals; drink tickets or small packets of tissues are especially coveted items when walking through Kamagasaki. After starting the day in front of the store, not yet open, with Hanada Masashi playing the familiar winter tune "Kitakaze Kozō no Kantarō" on the soprano sax, we started walking. Immediately Nana, giving out the drink tickets, was stopped by an old man asking to take a photo with her on his outdated flip phone—"I like sisters in kimono." Hanada kept playing pop hits from the 1950s through the '70s (kayōkyoku) to appeal to the men, one of whom stopped him and requested "Chanchiki Okesa," a million-seller hit from 1957. Hanada obliged. I did not often see people requesting tunes from chindon-ya in other areas, but it seems fitting in Kamagasaki, where singing songs from their youth at karaoke bars is the most popular form of entertainment. As we passed through the shopping arcade (shōtengai), many called out to us in passing. "Must be so cold today—take care not to catch a cold!" shouted one man in front of the public employment service. "What, you're advertising pachinko? Gambling's an obstacle of life!" joked another. Middle-aged women on their bicycles remarked, on several occasions, "Oh, so pretty!" "Beautiful! [*beppin san ya*]" to the two female members. I heard at least several men humming along to Hanada's saxophone, and a few people spontaneously started dancing. The troupe members told me that, a few weeks prior on the same gig, a couple of men ended up joining the troupe and kept following them for an hour, dancing. Within a couple of hours, most of the drink tickets had already been handed out—a testament to the exceptionally high frequency of social interactions between the locals and chindon-ya and the affective intensity of these encounters, compared to what I have observed in most other neighborhoods of Osaka. On the day welfare or pensions are paid, the whole neighborhood is even more lively; despite their low income, the men are in a good mood, and chindon-ya members say they receive far more tips (*goshūgi*) on those days in Kamagasaki than in any other neighborhood—however small in amount, or in whatever form (snacks, beer). While many of the volunteer social workers, journalists, international backpackers, and curious tourists who pass through the neighborhood are often perceived with suspicion, chindon-ya are well received as a rare form of live musical entertainment and an integral part of the neighborhood scenery in the otherwise socially and geographically alienated community of Kamagasaki.

At another time, Chindon Tsūshinsha worked a monthlong campaign to sell prepaid cell phones that was launched by NTT (Nippon Telegraph and Telephone) in Kamagasaki. NTT specifically targeted day laborers in Kamagasaki who often do not have the registered address, bank account, and/or credit card number required for a monthly phone contract. Every day during the campaign, Chindon Tsūshinsha was given 420 flyers, and two thousand candies with promotional wrapping, and was asked to walk through Kamagasaki to hold conversations with the locals. They spent most of their mornings near a public unemployment office, engaging with unemployed day laborers, who came up to the troupe to get candy and start conversations. Many showed interest in the cell phone plans, but then moved onto other topics just to have conversations with the members, particularly female members, seeking human interaction rather than business transactions. Hayashi said that the chindon-ya troupe, skilled at reaching out to the socially marginalized, would be the only advertisement medium through which the large corporations might establish a physical presence in this segregated neighborhood.[40] A case in point: chindon-ya's ability to gain acceptance by the locals and to relate to them was deployed by NTT not only to publicize its cell phone plan, but also to conduct an informal market survey among the day laborers on potential customers' ages and whether they previously knew about the particular prepaid cell phone plan. Chindon-ya's soundings invited conviviality with and among the Kamagasaki locals, forging a sense of affinity and intimacy through these unexpected encounters.

———

The imaginative empathy involved in chindon-ya's soundings calls into question not only the alleged incommensurability of money and sentiment, but also the interpretation of space as a physical enclosure onto which social differences are mapped. Chindon-ya practitioners' attention to the forces that create the particular site of performance and their creative improvisatory practices make explicit the otherwise intangible sentiments, forces, and relations that are in fact palpable in what constitutes everyday urban space. Contrary to a teleological narrative in which capitalist modernity abstracts lived urban spaces through urban development, privatization, regulation, and gentrification, chindon-ya's sounds embody and reproduce the historical understanding of streets as an always heterogeneous and socially dynamic space.

As chindon-ya's hibiki moves across the physical boundaries of apartment walls and segregated neighborhoods, they both make audible and disrupt such boundaries—ones that mark and contain social difference while delineating the public and the private. While studies of portable musical technologies such as car radios and the Walkman show how sounds transform public space into private space (Bull 2003, 2004), chindon-ya's sounds reframe the very location of public space. Their sounds, when reaching listeners who have been excluded from the labor force and marginalized geographically, move the notion of public space from the anonymous and abstracted physical streets to social relations themselves. Chindon-ya's imaginative empathy helps create the affective and acoustic resonances of hibiki, which in turn does the cultural work of producing sociality by drawing people into encounters in which they did not intend to

FIGURE 3.7 Chindon-ya's smiles, 2008. Photo by the author.

participate. As in the case of the housewives behind walls, or the day laborers in a segregated neighborhood, chindon-ya are tasked to not only bring nigiyakasa, but also to imagine and sense those who are invisible, marginalized, and living precariously.

However, the question arises: what is the cost of selling their smiles (figure 3.7)? While chindon-ya's sounds do the work of producing public intimacies by drawing people into unexpected social relations spanning class, ethnic, and geographical boundaries through hibiki, the fact that chindon-ya ultimately seek profit puts chindon-ya in an ambiguous position. Chindon-ya's soundings oscillate between those who are living with precarity, to whom they appeal through imaginative empathy, and the very capitalist market forces that alienate people like the day laborers, furītā, and chindon-ya themselves. Kawaguchi highlights how chindon-ya practitioners both capitalize on and struggle with this contradictory position in their everyday practices in order to make ends meet: "There are both positive and negative images [of chindon-ya]. It's a battle every day for us, figuring out how we navigate through them, and survive and sustain ourselves."[41]

This seeming paradox is precisely what propels the increasing demand for affective labor in the postindustrial economy, in which reification of sociality is the name of the game. But it would be hasty to consider chindon-ya as simply being co-opted by, or opportunistically valorizing, the logic of neoliberal capitalism. Chindon-ya's persistent commitment to the acoustic and affective production of sociality—inalienable and embodied "presences" improvised in every encounter—resists the terms of capital; and their distinctly relational and anti-individualistic aesthetic principles run directly against the assumptions of the liberal subject central to the neoliberal present.

The linguistic particularity about the ways in which listeners are socialized to *overhear* chindon-ya's sound may offer a clue here. Just as the overheard sound can become part of the listeners' soundscape and awareness without their necessarily actively taking part, I suggest that chindon-ya is riding the wave of the increasing demand for affective labor without necessarily taking part in the logic of the neoliberal present. Much in the same way that chindon-ya has internalized multiple histories and logics of time—vernacular histories of social marginalization, shifting modes of sociality through different capitalisms, and narratives of European and Japanese capitalist modernities (chapters 1 and 2)—chindon-ya's hibiki simultaneously works within multiple spatialities and modes of production, within the neoliberal economy and outside the logic of capital. Without accounting for or being accounted for by any single structural logic, chindon-ya gathers and articulates relations, histories, and forces by attending to the contingencies that inform the present moment. Chindon-ya's sounding, then, is "a circuit that's always tuned in to some little something somewhere. A mode of attending to the possible and the threatening, it amasses the resonance in things" (Stewart 2007, 12). Their hibiki resonates precisely within these open-ended potentialities, circulating both publicly and through intimate everyday lives.

In listening carefully to chindon-ya's hibiki, what we hear resounding in the streets, through windows, and into living rooms is an understanding of space that is actively produced through an articulation of social relations, histories, and affective dynamics that are otherwise silenced, contained, and regulated within physical boundaries. Through this dynamically produced sound-space, chindon-ya simultaneously contest the homogenizing discourse of abstract space, and work to stay relevant and financially sustainable in the face of the very economic forces that produced spatialized social difference in the first place. This dynamic and inclusive sense of space, and the open, animate circuit

of potentialities, is where we hear the economy of affect and political economy in the productive feedback loop of chindon-ya's sound business. In the
next chapter, I turn to how these potentialities of resonance have unexpectedly
gained traction among musicians and activists within politicized contexts beyond chindon-ya's traditional sound business of advertisement.

CHAPTER 4

Politicizing Chindon-ya

It was dawn, on a crisp cold day in December 2007. A bonfire in a used oil barrel provided warmth for a small crowd and the production crew from the national public television channel NHK. Multiple cameras were set up, including one on a crane. A dozen bright lights were mounted on tall scaffolding, flooding the courtyard of Nagata Shrine with harsh light. Here, in the southern part of Kobe, members of the Osaka-based band Soul Flower Mononoke Summit—dubbed a "vagabond/ascetic chindon band" (*fūkyō chindon gakudan*)—were getting ready to perform a short set. Usually a public space, the shrine courtyard was cordoned off with red-and-white-striped tape for the TV shoot, accessible only to the band, the crew, and a selected audience, including me. Starting with the famous Korean new folk song (*shinminyō*) "Arirang," the band played an assortment of songs of wide geographical and ethnic diversity: "Henoko-bushi" (Henoko song), an original tune dedicated to a politically contentious Okinawan beach where a new U.S. military base is planned to be constructed; "Mangetsu no Yūbe" (Evening of the full moon), another original song written after the 1995 Hanshin Awaji Earthquake that shattered the very neighborhood they were performing in; "Asadoya Yunta" (Asadoya song), an iconic folk song from Okinawa; and "Takeda no Komoriuta" (Lullaby of Takeda), a well-known lullaby from the Takeda neighborhood on the outskirts of Kyoto, where there is a large ostracized buraku community.[1] Considering that the rather conservative national public television channel tends to avoid the subject of ethnic minorities and is known for its complicity with the government, the selection of tunes seemed rather provocative.

This shoot was for a TV program that commemorated the thirteenth anniversary of the Hanshin Awaji Earthquake. The magnitude 7.3 earthquake hit the Kobe metropolitan area, about thirty kilometers (19 miles) west of Osaka and home to 3.5 million people, on the cold winter morning of January 17, 1995. The Soul Flower Mononoke Summit member Itami Hideko surmised that the consequences of the earthquake were profoundly social: "The first twenty seconds was a natural disaster. After that, the disaster was man-made."[2] The largest earthquake in postwar Japan at the time (now second, after the Great Northeastern Japan Earthquake of 2011, discussed in chapter 5), it left the southern part of Hyōgo prefecture in shambles. The quake claimed more than fifty-four hundred lives. Urban infrastructure was paralyzed, with electricity, water, gas lines, and the underground train system left inoperative. Fires engulfed densely populated areas, and many were left without homes and forced to live in temporary housing provided by the city for many subsequent years.

In the immediate aftermath of the earthquake, Soul Flower Mononoke Summit—an acoustic outfit of the popular rock band Soul Flower Union[3]—visited the disaster-affected areas to provide entertainment to the survivors who had lost their homes. For the visit, they replaced their electric instruments and microphones with chindon drums, *changgo* (Korean hourglass drum), *sanshin* (Okinawan three-stringed lute), accordion, and megaphones. The new instrumentation was necessary to be able to play without electricity at various *hinanjo*—shelters set up in school gyms, public parks, and tents, where survivors sought temporary housing. A successful rock band on a major record label then, the band at first had some reservations about visiting the shelters with unfamiliar acoustic instruments. But their reception exceeded their expectations, and Soul Flower Mononoke Summit quickly garnered popularity, especially among the elderly (figure 4.1). They frequented the disaster-affected areas almost every other day after their first visit on February 10, 1995, and before year's end had performed more than fifty "delivery live shows" (*demae raibu*).

A year later, Soul Flower Mononoke Summit independently released their first album, *Asyle Ching-dong*,[4] featuring songs that had entered their repertoire through their ongoing performances in Kobe. The first sounds one hears on the record are the distinct sounds of the uchikomi (percussion introduction) of chindon-ya: fast rhythmic patterns played on the bright, high-pitched, and metallic kane and chindon drums, followed by the three beats on the gorosu—just as a chindon-ya would start any song in their street routine. This is immediately followed by the full-volume, exuberant, and festive sounds of the ensemble (sanshin, changgo, accordion, chindon drums, percussion, clarinet, bass, and backup vocals) energetically playing the melody of "Fukkōbushi," or "Reconstruction Song," which was written after the 1923 Tokyo Earthquake to cheer up survivors. From the downbeat, the syncopated beats on the chindon percussion and lilting call-and-response of *ohayashi* (traditional festival and theater music) vocals evoke nigiyakasa, the liveliness of summer festivals that inspires dancing. Lead vocalist and band leader Nakagawa Takashi starts singing, modifying Soeda Satsuki's original lyrics to suit the Kobe disaster:

There's money in Tokyo's Nagata
There are songs in Kobe's Nagata
Arama, oyama,
Show them the real *matsurigoto* [festivity/politics]
Koreans and Yamatonchu [Japanese] all go through Arirang Pass
Nagata, chindon, way to go, way to go.

Even though the houses are burned down
Laugh, get angry, but we don't need tears, *Dekansho*[5]
Reconstruct Hanshin, way to go, way to go.
The spirit of Kobe people doesn't disappear, just wait and see
Arama, oyama,
Real people are right here
Reconstruct Awaji, way to go, way to go.
Dissolve Japan, way to go, way to go.

Contrasting two localities called Nagata—one in Tokyo, where governmental institutions are concentrated, and the other a disaster-stricken area in Kobe—the new lyrics sharply criticize the Tokyo-centric, official national construct of Japan ("dissolve Japan"), while festively celebrating the cultural plurality of Nagata, with its ethnically diverse immigrant population. Playing on the double meaning of the Japanese word *matsurigoto*, which phonetically means both politics and festival, the lyrics and the musical arrangement of the song locate "real" politics in the lively sound of chindon and the vibrant spirits of the diverse community of Nagata. The governmental power and money may be in Tokyo's Nagata, the lyrics imply; but the real politics happen in Kobe's Nagata, as the people of numerous heritages sing and dance to the lively sounds of chindon percussion.

Soul Flower Mononoke Summit's mobilization of chindon-ya after the 1995

FIGURE 4.1 Soul Flower Mononoke Summit, performing for
Mie Human Rights Festival, 2006. Photo by the author.

earthquake, both in its instrumentation and as a cultural trope, marked a significant shift in the way chindon-ya was perceived and practiced. As we will see,
the band was not the first to use chindon-ya in a non-advertisement context,
but the high profile of its activities in post-disaster Kobe laid the ground for
others over the next two decades to take up the chindon drums outside the
advertising business, investing it with new meanings and opening up new possibilities, both musical and political.

In earlier chapters I have focused almost exclusively on professional
chindon-ya practitioners who perform for advertisement purposes. This chapter and the next examine how chindon-ya's sounds have reached beyond these
origins. Among contemporary Japanese musicians,[6] intellectuals, artists, activists, record producers, and volunteer social workers, the cultural imaginary
of chindon-ya has generated a wide variety of creative projects: historical research, collaborations, new musical forms, publications, and political protests.
To distinguish the older style, which I simply call chindon-ya, from the recent
various offshoot practices, I call the latter "chindon-inspired," referring to con-

temporary cultural practices that draw on chindon-ya in some manner in their hybridizing practices.[7] I ask: What is it about chindon-ya that has appealed to this diverse and loose network of artists? What are some of the social, cultural, and historical forces that set the stage for the chindon-inspired practitioners to politicize this erstwhile advertising practice over the past two decades? What new possibilities have emerged from their interpretations of chindon-ya?

To explore these questions, I trace the ways contemporary musical offshoots of chindon-ya have emerged, developed, and become politicized since the early 1990s. In doing so, this chapter provides the historical context in which to understand the next chapter, a case study of the politicization of chindon-ya in the post-3.11 anti-nuclear-power movement. Three key themes that emerge from the "Reconstruction Song" lyrics guide my analysis in this chapter. The first is the crisis of public space, and anxiety around spaces physically and socially fractured through forces of corporatization and privatization; the second is the building of affective alliances across different registers of difference; and the third is the politics of festivity—the double meaning coded in the Japanese word *matsurigoto*. By walking through these themes, I argue that chindon-ya's historical associations with the street, the subversive narratives of street performers, and the festivity of nigiyakasa have enabled a new mode of social critique in neoliberal, post-disaster Japan.

A comprehensive survey of chindon-inspired musical projects lies beyond the scope of this chapter. Instead, I provide snapshots of several chindon-inspired practitioners who have mobilized chindon-ya in politically contested situations in Japan since the mid-1990s: Soul Flower Mononoke Summit; the Osaka-based zainichi Korean singer Cho Paggie; Okinawan folk singer Daiku Tetsuhiro; and the Tokyo-based band Cicala Mvta, led by the chindon-ya clarinetist Ōkuma Wataru. By examining their musical and discursive practices, I explore how these musicians' understandings of and experiences with chindon-ya have led them to assemble local and translocal social connections exceeding the original commercial contexts of chindon-ya, to adopt chindon-ya aesthetics in the creation of musical styles, and to link these styles to political aspirations, gesturing toward the multicultural question of Japan.

CHINDON-INSPIRED PROJECTS

Since the early 1990s, various chindon-inspired projects have emerged in non-advertisement contexts throughout Japan. The sounds and trope of chindon-ya have yielded some unlikely collaborations between chindon-ya troupes and other musicians, and unexpected relationships across places and times have been imagined and formed as a result. For instance, Osaka's Chindon Tsūshinsha was invited to perform with the Bosnian singer Jadranka Stojaković, and to record and tour with the Okinawan singer Daiku Tetsuhiro. The group also recorded an album with the brass band Ōsawa Gakutai, the last existing jinta band—the precursor of chindon-ya—in the rural area near Sendai, northern Japan (see chapter 2).[8]

Chindon-inspired musical projects did not simply involve musical collaborations between chindon-ya and other musicians. Starting in the mid-1990s, many non-chindon practitioners started to build their own chindon drum sets and incorporate them into their music, resulting in new hybridized musical forms. These musicians have also drawn on klezmer and Balkan Roma repertoire, free improvisation, Korean folk songs, and Okinawan folk songs, just to name a few influences. There have been several chindon-inspired musical groups run by freelance chindon-ya gakushi (melody players), such as Seto Nobuyuki, Nishiuchi Tetsu, Adachi Tomoshige, Hotta Hiroki, Hashimoto Takehide (Kizzu Kun), and Kimura Shinya, as well as groups such as Kabocha Shōkai (founded in 1991) and Chindon Brass Kingyo (founded in 1999), which are run by non-chindon-ya practitioners.

These chindon-inspired bands depart from chindon-ya significantly not only stylistically but also in terms of performance sites. While chindon-ya perform almost exclusively on the streets as an advertisement business, chindon-inspired performance sites include various non-publicity contexts, both on stage and in the streets. During my fieldwork, following some of these chindon-inspired projects led me to a recording studio in Tokyo, a small rock venue in Nagoya, a Buddhist temple in Kyoto, an anti-G8-summit protest in Hokkaido, an anti-military-base music festival in Okinawa, the Thames Festival in London, a music camp near Montreal, and a museum in New York City.

Alongside these chindon-inspired collaborations and musical formations, popular publications on chindon-ya have proliferated since the mid-1990s. Books on the chindon-ya troupe led by the legendary veteran Kikunoya Shimemaru—at ninety-two the oldest chindon practitioner until he passed away in 2010—have been published by his disciples and by journalists (Shimizu 1997; Kikunoya 2002). Oral histories of veteran chindon-ya have been published by a group of younger practitioners (Ōyama 1995; Ōba and Yada 2009), while the current generation of chindon-ya such as Hayashi Kōjirō and Hananoya Kei in

Osaka, Adachi Hideya in Fukuoka, and Kawachi Ryūtarō in Nagasaki have authored biographical books chronicling their own experiences in the chindon-ya business (Adachi 2005; Hananoya 2007; Hayashi and Akae 1986; Hayashi 1993, 2006; Kawachi 2016).[9] Ōkuma Wataru of Cicala Mvta wrote a book called *Rafu Myūjikku Sengen* [Declaration of rough music]: *Chindon, Punk, Jazz* (2001), which weaves together archival and genealogical research, as well as his own perspectives as a chindon clarinet player. Although a few scholars have authored articles, dissertations, and book chapters on chindon-ya, academic publications on chindon-ya remain scarce.[10]

Hayashi, Ōkuma, and members of Soul Flower Mononoke Summit have contributed numerous essays and interviews to other publications as well. One of these is the *Power of Sound* (*Oto no chikara*) book series dedicated to the theme of "street," published by the cultural collective DeMusik Inter. Founded in 1995, DeMusik Inter is a group of critics, writers, journalists, scholars, activists, and musicians who seek to publish writing that addresses contemporary social issues through musical practice. The Marxian manifesto that accompanied the group's founding promised the "creation of a counter-market" that can challenge the "overwhelmingly false reality of capitalism"; "collaborative regional studies of taishū music"; "pursuit of counter-histories of popular music"; "highlighting [of] the presence and creative input of the zainichi [resident] foreigners in Japan"; and the "interconnecting [of] musicians within and without Japan who are often restricted by small markets" (2002, 312–313). Politically driven, DeMusik Inter's publications position chindon-ya as a distinctly Japanese street practice worthy of critical attention, along with many other street-based musical practices from all corners of the world.

DeMusik Inter's investment in highlighting chindon-ya as a subversive sonic practice is rooted in concern with the "streets," the theme that runs through three out of seven of the group's publications between 2002 and 2005. Underlining DeMusik Inter's focus on the streets is a sense of crisis: a crisis of public space, propelled by forces of privatization, gentrification, and increasing legal regulations that criminalize cultural expressions on the streets.[11] The DeMusik Inter writers grapple with this sense of a crisis of public space through examination of various incidents in Japan: the 2003 eviction of the homeless and the removal of a makeshift open-air karaoke space (*aozora* karaoke) from the public park in Tennōji by the Osaka City Planning Committee;[12] the 2003 privatization of Miyashita Park in Tokyo by Nike, which displaced many homeless and youth skaters;[13] and the tightened policing of street performers in Shibuya

Park in Tokyo and the Abeno Shopping District in Osaka, just to name a few. Within this framework, chindon-inspired practices can be understood to have emerged amid the increasing anxieties and debates around the capitalist encroachments on public space in the 1990s and 2000s in Japan.

THE CRISIS OF PUBLIC SPACE

There's money in Tokyo's Nagata
There are songs in Kobe's Nagata . . .
Even though the houses are burned down
The spirit of Kobe people doesn't disappear, just wait and see

In chindon-inspired practices, *sutorīto* (transliteration of the English word "street"), *rojō* (on the street), *dōro* (road, often for cars), or at times *chimata* (busy town, public, society)—variations of the notion of "streets"—framed debates around public space. In some ways, this growing concern can be seen as an extension of the street observation studies movement of the 1980s (see chapter 1), as both share concerns with the effects of late capitalism that are subsuming inclusive, communal public life. But unlike the street observation studies, which took a passive, observational approach to documenting the residual traces of communal sociality in public space, chindon-inspired practitioners in the 1990s took a more interventionist stance and have incorporated global perspectives.

In DeMusik Inter's Power of Sound series, "the street" is seen both as a controlled public space and as a space with emancipatory possibilities. The 2002 publication subtitled *Sutorīto o torimodose* (Let's reclaim the street) opens with a quote from the manifesto by the Reclaim the Streets (RTS) movement in Toronto, Canada: "Our goal is to reclaim what belonged to us originally. 'Us' does not refer to a selected few, but all. We can be connected with one another beyond the 'government' and 'corporations.' . . . By uniting, we aim to reclaim people's power. Let's reclaim the street" (DeMusik Inter 2002, 6).[14]

The Reclaim the Streets movement started initially as an anti-car movement in the UK in the early 1990s. Aspiring to communal ownership of public space through festive occupation of the streets, the movement quickly became a global phenomenon. Various forms of nonviolent direct action—spontaneous rave parties, festivals, gardening, etc.—in carnivalesque refusal of the technocratic rationalization of public space, took place to protest the corporatizing and privatizing forces of neoliberal capitalism. The slogan on the UK-based website of this "disorganization" reads: "Ultimately it is in the streets that power must be dissolved; for the streets where daily life is endured, suffered and eroded, and where power is confronted and fought, must be turned into the domain where daily life is enjoyed, created and nourished."[15]

Echoing RTS's anxiety over the global dispossession and reterritorialization of public space, DeMusik Inter writers and musicians seek their way out of abstracted space in postindustrial Japan through musical sounds.[16] These public intellectuals, scholars, and artists have looked to musical sounds on the street as a way of revealing and contesting allegedly public—but in reality dispossessed—spaces across Japan. Among the musical practices examined in DeMusik Inter from many different corners of the world, from Mexico to New York, Beijing, Jamaica, Germany, and Ghana, chindon-ya is positioned as a distinctly Japanese street-based musical practice that has persisted throughout the shifting geographies of modernity. The historical resilience of chindon-ya's playful and quotidian sonic presence captured the attention of DeMusik Inter's authors and musicians as a possible way of responding to the crisis of public space in Japan.

The understanding of space that emerges from chindon-ya practice sheds light on the connection between chindon-ya and the crisis of public space espoused in these writings. In Hayashi Kōjirō's essay in one of DeMusik Inter's Power of Sound volumes, titled "My Wanderings, Random Thoughts on Chindon Life" (*Waga hyōryū no chindon seikatsu zakkan*), Hayashi defines what the street means for chindon-ya: "Everyone, aren't you assuming that the street is a public, clear and transparent space that doesn't belong to anyone? Quite the opposite. In reality, it's the space of a complex ecological system, entangled organically with various human relations and relations of interest" (DeMusik Inter 2002, 1).[17]

As I have shown in chapter 3, Hayashi's conceptualization of public space, deeply rooted in the everyday street routine of chindon-ya, challenges both the notion of "public" as anonymous, and "space" as a physically delineated, socially and politically neutral surface. Instead, Hayashi puts forward an understanding of public space as an articulation of social relations, renewed and transformed through each step, each sounding, and each encounter. Some of the chindon-inspired musicians and writers seem to find inspiration in this social, spatial, and aural negotiation process inherent in chindon-ya's profession that creates a new type of sociality by bringing together people, sounds,

FIGURE 4.2 TCDC's bass drum
with chindon-ya stencil art. Photo by the author.

and materials where they are not expected or designed to be. A rather extreme
example is a "sound demonstration" (sound demo) group called TCDC (Tran-
sistor Connected Drum Collective), a group of street political protesters based
in Tokyo. Explicitly against the increasing regulation of the streets, sound
demo sought to occupy public space by turning street protests into mobile
rave parties with speakers loaded on a truck.[18] Although TCDC does not incorporate chindon instruments, costumes, or repertoire, leader Oda Masanori
explicitly acknowledges its indebtedness to chindon-ya, calling the group an
"antiwar chindon-ya" (Oda, quoted in DeMusik Inter 2005, 123). He claims the
group is a "complex constituted by patchworks of cultural memories including
chindon-ya." The logo of the group from the TCDC website clearly shows a typical chindon drum player, again drawing a conceptual parallel to their perception of chindon-ya (figure 4.2).[19]

The key to understanding how particular aspects of chindon-ya have been mobilized in order to offer such a critique of the crisis of public space is the notion of *bachigai*. As I illustrated in the previous chapter, because chindon-ya are always out-of-place, they must continuously and actively work with the contingencies of each particular place they walk through in order to create space to belong (*ibasho*), at least temporarily. The deliberately subversive choice to engage in this historically sedimented, visibly and aurally idiosyncratic performance, I suggest, reflects chindon-inspired artists' desire to produce this provisional space where the itinerant and marginalized can stay awhile within public space that is otherwise not hospitable.

Soul Flower Mononoke Summit's efforts to visit and perform in disaster-stricken Kobe are one such example. In an interview reflecting on the new performance skills and perspective they gained through performing acoustically at shelters in Kobe in 1995, the leading figures of the band, Nakagawa Takashi and Itami Hideko, contrasted two Japanese terms referring to public space: *sutorīto* and *chimata*. Itami told the interviewer that the transliteration of the English word "street," *sutorīto*, sounds dead to her; by contrast, the word *chimata* "feels alive. Feels like there are people. When you say 'sutorīto,' it feels like there are no people" (Takahashi 1996, 7). *Chimata* has several meanings: forking paths, border, town street, in the middle of a town, society, or where things get done. Itami's distinction opposes the abstraction of space implied by the borrowed English term "street" to the sociality and liveliness inherent to the indigenous notion of *chimata* as public space. Nakagawa continued: "It's very difficult to [get music to] resonate in chimata. The structure [of chimata] is complex. Just within Japan, there are places like Roppongi [a neighborhood in Tokyo known for foreign capital and nightclubs], fishermen's towns, agricultural farms—there are so many complex stratifications . . . and in this space called Japan, what is 'popular music' that reverberates in chimata? . . . What kind of soil is Soul Flower Union from? It's chimata music. . . . We're intending to let [our music] resonate in chimata" (1996, 7). By choosing the term *chimata* (public space/society), Nakagawa foregrounds an understanding of public space as inherently socially and sonically produced—akin to the production of hibiki, the acoustic and affective resonances discussed in the previous chapter. By aspiring to "let [their] music resonate" in chimata, Soul Flower Mononoke Summit reveals an understanding of resonances as sounded and spatialized sociality.

Nakagawa's comment above also highlights another key theme that made chindon-ya relevant to post-disaster Kobe: the unevenness of public space. Nakagawa's reference to chimata as a space of "complex stratifications" highlights the issues of spatialized difference—the depopulated rural towns dependent on public subsidy contrasted against the urban center of global capital flows, for example—that often go unacknowledged in the perceived notion of public space as anonymous or transparent. Just as Chindon Tsūshinsha members produce acoustic and affective resonances through imaginative empathy that attends to the politics of inclusion and exclusion in their street routines (see chapter 3), Nakagawa aspires to produce hibiki in disaster-stricken Nagata that simultaneously makes audible and embraces the difference within chimata / public space.

This was particularly a poignant issue in post-disaster Kobe, and in the Nagata area in particular. Nagata ward was one of the hardest-hit areas. Over 60 percent of the fire damage and 30 percent of the housing destruction from the earthquake were concentrated in this district, and sixty-six hundred people, almost half the population of Nagata, were forced to evacuate to various shelters. One factor in the disproportionate destruction in the area was the fact that Nagata had a high concentration of nagaya—decades-old, one-story wooden houses. Nagata escaped U.S. bombing attacks during World War II and thus retained the appearance of a prewar plebeian neighborhood consisting of small wooden houses built in tight quarters. Nagata was known for back alleyways so narrow that cars could not get through. Many of these nagaya houses did not withstand the strong quake, and they were particularly prone to fire.

Before the earthquake, Nagata was known as a working-class neighborhood of ethnic diversity. Small-scale industrial factories producing rubber, shoes, and matches sprang up in the neighborhood in the 1920s, attracting manual laborers and many foreign-born residents and zainichi Koreans. Migrants from Okinawa also came to Kobe to settle, while others traveled farther from the port, to Hawaii and beyond. Today, the official website for Nagata Ward is available in Japanese, English, Chinese, Korean, Spanish, Portuguese, Tagalog, and Vietnamese, reflecting its large population of foreign-born residents and zainichi Koreans.[20]

In the aftermath of the earthquake, language barriers and the lack of social support systems made conditions even harder for the immigrant communities in Nagata. Many struggled to gain access to welfare and support services. There was also the dark shadow of the massive persecution of Koreans in the aftermath of the 1923 Tokyo earthquake—mass hysteria and xenophobic fear of looters led to a massacre of Koreans. The earthquake revealed the fault lines of social barriers, marginalization, and discrimination that affect foreign-born residents and zainichi Koreans.

Another group particularly affected by the 1995 disaster was the elderly. *Kodokushi*, or solitary death, became a serious problem. Even after surviving the disaster, over one thousand elderly people died alone in the region between 1995 and 2012.[21] After several months of living in school gym shelters, many moved into temporary housing (*kasetsu jūtaku*) for up to five years.[22] Isolated from their families and the neighborly social networks that supported them before the disaster, and lacking proper home insulation or heating, many elderly people struggled to maintain good health, both physical and mental. The solitary death toll continued to rise even after many elderly people were provided with government-sponsored apartments in high-rise buildings. The public relocation was done on a random, lottery basis, which did not take into consideration how the tight-knit social network that once existed in Nagata or that developed in the years of temporary housing was fragmented. Having lost these networks of care and sociality, over seven hundred elderly people were found dead in the following several years.

These geographies of class, ethnic, and generational difference in the Nagata neighborhood informed the choice of musical instruments used by Soul Flower Mononoke Summit—chindon drums, the Korean drum *changgo*, and the Okinawan lute *sanshin*, especially—and the selection of tunes for their TV shoot in Nagata shrine reflected this. "Arirang" and "Asadoya Yunta" were enthusiastically received by ethnic Koreans and Okinawans in Nagata as if they were their own anthems, while these songs were also familiar to the rest of the audience as iconic Korean and Okinawan pieces. The references to the Arirang Pass and Korea in the updated version of the "Fukkōbushi" lyrics also refer to this little-known history and geography of difference in Nagata. The prewar and postwar *hayariuta* (popular songs) were selected out of Itami's concern for the elderly people. She said: "Many grandmas and grandpas withdraw into their houses, not wanting to be a burden on other people [*meiwaku no kakaranai yōni*]. We were worried that people might think we would be a nuisance, but we wanted to invite them outside."[23] Her choice to pick up the chindon drums for the occasion was also directed at the older generation, for whom chindon-ya's sounds are integral to their childhood memories. As with chindon-ya's street routine, Itami hoped for the sound of chindon drums and kane to lure the elderly out of insular, isolated lives in the shelter or temporary housing and to provide a temporary respite.

In post-disaster Kobe, the crisis of public space was particularly dire. Such space was physically obliterated, only to be rezoned and reterritorialized through state-designed urban redevelopment plans that failed to recognize the importance of the neighborly social networks for the single-occupying elderly. Activists on the ground and Itami and Nakagawa attributed the so-called solitary deaths among the elderly who were relocated into the newly built public housing projects to the top-down reconstruction plans that rested on a conception of public space that ignored the preexisting social relations.

Soul Flower Mononoke Summit repurposed the techniques of chindon-ya's affective labor in this post-disaster context. Their chindon-inspired sounds echoed across town, as if to produce the dynamic sociality and working-class solidarity that once existed in the back alleyways of the Nagata neighborhood, and to offer a poignant sonic critique of top-down reconstruction plans. Such plans overlooked the social relations that constituted the neighborhood and sustained the livelihood of the residents, and instead rested on the conception of public space as a Cartesian grid to be territorialized—precisely the spatial assumptions that DeMusik Inter seek to problematize.

Sounding across, and against, the crisis of public space in Nagata, Soul Flower Mononoke Summit's sound highlighted the unevenly spatialized difference of Nagata, particularly audible in the sounds of the instruments that indexed ethnic, class, and generational differences among local residents. Playing with and reworking the meanings of out-of-placeness implicated in the trope of chindon-ya was a key theme that animates chindon-inspired projects like theirs; the spatial difference as bachigai was mobilized to respond to the particular social and affective dynamics of the town. Chindon-ya's bachigai difference is not only spatial, however, but also temporal (chapter 2). As I will show next, the historical associations of chindon-ya with the socially marginalized and the subversive narratives of historical street performances played a role in the politicization of chindon-ya.

SOUNDING OUT AFFECTIVE ALLIANCES

Koreans and Yamatonchu [Japanese] all go through Arirang Pass
Nagata, chindon, way to go, way to go . . .
Reconstruct Hanshin, way to go, way to go.
The spirit of Kobe people doesn't disappear, just wait and see
Arama, *oyama*, real people are right here
Reconstruct Awaji, way to go, way to go.
Dissolve Japan, way to go, way to go.

Recounting his experiences in the early days of Soul Flower Mononoke Summit, Nakagawa told me that he was once affectionately scolded by an elderly woman in Nagata, who said several songs he sang were too old, even for her. The songs the band sang and have recorded on albums include popular songs from the 1900s through the 1920s; Nakagawa commented that you would have to be a hundred years old to know some of them. While some chindon-ya practitioners saw this as an ineffective or misguided effort to engage the target audience, this point wasn't lost on the Soul Flower Mononoke Summit members. Unlike chindon-ya, for whom the selection of repertoire was first and foremost motivated by the need to maximize the reach of affective resonance to those who may be overhearing their sounds (chapter 3), chindon-inspired practitioners like Soul Flower Mononoke Summit carefully selected tunes in part to deliver particular political messages to those who have chosen to listen.

Soul Flower Mononoke Summit's repertoire consisted mostly of traditional folk songs from various regions and ethnic minorities, popular songs from the 1920s and postwar period, and many *sōshi enka*—political and social satire songs sung by young activists (*sōshi*) on the streets in the 1880s. This genre was closely connected with the Liberty and Civil Rights Movement (*Jiyū minken undō*), a social and political movement that began the transition from the post-Edo government toward constitutional government and political democracy.[24] Each album the band has released includes at least a few sōshi enka, penned primarily by the father of the genre, Soeda Azembō (1872–1944), and his son, Soeda Satsuki (1902–1980), who wrote the lyrics for "Fukkōbushi" described above. Although it is a vocal genre that has little in common with chindon-ya in terms of instrumentation, many sōshi enka tunes entered chindon-inspired artists' projects because of their associations with the street and with subversive politics.

The most accepted narrative about the earliest form of enka is that it was a kind of political public speech turned into a song form during the Liberty and Civil Rights Movement in the 1880s.[25] After the fall of the Edo government and shogunate, Japan saw dramatic political turmoil. Under the repressive measures of the new Meiji government, which prohibited any public speeches and meetings against the government, the activists resorted to songs as a means of public political expression and circulation. Soeda Azembō, an important enka writer and singer who almost single-handedly established enka as a genre, defined enka as "songs of the street, born on the sidewalk, that flowed from the bottom of society" (quoted in Soeda 1963, 1). Soeda wrote: "Every public speech gathering was crushed by the police. Thus the alternative was to go out to the streets and sing. Also, there was an idea that it would be more appropriate to use songs and storytelling that are more accessible to the people rather than formal speech, in the spirit that the principle of democracy needed to take root within the masses" (Soeda, quoted in Kimura 1987, 26).

Activists at this time wrote satirical songs critical of the government that were often informed by socialist ideologies. Soeda, too, was involved with the socialist movement, becoming a city councilor for the socialist party in 1908, albeit temporarily. Soon he went back to the life of a poet and a songwriter, prolifically producing songs written from the critical viewpoint of the lower class on issues of class and union organization, in a language familiar to the working classes. Biographer Kimura argues that Soeda's musical activism sprang from his background: he lived in poverty and on the street throughout his life, and the only stable residence he had with his son was in a terrace house in Shitayaku, one of the biggest slums of Tokyo. By reinterpreting and updating the historical memory of Soeda's sōshi enka tunes, Soul Flower Mononoke Summit is alluding to a historical parallel between the turn of the century, when lifeways and the mode of production were radically reorganized under industrial capitalism on the one hand, and the 1990s, when the nation's neoliberal turn was producing structural reform in both the workplace and social life, on the other. Such layering of historical socialities onto the contemporary moment within musical projects provided a way for chindon-inspired practitioners to forge affective alliances, both within the imaginative realm across historical moments and among a loosely networked cohort of musicians across Japan with disparate political aspirations—some of whom I will briefly introduce below.

Ōkuma Wataru and Cicala Mvta

In the liner notes for Soul Flower Mononoke Summit's album *Asyl Chindon* (1995), Tokyo-based chindon clarinet player Ōkuma Wataru suggests that the group's inclusion of older songs, especially sōshi enka, is not a coincidence or mere nostalgic preference. Rather, he writes, a "bundle of collective memories" beckoned the band to revisit these songs. Although chindon-ya and sōshi enka were not contemporaneous, Ōkuma draws an imaginative connection between chindon-ya and street performances at the turn of the century: "Chindon-ya established its style in the 1920–30s, as if to care for the various street performers including enka singers on their death beds."[26] Thus situating chindon-ya historically, Ōkuma views chindon-inspired projects as breathing new life into the repertoire that had been forgotten or silenced for over a century—a kind of a eulogy for the subversive, antigovernment politics that these historical performing-arts practices on the streets represented.

Ōkuma pays homage to Soeda Azembō's legacy in his own musical projects. The name of his chindon-inspired band, Cicala Mvta, comes from a poem in Italian that is carved on Soeda Azembō's tombstone:

> A CICALA-MVTA CHE CANTAVA
> E LA SVA MOGLIE CHE L'AMAVA
> [To the mute cicada that used to sing
> And his wife that loved him] (Kimura 1987, 9)

Cicala Mvta: a mute cicada. This somewhat enigmatic phrase in Soeda's epitaph is based on his pen name Azembō, which means "*A* (mute) *zen* (cicada) *bō* (monk, or kid)." Although Soeda's direct involvement with the Liberty and Civil Rights Movement has been contested,[27] and the connection between the sung-political speeches of enka and chindon-ya is largely spurious or imaginative at best, the rich and vibrant second life enka has enjoyed as part of the chindon-inspired musical expressions of the 1990s attests to the tangible and concrete ways in which chindon-ya's sound has become a fulcrum point for creative expressions of historical affective alliances. With the already richly imaginative genealogical performances of chindon-ya practitioners who have invested chindon-ya with historical meanings (see chapters 1 and 2), chindon-ya as both a musical and discursive trope offered intellectuals, artists, and activists new possibilities to create further historical resonances, activating the subversive narratives of sonic practices on the streets—like a diffractive ripple effect.

FIGURE 4.3 Ōkuma Wataru (*right*, clarinet) and Kogure Miwazō
(*middle*, chindon drums) of Jinta-la-Mvta at an anti-nuclear-power rally.
Photo by the author.

Looking at performing arts on the streets as a source of antiestablishment
politics is not new. Historian Yoshida Mitsukuni (1969) points to the contestatory possibilities that the domain of amusement, entertainment, and pleasure
provided for the otherwise socially marginalized and oppressed during the
late Edo period. This widely accepted narrative accounts for the fall of feudal
oppression and the status system as the popular culture of the merchant class
gained power with the rise of commercialism.[28] For example, newspaper hawkers and *saimon uri* (blessing prayer vendor) performers, who sang the news
while accompanying themselves on the shamisen, were subject to constant
state pressure and censorship, as they often voiced satirical and critical views
of the powerful (Matsumiya 1968, 349–51). Street performers have historically
been an oppositional force against the governmental power, which enforced an
extremely strict status system that oppressed those performing on the streets
(chapter 2).

As Ōkuma and others situate chindon-ya among the prevalent narrative of historical street performing arts as contestatory, it gains a subversive valence by association. In the 1990s, with the romanticized undertone of the streets as a site of resistance, and sparked by the global Reclaim the Streets movement, chindon-ya for some became a trope that wove together fragments of desire for the subversive possibilities against the forces of privatization, corporatization, and criminalization that caused the crisis of public space. Building historical affective alliances, chindon-inspired practices amplified the various historical meanings and associations that cohered around the trope of the streets. The sounds and cultural imaginary of chindon-ya, in other words, enabled chindon-inspired artists to reclaim the streets before they became "sutorīto," activating the long historical lineages of sonic street activism distinct to Japan. In 2004, Ōkuma formed an offshoot band of Cicala Mvta called Jinta-la-Mvta, specifically aimed toward street-based gigs at protests (see figure 4.3). An acoustic, compact, and mobile version of Cicala Mvta, Jinta-la-Mvta became increasingly active at various political rallies, events, and protests; the next chapter will dive deeper into their work in the post-3.11 disaster Japan.

Daiku Tetsuhiro

Soul Flower Mononoke Summit's attempt to refashion chindon-ya and reinterpret prewar and postwar popular songs did not emerge out of nowhere. It was the album *Uchinā Jinta* (Okinawan jinta) by Daiku Tetsuhiro, a famed singer of traditional folk songs from Ishigaki island in the Okinawan archipelago, that inspired the band to reactivate these decades-old songs—the same album that sparked my initial interest in research on chindon-ya (see prologue). Born in 1948 as a Yaeyama native (a cluster of islands including Ishigaki), Daiku Tetsuhiro is a chief voice of local traditional music (figure 4.4). Having won numerous competitions, Daiku holds licenses to teach traditional songs from both Okinawa and the Yaeyama islands, and has been awarded Intangible Cultural Heritage status by Okinawa prefecture. Now living on Okinawa, Daiku frequently travels to teach at the twelve Okinawan music schools he has founded across Japan, while also touring abroad as a musical ambassador of Okinawa prefecture.

Daiku won his reputation as a maverick in 1994, when he defied the expectation that traditional singers should sing exclusively Okinawan songs, and instead put out *Uchinā Jinta*, which mostly contained popular songs from mainland Japan from the 1910s to the 1960s. Released on Off-note Records—the same label that put out the jinta band in Ishinomaki (chapter 1)—the album was the first musical recording project to integrate chindon drums in rearranging and reinterpreting sōshi enka and popular songs. Hosokawa Shūhei called this unusual selection of older, forgotten tunes from mainland Japan a kind of *mushiboshi*—an "airing out" of old, forgotten songs. Just as in the seasonal tradition in which one takes out old clothing and books to dry in order to prevent mold and insects, the chindon-inspired project sent a breeze through once-forgotten songs and produced new meanings by articulating them with the present.

Now considered one of the most influential records among chindon-inspired musicians, the album features Daiku's straight and broad voice cultivated within the Yaeyama island folk tradition backed by chindon-ya practitioners from the all-female family troupe Takada Sendensha, as well as musicians from the Tokyo jazz and improvisation scenes, some of whom had worked part time as gakushi (melody players) for chindon-ya troupes. The 1992 release of the album *Tokyo Chin Don* by Shinoda Masami provided a crucial backdrop for *Uchinā Jinta*. A double album of field recordings and studio recording, *Tokyo Chin Don* led to Takada Sendensha's sounds circulating and catching the attention of many musicians (plate 11). As a result, veteran chindon-ya practitioners from the troupe Takada Mitsuko and Hasegawa Yachiyo were invited to play chindon drums and gorosu on Daiku's album; they were brought in to the project by clarinet player Ōkuma Wataru, who had worked for Takada Sendensha's family chindon business for quite some time.

Music critic Hirai Gen describes Daiku's *Uchinā Jinta* as a "Pandora's box" of old songs from mainland Japan, reinterpreted in the voice of a singer from the geographical periphery, backed up by a distinctly hybridized instrumentation of chindon drums, other percussion, sax, accordion, clarinet, tuba, violin, and various horns. Daiku told me that his selection of tunes for the album wasn't arbitrary, but emerged from a process of remembering songs he grew up listening to his grandfather sing in Yaeyama. These old Japanese songs traveled all the way to Yaeyama and became part of Daiku's childhood soundscape, and continue to live in his memory while losing their currency in mainland Japan. These are the sounds through which he knew the world, his place in Yaeyama, and his view of mainland Japan from the small island. While Daiku took a rather nonchalant attitude toward reworking the songs, he politicized the process of recording the songs in 1994 by professing to me in an interview that the album was driven by a longtime grudge he held against mainland Japan. At age twenty-two, he advanced through the ranks of a nationally televised regional

FIGURE 4.4 Daiku Tetsuhiro (*middle*), playing with
Chindon Tsūshinsha, Nagoya, 2006. Photo by the author.

traditional folk song (*minyō*) competition for eight weeks. The first prize was a
major record deal. Just two weeks before the final round, he was booted from
the competition by the judges, who criticized and humiliated him for his "in-
comprehensible" Okinawan accent. Daiku told me that behind the record was
an anger he has lived with for decades. "Japanese listeners, listen to me sing
Japanese songs that you don't even remember."[29]

Claiming such old Japanese songs as his own, Daiku challenges the marginalized difference ascribed to Okinawa. Once an independent kingdom called
Ryūkyū, Okinawa was invaded by the Satsuma domain of Japan in the seven-
teenth century, and subsequently became a colony under direct Japanese rule
in 1872. In 1945, the island became the site of the bloodiest and largest battle between Japan and the United States in the Pacific theater, killing more than one
hundred thousand civilians and wiping out one-third of the population. Subsequently, Okinawa was occupied by the United States between 1945 and 1972.
Even after the "reversion" of Okinawa to Japan, the U.S. military has remained
in Okinawa on an indefinite basis under the U.S.-Japanese Treaty of Mutual
Cooperation and Security. Thus, Okinawa has long been in a doubly subju-
gated position through its neocolonial relations with mainland Japan and the
United States. Today, however, Okinawan difference is often representationally
abstracted and naturalized through the distance—almost one thousand miles
away from Tokyo—and the colonial traces concealed within mainstream representations of Okinawa as a paradise and a vacation destination.[30]

In his album, Daiku sonically challenges the geographically naturalized difference ascribed to Okinawa; the challenge is audible in the selection of repertoire and his Okinawan accent. In so doing, Daiku also reveals the historical struggles and oppression that pass unnoticed together with these old songs—remnants of colonial reach and assimilationist policies that repressed Okinawan difference. Even though the lyrics may not be inherently political, the act of singing these mainland songs, which were forgotten among most mainland Japanese listeners, becomes a mode of social critique, highlighting Japan's histories of colonialist violence.

None of the musicians or producers of the album could have predicted the kind of ripple effects the album would produce the year following its release. The year 1995 in Japan, as I discussed in chapter 3, was marked by tumultuous events that threw into question the routines and values of everyday life, while exposing the unevenness and contradictions within the persistent official discourse of national homogeneity. The Hanshin Awaji Earthquake (January 1995) unveiled the vulnerable lives of the zainichi populations and immigrant communities; and the gang rape of a teenage girl in Okinawa by U.S. military servicemen (September 1995) sparked a protest movement against the U.S. military and the Japanese government in Okinawa. The exposure of these fault lines in Japanese life brought with it a new critical questioning of the status quo.

Within this climate, Daiku's chindon-inflected album became a musical catalyst of sorts. The musical work of "airing out" old songs, made politically poignant through Daiku's particular lived experiences as a Yaeyama native, resonated strongly with mainland musicians who shared a similar critical gaze toward the government. Given this confluence of musical and social forces that emerged around 1995, it is not surprising that Soul Flower Mononoke Summit's first album, inspired by Daiku, explicitly interrogated the issue of "Japaneseness." Nakagawa states that the theme for their first album was the question "What the hell is Yamato [mainland Japan]?"[31] By using the term "Yamato," which emerged in the nineteenth century to refer to the settlers of mainland Japan in contrast to ethnic minorities, he highlights the silenced Others within the country—the indigenous Ainu, Okinawan islanders, zainichi Koreans and Chinese, buraku communities, and others. Others within the network of musicians in Osaka joined in, amplifying and diversifying the voices that were gaining volume in the 1990s. A seemingly disconnected network of musicians started to come together in sounding out a kind of affective alliance of difference marked by itinerancy, history, class, and ethnicity.

FIGURE 4.5 Cho Paggie. Photo by Hiromasa Mori.
Courtesy of Cho Paggie.

Cho Paggie

Cho Paggie, a zainichi Korean singer born in Osaka in 1956, was another musician who followed suit in integrating chindon-ya sounds into politicized musical projects (figure 4.5). Affectionately known as Pagi-yan, Cho has a wide
repertoire, comprising Korean folk songs, blues, and rock. In addition to being
an active performer, doing more than one hundred shows a year, Cho works
as a lecturer and writer to inform audiences about issues in education, human
rights, and Japan-Korea relations. He is a vocal critic of the discriminatory policies around ethnic Koreans in Japan, who are barred from voting or seeking
government jobs regardless of their generation or birth in Japan. In the aftermath of the 1995 earthquake, Cho collaborated with Soul Flower Mononoke
Summit and released a live album titled *Garlic Chindon* in 2000, featuring
members of Chindon Tsūshinsha.

Cho's answer to my question about how he came to incorporate chindon
sounds into his album—that he wanted to be "strange," just like chindon-ya—
warrants revisiting here. For a Korean Japanese singer marked by ethnic difference, musical rearticulation of his difference along with that of chindon-ya is
politically provocative. Cho's affinity with chindon-ya, explicitly and implicitly,

stems from the various historical and affective parallels that he is able to make audible between his difference as a zainichi Korean and other forms of marginalized difference that chindon-ya has absorbed. The always-already hybridized sounds of chindon-ya evoke both the traces of Western imperialism and Japan's own colonial past (chapter 1), which in turn resonate with the colonial relations between Korea and Japan of which Cho is a product. In playing with chindon-ya sounds, then, Cho marks his own difference as inherently constitutive of Japaneseness, along with other forms of historical and social difference evoked by chindon-ya.

Chindon-ya's historical association with the socially castigated and bachigai difference (out-of-placeness) is also one of the reasons why Soul Flower Mononoke Summit member Itami Hideko came to play chindon drums. She was raised with a sensitivity and concern for ethnic difference and generational gaps, she told me. She described the house where she grew up in Yamasaki, Osaka, as close to buraku areas. Her grade school was part of the environment that nurtured her sensitivity to ethnic difference: her third-grade music teacher burned government-issued music textbooks and instead instructed his students, including Itami, to sing South and North Korean songs from handmade music textbooks.[32] This was a radical act of condemning the homogenizing education system that promoted the nationalist and monoethnic conception of the state. Itami recalled that she considered her teacher's act to be appropriate, as her diverse classmates included zainichi Koreans as well as students with buraku background. This experience informed her later efforts to musically forge affective alliances across various forms of marginalized difference.

In addition to chindon-ya's historical roots, its musical sounds were key to Itami's adaptation of chindon-ya for her politicized musical projects. Chindon drums, for Itami, bypassed various hierarchical limitations set in place for other traditional instruments. Instead, their malleability enabled Itami to create new possibilities while retaining historical, familiar, and popular sonorities and associations in listeners' ears. "It's hard to approach *minyō* [traditional folk] genres because of stylistic difference and hierarchies [between masters and disciples, for example]; in contrast, chindon-ya seemed cool."[33] Itami has rearticulated her imaginary of chindon-ya with forms of ethnically marked difference that have not been necessarily historically associated with chindon-ya before.

For Cho and Itami, the sounds, instruments, and historically sedimented meanings of chindon-ya are means of highlighting, and articulating, different kinds of social difference and uneven relations that are often subsumed under the dominant discourse of Japan as a homogeneous nation. The ripple effects of Daiku's album led to the building of affective alliances among musicians from various backgrounds with distinct political concerns—concerns about U.S. militarism in Okinawa and Japan, the vulnerability of working-class residents in Nagata, human rights concerns around zainichi Koreans, and others. When Cho, Itami, and Daiku mobilize chindon-ya's sounds in gesturing toward the questions of ethnic minorities and colonial histories of Japan based on their lived experiences, they are reactivating and reworking the latent histories of marginalization and contestatory possibilities of street musical performances. In so doing, they make audible the complex articulation of the buraku issues, class politics, questions of ethnicity, and colonial histories of Japan—thereby raising the multicultural question of Japan.

Here I follow Stuart Hall's adjectival use of the word "multicultural"—rather than multicultural*ism*—to highlight the fact that, although some of the chindon-inspired musicians are marked by ethnic difference, it is not simply the ethnic plurality of Japan that these chindon-inspired sounds highlight.[34] In Hall's formulation, the multicultural question resists an essentialized notion of ethnicity as a unit of segments composing a society, and instead refers to the messiness of the process of "cultural pluralization" in which people are not formally fixed into groups (2000, 210).[35] The multicultural question, then, is not about the mere celebration of particularity and multiplicity within a given practice or geographical territory. Instead, it urges us to understand how the presumed homogeneity of a society is in fact inextricably constituted through the silenced production of difference (Hesse 1993, 172). This understanding of the multicultural is particularly pertinent to the Japanese case, as the terms "ethnicity" and "race" have entirely different histories, meanings, and connotations in Japanese, inflected as they were by the distinct histories of the feudal status system of the Edo period and the rise of capitalist consumer economy and attendant class politics (chapter 2).[36] While it is beyond the scope of this chapter to delve into the historical analysis of Japanese registers of difference, it is important to note how chindon-inspired musicians' sounds compel us to understand Japan as not a repository of multiple ethnic groups, but rather as a dynamically produced space that is constituted through overlapping and shifting histories of social differences and power relations.

In the aftermath of events that afflicted the national psyche in 1995, Daiku's chindon-inspired album thus had the unexpected consequence of giving rise to an emergent musical trend among mainland musicians and listeners alike, and this album remains to this day the best-selling album released by the Off-note label. Chindon-ya's resonances, integrated in these chindon-inspired musical projects, stirred up musical sensibilities and political concerns, and helped forge affective alliances among musicians orbiting around the cultural imaginary of chindon-ya. While these practitioners do not self-consciously identify as part of a unitary network or a singular cause of multiculturalism, an unexpected convergence of events led chindon-ya to serve as a sonic thread that articulates a loose, provisional, and shifting network of musicians, intellectuals, artists, and activists with a wide variety of backgrounds and political investments— not through concerted and organized efforts, but rather through unanticipated connections and individual collaborations. Without forming a coherent movement, these chindon-inspired musicians occasionally intersected with one another while attending to their own specific and local concerns. Their musical sounds gestured toward the multicultural question of Japan, foregrounding not preexisting categories of social differences, but rather possibilities and improvisatory practices that forge alliances—such as those between musician activists, day laborers, zainichi Koreans, anti-U.S. military activists in Okinawa—and the pleasure and festivity that often accompany such creative alliances.

MATSURIGOTO: POLITICS OF FESTIVITY

Arama, oyama, Show them the real *matsurigoto*

The emergence of the politicized chindon-inspired projects must also be understood within the shifting climate of the Japanese Left. Chindon-inspired practices amplified already latent changes within contemporary social movements in Japan—namely, a turn away from the oppositional politics of indignation toward a new politics of festivity. The 1980s and 1990s were a moment of self-reflexivity for the Japanese Left, after the so-called "failure" of the Left in the 1970s to stop the government from renewing the controversial security treaty with the United States. In his analysis of the 1990s Left, cultural critic Mōri Yoshitaka (2009) lists festivity (*shukusaisei*) as one of the strategies that has informed leftist political expressions as new generations assessed the limitations of the approaches taken by the previous generation and sought creative means of political expression. Within this context, the influence of the Reclaim the Streets movement was not insignificant. The emergence of sound demo in Japan in the wake of the Iraq War followed the global trend of bacchanalian occupation of the streets as a means of contesting the technocratic and capitalist encroachment on public space. Colorfully dressed, the younger generation turned from the prior generation's oppositional politics, which was often characterized by verbal expressions of indignation, masculinity, and at times physical violence. Instead, artists and musicians started to host music and arts festivals in lieu of rallies and street protests in which participants shouted slogans and held fists in the air.

Chindon-ya became an effective tool for producing this politics of festivity in a distinctly localized and familiar cultural form. In 2006, Itami Hideko, in collaboration with other musicians from Tokyo and Okinawa, held the first annual festival, called the Henoko Music Festa, to contest the imminent construction of a new U.S. military base in northern Okinawa. Consciously organized as a new mode of political expression, the festival marked a significant strategic departure from previous protest activities on the Henoko beach. The new protest culture foregrounded musical sounds instead of verbal expressions of political discontent that characterized the previous political protests. A wide array of musical sounds—from free jazz to Okinawan folk music, reggae, Irish music, hip-hop, African dance, rock, and of course, chindon-inspired music—resounded across the contested beach. Itami speculated that previous generations' demonstrations of discontent and anger were not only ineffective but also turned younger generations away.[37] The organizers emphasized the importance of "partying," "shaking bodies," "laughing," and "having fun" with music, instead of "sitting still," "shouting" and "giving speeches."

The political efficacy of festivity, partying, and pleasure has been discussed in many case studies, from block parties in the 1970s South Bronx to New Orleans brass bands.[38] Notably, in her work on *soca* in Trinidad, Guilbault (2010) coined the term "the politics of pleasure" to highlight the significance of pleasure as a crucial political force. She asserts that the political can be articulated not only through words or in state politics, but also through pleasure and personal enjoyment. While the politics of festivity may be found in many other places, it has a distinctly localized genealogy in Japan. For instance, various Okinawan traditional festivities have been mobilized as frameworks for social critique and political expression.[39] Likewise, the double meaning of the Japanese word *matsurigoto*, which phonetically means both politics and festival, has been popularly referenced by many organizers and activists as they have sought to ground inspirations from 1990s radical Left activists in the Japanese context. Although the political philosopher Maruyama Masao cautions against conflating the two notions,[40] the popular perception of a shared etymological origin between the Japanese words for "politics" and "festival" has often been valorized by activists who mobilize this distinctly Japanese concept in their attempt to transform the political from the antagonistic to the agonistic, from indignant expression to lively celebration.[41]

Of particular interest to my analysis of soundings within this new festive modality of political expression is the related notion of *nigiyakasa*, which evokes a dynamic and spirited sociality as well as the raucous sounds that characterize festive gatherings (see chapter 3). As an embodiment of nigiyakasa, chindon-ya was thus transposed productively to the politics of festivity. Perhaps wary of the possible contradiction inherent in critiquing the global forces of neoliberalism through the global network of protest expressions primarily centered in Europe and North America, artists-activists like Soul Flower Mononoke Summit and Ōkuma Wataru found a distinctly local expression in chindon-ya, whose sounds evoke not only subversive politics through historical associations, but also the liveliness that is central to the politics of festivity.

Unlike emulation of the Reclaim the Streets tactics from the UK, integration of chindon-ya did distinctly local work in at least three ways. First, chindon-inspired practitioners' turn to this distinctly Japanese practice is not based on a market-driven, self-exoticizing impulse. Rather, it is in the footsteps of the leftist intellectuals of the 1960s who sought to mobilize "indigenous" (*dochakuteki*) populist culture in an attempt to critique the earlier model of political organization based on Western, elitist cultural forms. In the 1960s, leftist intellectuals romanticized popular culture (*taishū bunka*)—the recorded popular music of enka being a case in point—for its rootedness among the marginalized, lower-class "masses."[42] This was a reactionary move away from the previous generation of left-leaning activists that upheld Western choral music (*utagoe undō*) as the emblem of the masses, denigrating "melancholic" and "dark" indigenous popular music. Similarly, the chindon-ya resurgence of the 1990s among leftist intellectuals, artists, and activists reflects a self-reflexive stance that critiques their own elite position. Instead, as Mōri points out (2009, 7–32), the "street philosophy" that emerged in the 1990s was an intentional turn toward the do-it-yourself spirit, embodied practices, and pleasure.

Second, as we have seen in Soul Flower Mononoke Summit's work in multicultural Nagata, chindon-inspired musical activism in the 1990s was about not only reclaiming public space, but also articulating the histories of status-based marginalization with those of ethnically marked difference today. As chindon-ya evokes precapital histories of marginalized difference and working-class solidarity and sociality in modern Japan (chapter 2), it serves as an effective means for intellectuals, activists, and artists to foreground the continuity and new articulations of different forms of oppression and discrimination. It was no coincidence that the post-disaster activities of Soul Flower Mononoke Summit focused on the low-income neighborhood of Nagata, where not only the impact of the disaster—both natural and manmade—was disproportionately severe, but also the histories of marginalized difference are spatialized. In line with the do-it-yourself, on-the-ground effort that sought to bridge the gap between the previous generations of leftist activists and the exploited working class today, the band also makes frequent appearances at festivals in the day laborers' towns known as *yoseba* in Yokohama and Osaka. Jinta-la-Mvta has also performed at summer festivals in Tokyo's San-ya neighborhood, one of the oldest and largest day laborer communities in Japan. As chindon-inspired musicians' juxtapositions of imagined historical layers activate memories latent in the streets, long histories of status-, ethnicity-, and class-based marginalization are stirred up within their sounds.

Third, the chindon-inspired activism around the crisis of public space was not simply a temporary refusal of the technocratic rationalization of public space as exemplified by Reclaim the Streets, but instead presented a radically different conception of spatial politics. While festive and spontaneous occupation of the street by Reclaim the Streets is a strategic reversal of the dominant spatial logic, chindon-inspired practitioners' performance puts forward alternative ways of conceiving and living the public space that are—and have been in the past—possible in Japan. Through the old, forgotten songs and memories evoked by the sounds of chindon percussion, these performers evince the historical incongruence between the sounds that once were heard on the streets and the streets that no longer allow them to reverberate. The temporary denial of the absolutist conception of space is inherently predicated upon, and ultimately reproduces, the dominant logic itself. Instead of engaging with this logic, chindon-inspired practitioners foreground a historically grounded, entirely different understanding of space—that it is to be produced through an articulation of social relations, histories, and soundings.

————

The recent politicization of chindon-ya was not a coherent movement that can be attributed a singular logic. Rather, it emerged through a loose assemblage of incidental personal connections and imaginations. A confluence of disparate musical, historical, political, and cultural currents in the 1990s informed this process: the global movement of Reclaim the Streets that responded to the crisis of public space; self-reflexive Japanese leftist activists and intellectuals seeking to embrace and embody taishū bunka and the politics of festivity; devastating calamities afflicting national sociality; and critical voices that posed a "multi-cultural" question of Japan.

The various political interests and musical sensibilities of the chindon-inspired musicians have coalesced messily, but are held together by the force of memories, narratives, and perceptions of chindon-ya. Chindon-ya, with its polysemic, memory-evoking, and affectively charged potentialities, became a catalyst that activated the sedimented subversive possibilities of street performing arts as well as colonial histories of Japan, while also helping to produce affective alliances. Although historically a commercial enterprise, chindon-ya, through its emergent poetics and politics, unexpectedly created tangible effects in socially and politically contested situations—sounding out the "real matsurigoto."

CHAPTER 5

Resonances of Silence

On April 10, 2011, just one month after the devastating magnitude 9.0 earthquake, tsunami, and subsequent nuclear crisis in northeast Japan, over fifteen thousand people took over the streets of the Kōenji neighborhood of Tokyo in an anti-nuclear-power protest. This was one of the first events of what would become a nationwide antinuclear movement, which has grown into a series of the largest street demonstrations Japan has seen since the 1960s. In the following years, various forms of street protests have taken place, from occasional large street demonstrations (or *demo* in Japanese) to weekly antinuclear rallies in front of the prime minister's residence and more localized smaller events, such as town meetings, kite-flying gatherings, and folk dance festivals.[1]

Leading the April 10 protest was the raucous sound of chindon-ya. Costumed in bright-colored kimonos, six chindon-ya performers walked, twirled, and smiled while playing chindon drum sets that were adorned with colorful paper umbrellas. They were followed by a group of instrumentalists playing melody—a wide array of tunes, from recognizable Japanese popular songs to "Amazing Grace" and "Ppurip'a" ("Root," or "Radical," a Korean adaptation of "When Johnny Comes Marching Home")[2]—in unison on the clarinet, saxophone, tuba, and harmonica. Some of them were dressed in ostentatious costumes with comical wigs and hats, while others were in everyday clothing. A couple of electric guitarists provided a harmonic underpinning to the melody, carrying small portable amplifiers on straps slung across their shoulders. What was notable about their appearance at this particular antinuclear rally on April 10, 2011, however, was that these chindon-ya musicians weren't hired by any client to advertise businesses—they were voluntary participants of the first demonstration after the disaster, alongside thousands of other citizens. The chindon-ya performers walked along with the fifteen thousand participants to voice their anxiety around the precarious condition of the nuclear power plant in Fukushima and their desire for a nuclear-power-free economy.

The festive sounds and vibrant colors of chindon-ya performers provided a stark contrast to the solemn and dark atmosphere that had pervaded Tokyo city streets for the month since the triple disaster on March 11. Faced with the catastrophic devastation shown daily on TV, reports of an increasing death toll,[3] and uncertainty around the precarious state of the nuclear crises at the Fukushima Daiichi Plant, many Tokyo residents experienced confusion, frustration, fear, and paralysis. In the name of national mourning and energy-conservation efforts, many businesses and individuals observed the social convention of silence and frugality called *jishuku*, leaving the streets dimmer, quieter, and emptier than usual.

Amid this silence of jishuku, how did these chindon-ya practitioners choose to festively sound out against the government's energy policies and its much-criticized reactions to the disasters? How did chindon-ya, an erstwhile commercial practice, become a sonic marker of the mass antinuclear movement in the spring of 2011? Although there had been precedents for the political mobilization of the chindon-ya aesthetic (chapter 4), it was not until post-3.11 that I witnessed chindon-ya practitioners, most of whom had previously refrained from being involved in protests, becoming prominently present and recognizably emblematic of a particular political movement. I suggest that the particular traction that chindon-ya has gained in post-3.11 Japan must be understood in a specific historical, geographical, and sonic conjuncture—particularly by listening to the weighty silence against which the musicians sounded their instruments.[4]

This chapter is a case study that looks closely at the politicization of chindon-ya, offering a framework in which to understand the role of sound in political interventions against socioeconomic precarity in neoliberal and post-disaster Japan. Focusing on the forms of sociality that are produced at these antinuclear street protests, I explore the tension between the resonances of street protests and socially reinforced silence to understand how chindon-ya has gained political traction in the anti-nuclear-power movement in post-3.11 Japan—in a much more audible and visible way than many other instances of the politicization of chindon-ya I described in the previous chapter. Contextualizing the antinuclear protests within a larger arc of social movements in postwar Japan, I first discuss how the popular imaginary of chindon-ya has informed its political efficacy at street protests. Then I shift my focus to the forms of sociality at these antinuclear street protests to examine how the particular logic of chindon-ya's musical labor was transposed from the commercial to the political.[5] Third, I examine the silence of jishuku. Taking silence as not simply a metaphor for political oppression but as an active auditory condition of quiet, I ask what the consequences of the silence were, and what kinds of understanding of sociality and precarity emerge from listening carefully to the silence. Finally, I zero in on the silence of jishuku and the sounds of chindon-ya at a politicized folk dance festival. Listening to them together, I argue, reveals emergent modes of political expressions, enabling a broader-based movement toward, and beyond, what anthropologist Marc Abélès calls "the politics of survival" in post-3.11 Japan. In so doing, I foreground not only the significance of the nondiscursive sounds in analyzing music in social movements but also the necessity to avoid unreflexively reducing sounding to an oppositional political move. By closely attending to resonances, local ontologies, and sedimented histories, I situate the political affordances of chindon-ya in the very relationality—necessarily contingent and ephemeral—between sound and silence.

CHINDON-YA AT STREET PROTESTS

To explore how chindon-ya has been mobilized in recent antinuclear street protests, it is important to first understand how chindon-ya is situated in the Japanese cultural imagination. As I have shown in the previous chapters, the popular imaginary and representation of chindon-ya today largely has its roots in the 1950s, the period that is considered to be chindon-ya's heyday, when they were familiar sights and sounds on small neighborhood urban streets. Even though their physical presence has become rarer in the recent few decades as they became replaced by other advertisement practices, chindon-ya as a cultural trope have persisted in popular media.

This popular perception of chindon-ya proved especially effective for the recent antinuclear demonstrations, which drew a large number of people who had never participated in street protests before. This is significant, as deeply rooted prejudices against demo have kept the general public from participating in street rallies since the student protests of the 1960s, which were often confrontational and violent. During the street demonstrations of that era, called the ANPO struggles (ANPO is the Japanese abbreviation for the Treaty of Mutual

Cooperation and Security between the United States and Japan), many activists and students took to the streets and university campuses to oppose the government's plan to renew the security treaty with the United States, extending Japan's neocolonial dependency on U.S. military bases. Perhaps it is no coincidence that the fear of allowing Japan to fall under the U.S. nuclear umbrella was one of the main concerns that had led to the massive protests against the Japanese government's renewal of the interdependency on the U.S. military hegemony at that time.[6] The protesters were met with violent suppression by the police, cementing the popular perception of demos as dangerous, sectarian, and perhaps ultimately futile, as the treaty was signed despite the massive dissent.

The demo constituencies on the Japanese streets started to shift in the early 2000s, when a new form of political protest called "sound demo" turned street rallies into mobile rave parties through the use of trucks loaded with sound systems. Inspired by the international Reclaim the Streets movement that started in the UK in 1991 (chapter 4), sound demos attracted new participants, largely youth with diverse tastes and socioeconomic backgrounds (DeMusik Inter 2005, 122; Hayashi and McKnight 2005, 94).[7] Even then, however, the outreach of this new form of sound demo was largely limited to countercultural youths who shared concerns around the shifts in the flexible and globalized labor market, the U.S. invasion of Iraq, and the neoliberal order of then prime minister Jun'ichiro Koizumi and Tokyo governor Ishihara Shintarō.

It was not until the antinuclear demos in the spring of 2011 that a significantly wider spectrum of society started to participate in street protests, many of them for the first time. Indicative of this demographic shift in demo participants was the issuing of a "demo for first timers" brochure that served as a how-to guide for people with no experience partaking in street protests (figure 5.1). The illustrated booklet, made available for free download online, is written to be accessible for people from three-year-olds to adults, showing what to expect at a street protest, what to bring (e.g., snacks, water, homemade flyers or signs, musical instruments), and putting forth an inclusive picture of who can participate and how. This brochure indexed the changing image of demo and the widening demography of participants in antinuclear rallies.

Chindon-ya's appearance at the antinuclear street protests in 2011 was part of the volunteers' and organizers' effort to appeal to a wider audience by transforming the cultural stigma of demo. To further encourage participation from citizens, and to undo the persistent and widespread assumption that demon-

さあ、デモがはじまった。あちこちで、いろんな声がするよ。音楽も
きこえる。いつもと違う景色見えてくる。これがひとりじゃないという
こと、みんなと一緒にいるということ。これがデモ。

プラカードはよく見えるようになるべく上にあげよ
う。声をだしてもいいし、ださなくてもいいよ。疲れたら
ゆっくり歩けばいいし、おしゃべりしながら歩いてもい
いね。前や後ろを見て、おもしろそうなことしているひと
がいたら、見に行ってみよう。そうすれば、デモがもっと
楽しくなるし、次もまた行きたくなるかもね。

FIGURE 5.1 "Hajimete no demo" (Demo for first timers), brochure excerpt. irutoirato-
sononakamatachi, https://activism3cream.wordpress.com.

strations are for combative activists with political affiliations, some antinuclear
movement organizers strategically embraced chindon-ya. A familiar trope,
chindon-ya provides a cultural framework for citizens who have never engaged
in street protests. Immediately recognizable to the bystanders aurally and visually, chindon-ya embodies the familiar and the everyday amid the otherwise
intimidating spectacle of street demos accompanied by a large number of police
forces. In this light, chindon-ya both indexed the diversifying demographic of
the post-3.11 antinuclear demo participants and served to update the public
perception of demo culture from masculine, violent, and sectarian to inclusive,
peaceful, and diverse.[8]

While chindon-ya was effectively mobilized to cater to the shift in the demographics and public understanding of street protests, its relevance within
the social movement was not merely symbolic. I suggest that the logic of
chindon-ya's musical labor as an advertisement enterprise and the historical
specificity of post-3.11 Japan must be closely examined to understand how
chindon-ya's sound might be signaling new political possibilities in contemporary Japan.

CHINDON-YA'S MUSICAL LABOR:
AFFECTIVE AND ACOUSTIC RESONANCES

Over a cold beer after one of the many street protests in which I played with chindon-ya performers in the summer of 2012, Hattori Natsuki, a guitarist who often joined the chindon-ya performers at demonstrations, said: "There are ways to play so that we'll be heard, without annoying people. We have to make sound so that they'll take notice. We have to play like that." As I have demonstrated in chapter 3, Hattori's comment echoes what the members of Chindon Tsūshinsha have repeatedly emphasized to me as the core principle of their commercial work: the need to sound their instruments in a way that "resonates with listeners' hearts" (*kokoro ni hibiku*). This core principle of chindon-ya's musical labor has been productively transposed to the political realm. One drummer who regularly participates in the street demonstrations tweeted: "I think there are some demo participants who have mistaken sound as a goal in itself as a way to release one's ego. There's a big difference between the objectives of those who want to express themselves through the nuclear problem and those who truly consider everyone affected by the problem."[9] Underneath this rather stoic critique against his own cohort is the professional demand for chindon-ya musicians to be imaginatively empathetic to potential listeners so as to elicit maximum social interaction among the otherwise uninterested.

Attentiveness to the affective dynamics of the streets is another aspect of chindon-ya practice that translated well to street protests. At one march, a sound truck driving right in front of the chindon-ya group used excessively loud speakers to make aggressive comments toward the secret police, who were on the sidewalks taking notes. The woman in the truck yelled through the speakers: "You dirty dogs, we know you are out there, go home!" To this, Kogure Miwazō, the chindon drummer central to Jinta-la-Mvta, voiced her disapproval: "That kind of rough and coarse voice makes everyone feel unpleasant. There were some police who were nice to us along the road. I don't like that sound of anger. That's why I used to hate demonstrations and never joined until this year." Noting the visceral response that the amplified voice of antagonism against police incited in her, Miwazō highlighted how the affective response to the "sound of anger" that typified the previous protests was a deterrent to her own participation in demonstrations.

The affective resonance of chindon-ya's sound has a tangible effect not only on listeners, but also on the performers themselves. A member of the drum group TCDC, the street-protest collective inspired by neo-chindon-ya aesthetics, told me that the materiality of chindon-ya sound is the mobilizing force for members' sustained participation in protests: "I keep coming back because I want to be in the middle of our sounds. Playing together and feeling the sound in my body makes me feel that I'm part of a much larger movement."[10] It is this sense of co-presence through the shared experience of self-reflexive sounding, hearing, and embodying sound that produces sociality at demonstrations. Through these acoustic and affective resonances, street protests become a site of social encounters—and it is such sociality that motivates the continued participation of the weekly protesters.

The production of acoustic and affective resonances requires a wide variety of performance skills. Some of the skills chindon-ya performers can easily transfer from their advertisement routine to protests are their extensive repertoire and their ability to play widely recognizable tunes catering to specific demographics. For instance, Jinta-la-Mvta (figure 5.2), the chindon-inspired group I performed with at numerous rallies over the past few years, was often asked by the organizers to walk and perform in the "family area" or "family bloc"—a section of the march designated for young parents and small children that is typically placed early in a rally. While walking along the streets with young mothers holding hands with their children or pushing strollers, Jinta-la-Mvta often selected tunes that were familiar to children. One of the repeated songs we would play in the family bloc is "Anpanman March," a theme song for a popular TV cartoon show *Anpanman*.

> Oh, yeah, we can feel the joy of our precious life
> Someday we will live without a heartache
> Have you ever wondered why we were born
> What it is we're meant to be
> We can find an answer on our own
> Let's find it, you and me
> Any time, anywhere, do your best
> Listen to your heart; be honest
> And then you can go far with a smile on your face.[11]

While the cheerful and catchy melody makes the tune widely popular among children, the lyrics' philosophical messages about the simple joy of being alive and the importance of personal integrity in the face of challenging circumstances have inspired and captured the imagination of many adults.[12] Coinci-

FIGURE 5.2 Jinta-la-Mvta members at an antinuclear rally in Tokyo,
July 29, 2012. Photo by David Novak.

dentally, many children and adults in the disaster-affected areas requested the song, making it simultaneously an anthem for the survivors of the disasters and for the antinuclear movement.[13]

As a sonic practice that negotiates social relations on the streets, chindon-ya is well poised to maneuver spatial dynamics during street demonstrations as well. While performing during the rally, chindon-ya members refused to simply be a spectacle to people on the streets observing the protest from the sidewalk. They were constantly weaving in and out of the demonstration route regulated by the police officers, moving between the street and the sidewalk, chatting with bystanders and inviting passersby to join the rally—precisely the kind of spatial negotiations chindon-ya practitioners navigate in their usual street advertisement routine. In doing so, chindon-ya unsettled the temporal and spatial demarcations that have historically contained street protests as the disturbance of everyday life and public space, while erasing the social barriers between the demo participants and passersby. By blurring the temporal line between the everyday and the extraordinary, obscuring the difference between participants and spectators, and revealing the porousness within the spatial dynamism of the public space, chindon-ya's commercial routine transposes productively to the mode of political expression.

But why did chindon-ya gain traction in the spring of 2011 in particular? In order to examine the particular political valence chindon-ya sounds have gained in the recent anti-nuclear-power movement, I suggest that we also need to listen to their sounds at this historically, geographically, and sonically specific conjuncture. I now turn to the silence of jishuku, against which chindon-ya sounded out their instruments as I described at the beginning of this chapter. Instead of understanding jishuku as a lack of soundings, I follow Eugenie Brinkema's reformulation of silence as a "regime of near-inaudibility," which postulates silence as not an absence of sound, but intensity in suspension (Brinkema 2011, 224–25). I am interested in the affective registers of the latent stirrings that mark the notion of nationally mandated silence; put another way, I want to listen to the resonances of the silence of jishuku. While silence has often been analyzed as a sonic metaphor for the suppression of differences or voices,[14] I suggest that we listen carefully to the historical resonances of the silence of jishuku itself to understand the political potency of chindon-ya's presence in the antinuclear protests in post-3.11 Japan.

SILENCE OF JISHUKU

"Let us dedicate a silent prayer to the victims of the disasters," one of the organizers announced through a handheld speaker to the thousands of protesters who gathered in Hibiya Park, Tokyo. It was exactly one year after the disaster, March 11, 2012. Together with the members of Jinta-la-Mvta, I was waiting for our turn to start the one-year-commemoration antinuclear rally. Many of us chose to dress in black that day, instead of the usual dress code of bright yellow—the symbolic color of the anti-nuclear-power movement. After a minute of silence, we plunged deep in conversation, noting the absence of familiar faces in the crowd, and discussing how many seemed to have decided not to participate that day, choosing instead to observe the day in silence at home. A young man, dressed in black, walked up and stood right by us, quietly demanding attention. When we turned to him, we saw that he was holding a sketchbook in his hands. It read in broken English: "I want to pray. Please silent." He stood there in silence, with a stiff expression on his face (figure 5.3). I sensed uneasiness among the chindon musicians, who had already shared with me their dilemma between their urge to pay respect to the dead in silence and their urge to voice their antinuclear message even louder on this particular day. After a few minutes, the march started, and we climbed up on the back of a truck to play.

It was a poignant moment of silence that spoke volumes about jishuku—the larger, more sustained, and nationalized form of silence performed in response to the disaster. Jishuku, spelled with the two Chinese characters *ji* (self) and *shuku* (reverence, lack of sound), is a form of self-restraint from activities considered unessential or selfish. It is pervasively practiced by individuals, businesses, and private and official institutions, and for several months on end. The voluntary agency implied in this social convention of jishuku has been subject to contestation. Though small in number, citizens, journalists, and scholars specializing in fields from religion to law were quick to point out the contradictions within the word *jishuku*.[15] Suggesting that jishuku was in fact externally prescribed, journalists coined the term *tashuku*; by replacing "*ji*" with "*ta*" (other, external), they revealed how jishuku was a repressive practice imposed upon citizens, sometimes against their will or to their discomfort (Hōgaku Seminā editorial team 1989, 161).

Behind the notion of jishuku, one can hear an echo of Asia-Pacific wartime austerity efforts demanding individual sacrifice in solidarity with others suffering for a national cause. Matsudaira Tokujin, a legal scholar, has shown that the word was created during World War II in the context of a regulated economy modeled after the Nazi Germany policy of total war, which demanded individual responsibility for the continuation of the collective even when that meant contributing your own life. Jishuku was a militaristic and government discourse that became a social custom through imperial ideology and social conformity (Matsudaira 2013, 88). After the 3.11 disasters, in the name of jishuku, many TV programs and commercials were withdrawn, cherry blossom picnic parties and summer festivals were canceled, pachinko parlors stopped blasting music and announcements, and performances and advertisements in public space were informally banned, leaving the streets dark and quiet.

Such nationwide jishuku was a rare occurrence in postwar Japan, preceded only by a similar ban after Emperor Hirohito's passing on January 7, 1989. The death of the emperor, who had been ill with duodenal cancer for over three months, marked the end of the Shōwa era (1926–1989). That day, Japan fell into silence. The news broke on TV channels, which promptly took special measures to withdraw all commercials and dedicated the following forty-eight to seventy-two hours to special programs reflecting on the life of the emperor.[16] This was

FIGURE 5.3 Man silently demanding silence at the one-year commemoration of the 3.11 disaster at the antinuclear rally in Hibiya Park, Tokyo, 2012. Photo by the author.

followed by a month of programming that excluded entertainment, performing arts, and music.[17] National flags flew at half-mast, with a black cloth covering the round golden tip of flagpoles. Shops and public offices were closed. People remained indoors, glued to the TV. Stores stopped playing recorded music and sales pitches from the speakers. The streets were unusually quiet.

This silence had been anticipated since the first news of the emperor's declining health broke in September the previous year. Though the cancer diagnosis was not publicly revealed until after his death, a sense of somberness and solemnity lurked in the everyday lives of Japanese citizens for several months leading up to the emperor's passing. A daily announcement of the emperor's condition became a staple on the radio and TV news, rendered eerily intimate by quantitative data on his pulse, temperature, blood content of his stool, and amount of blood transfusion, given as routinely as if it were a weather report. After the initial announcement of the emperor's ailing health in September 1988 until the time of the funeral in February 1989, many public events were canceled in reverence of the emperor, from small local festivals and sports festivals to the victory parade for the sumo champion, annual music awards, international fashion shows, and the New Year's performance of kabuki theater. Without any formal mandates or legal regulations, sound, gestures of festivity, and performance in public spaces were discouraged. Many sounds disappeared from public space, from the bass drums of the cheerleading team in the university league baseball games to right-wing sound trucks,[18] Christmas jingle bells, and, of course, chindon-ya, the epitome of commercialism, festivity, and sound and performance in public space.[19]

In these two affectively charged historical moments of 1989 and 2011, the disappearance of chindon-ya's sounds, together with other sounds of commercialism and merriment in public space, was a silence pregnant with questions. Just how did Japanese citizens come to participate in this voluntary practice of sonic abstinence? How voluntary is this silent practice of self-restraint? On what kind of social logic was this silence based, and what might it tell us about the particular sociality produced at these moments of national crisis?

Some cultural critics and journalists interpreted jishuku as complex processes and mechanisms of social management, reminiscent of the Foucauldian notion of governmentality. They argued that an ensemble of institutions from mass media, local and national government, the police, right-wing organizations, and private organizations created conditions in which the majority of citizens, arguably willingly, participated in the act of self-silencing, without formal technologies that forced them to do so.[20] Others pointed to the binding power of social custom and the moral aesthetic of consensus and conformity as the driving force behind jishuku. Many of these writers seemed unable to resist the allure of the explanatory power of nihonjinron, a persistent and popular postwar discourse that essentializes Japanese cultural exceptionalism.[21] Although they were critical of the nationalist tendencies behind jishuku, these writers nonetheless fell prey to reductively diagnosing the silence of jishuku as a symptom of a uniquely Japanese notion of social collectivity or community (*kyōdōtai*), attributing it to notions like "excessive conformism" (Funakoshi 1990), "friendly authoritarianism" (Davidson 2013, 3), *seken* (world-space) (Abe Kin'ya 1995, Kōkami 2009), and *kūki* (air) (Kōkami 2009, Yamamoto 1977). These terms are purported to refer to an inherent pattern of Japanese sociality that explains how citizens embrace the jishuku mandate without external coercion. The latter two Japanese terms in particular were frequently invoked in interviews and writings on jishuku. For example, an owner of movie theaters in Tokyo, who was asked why he decided to follow the jishuku order, answered: "I didn't do it out of consideration for the emperor. It's not because I'm scared of the right wing and mass media. . . . I guess it's *seken* [literally, "world-space"] in general [that made me follow the jishuku order]." *Asahi Journal* shuzai han (1988) argues that seken is a "native" concept of Japanese sociality or worldview, as opposed to the notion of *shakai* (society), which was coined in the late nineteenth century to translate the English word "society" (Abe 1995). *Seken*, unlike *shakai*, which defines society as a collection of individuals, refers to social relations that have an immediate impact on oneself, thereby highlighting one's embeddedness within a social circle and a sense of obligations required to maintain these relations. *Kūki* is used almost interchangeably, referring to the fluidity and flexibility of the inescapable social relations that govern one's social conduct. The presence and demands of the social collectivity can be tautologically defined through these notions, which signify a ubiquitous social space that is invisible, nebulous, and yet omnipresent—like the air.

Neither the notion of governmentality nor the essentialist characterization of the Japanese social order alone is enough to account for the prevalence and consequences of jishuku, however. Here, I suggest a third perspective to bring them together by paying particular attention to the role that affect plays in the logic of jishuku. Referring to the feedback loop between state forces, private forces, and social expectations held by individuals that produced and maintained jishuku, literary and cultural critic Akatsuka Yukio argues that jishuku works as if it were a "phenomenon of resonance" (1989, 149). Understanding the silence of jishuku as a kind of resonance is helpful in examining how various technologies of social management, the cultural imaginary of Japanese sociality, and affective rhetoric have been articulated together in the practice of jishuku, and what kinds of sociality and histories are audible within the silence.

The aforementioned spatial metaphors of *seken* (world-space) and *kūki* (air), which refer to senses of social collectivity, offer a key to examining the particular intensities of affective and social resonances within the silence of jishuku. Instilled in this air at the two specific historical moments of jishuku in 1989 and 2011 was the affective power of mourning and yearning for sociality. Examining the jishuku practices in post-3.11 Japan, Matsudaira asks why so many citizens sought in jishuku a proof of *kizuna* (affective bond, human connections). Chosen as the word of the year by popular vote, the notion of *kizuna* became the unofficial slogan for the disaster relief efforts, various charity events, national media coverage, and political campaigns, evoking a sense of human connection, from familial relations to the national (Matsudaira 2013, 86).[22] The rhetoric of human connection was a powerful mobilizing force behind jishuku, especially for a nation violently shaken by the disasters that revealed the ephemerality, fragility, and consolatory power of human connections. In this context, the silence of jishuku was represented, heard, and felt as a way of implicating oneself in the lives of those who were affected by the disaster, vicariously sharing the pain and losses suffered by them.

Both after the death of the emperor and after the disaster, jishuku was a sonic performance of national mourning and social embeddedness. Both were moments of national crisis, in which Japanese sociality was deeply fragmented— through the death of the national symbol in 1989, and through the devastation of people, region, and a power plant that supplied much of the capital's electricity demand in 2011. Jishuku, then, was an attempt to suture fragmented national sociality through silence, previously in the name of imperial nationalism, and today, disaster nationalism. In the resonance of jishuku, we hear the various forms of nationalist projects, which hailed citizens as state subjects through the affective rhetoric of mourning, empathy, and solidarity.

Jishuku was not simply a top-down state project, however. The silent production of nationalist sociality was filled with tensions—much like the moment of nervous restlessness between the young man who mutely insisted on silence and the chindon-ya musicians at the one-year anniversary antinuclear rally. As the political, social, affective, and economic consequences of jishuku spun out in interconnected and unexpected ways, new currents emerged from the resonances of silence. Among many sources of agitation were those whose livelihoods were constrained by the economic side effects of jishuku measures, including chindon-ya. As I describe below, the tensions within the resonances of silence created unanticipated receptions, reactions, and resistances in return.

SOUNDING OUT THE POLITICS OF SURVIVAL

The moments of silence in public space in both 1989 and 2011 severely affected the livelihood of chindon-ya practitioners, along with various street vendors (*rotenshō*), whose income depended on commercial activities and performances on the streets.[23] When reflecting on their careers, veteran chindon-ya—those who had witnessed the economic upturn of the postwar recovery as well as the decades-long downturn beginning in the early 1990s due to the burst of the economic bubble—often refer to the first few months of 1989 as the most damaging time for the chindon-ya industry.[24] After the emperor's declining health was made public, all business opportunities for chindon-ya were canceled. Veteran chindon-ya Takinoya Hihumi, who recently passed in his nineties, was so pessimistic about the future of the chindon-ya business at the time that he considered switching careers, taking up a part-time job working for a lunchbox shop. In her book *Chindon* (2009), Hiromi Ōba describes the impact the death of Emperor Hirohito had on the chindon-ya industry: "What gave the kiss of death to the surviving chindon-ya was the death of Emperor Shōwa [Hirohito]. From 1988 and 1989, entertainment and publicity were self-censored, and all of Japan became quiet as if a flame had gone out. Chindon-ya in Tokyo lost all their jobs for that year, and since this time, the number of chindon-ya troupes declined to fewer than twenty. Particularly, the self-censoring of the pachinko [slot machine] industry, which was the largest client for chindon-ya, was lethal to chindon-ya" (Ōba and Yada 2009, 357–58).

Though the impact of the jishuku movement varied slightly between Tokyo and other regions,[25] nationwide, the chindon-ya industry faced an unprecedented sense of crisis at this time. The long-term economic downturn that began in 1990 further aggravated this crisis, as fewer small business employers were able to afford chindon-ya.[26]

The chindon-ya industry faced a similar struggle again after the catastrophic earthquake, tsunami, and nuclear crisis of 2011. Chindon-ya was one of the sectors directly affected by the social convention of jishuku, as it discouraged performance of festiveness and commercialism in public spaces.[27] Following the triple disaster, clients canceled chindon-ya gigs scheduled for the following few months. According to a report, one chindon-ya troupe appealed to the government to claim the financial damage caused by the disaster, estimating a loss of $370,000—approximately 30 percent of their overall income. As a result, jishuku observed by chindon-ya's employers forced chindon performers to take up part-time jobs, joining the growing population of the irregularly employed or the underemployed who survive by stringing together various part-time jobs. Kawaguchi Masaaki related to me in an e-mail in April 2011 the impact the disaster had on the chindon industry: "I've never seen it this bad since we started our business in the 1980s. We all have had to find part-time jobs. We may not be in business by the time you come back to Japan this summer." Jishuku brought another blow to the chindon-ya industry in April 2011, when it was announced that the annual chindon contest in Toyama was canceled. This contest provides a sizable income and an opportunity for chindon-ya throughout the country to gather. Having lost the symbolic and financial pillar of business, chindon-ya practitioners had been at a loss.

Consequently, chindon-ya's affective labor—which has always been precarious throughout its history—became aligned with the contemporary struggles of those who are called *purekariāto* (precariat) in Japan.[28] The term "precariat" was popularized in Japan by activist-author Amemiya Karin in 2007, who drew it from the work of Michael Hardt and Antonio Negri on affective labor (2001, 293). A combination of the words "proletariat" and "precarious," precariat refers to the chronically underemployed or working poor (particularly youth), who are deemed socially and biologically unproductive and psychically and physically unable to survive in the postindustrial economy.[29] With the erosion of lifetime or regular employment, postindustrial Japan's demand for flexible labor has produced an unusually large number of people who are underemployed and living precariously.[30] Identifying the proliferation of the precariat as a contemporary Japanese social malaise, anthropologist Anne Allison mobilizes the term "precarity" to characterize the pervasive sense of fragmented sociality in Japan: a condition of being and feeling insecure in life that extends one's disconnectedness from a sense of social community (Allison 2009a, 92; 2013, 9).[31]

As chindon-ya felt at a loss in 2011, facing this deep sense of precarity, so did many Tokyo residents. Immediately after the 3.11 disaster, in the vacuum of reliable information and in fear of radiation exposure, many stayed home, without knowing what information to trust, how to feel, and with whom to share their confusion. Amid widespread, paralyzing confusion, a group of precariat called Shirōto no Ran (Revolt of Amateurs) announced its plan to protest on the streets under a blunt slogan with a comical overtone: "*Koee! Abunē! Genpatsu Yamero!*" (Dangerous! Terrifying! Stop nuclear power!) (figure 5.4). This emotionally charged call for action mobilized fifteen thousand people, a turnout far exceeding the organizers' initial expectation of a couple of thousand.

Part-time chindon-ya performer Midori Ishida told me that she felt relieved when she read the slogan, which reassured her that she wasn't alone in her confusion, fear, and frustration. Ishida continued: "I stayed at home as much as possible, because we really didn't know how it would impact our health. Everyone was staying home and feeling kind of scared and depressed. In the jishuku mood, we didn't even know what would be appropriate to say."[32] She then explained why she decided to put a call out to all her chindon-ya colleagues in the Tokyo area to join the march: "We lost our livelihood to jishuku. We didn't know what was going on with radiation. We were frustrated. We just wanted to make sounds against the jishuku order."[33]

Thus, the presence of chindon-ya at the first antinuclear protest after the disaster was not merely a cultural trope to mobilize a diverse crowd or spectacle adding to the politics of festivity. They were protesting not only the antinuclear policy but also the resonances of jishuku, unsettling the convention that precluded affective responses of fear, frustration, and confusion. As a form of affective labor grounded in the production of sociality, chindon-ya's soundings revealed the repressive and alienating effects of the nationalizing silence of jishuku.

Further, and more important, in sounding out within and against the silence of jishuku, chindon-ya produced a new sociality among constituents. Forced out of work by the silent logic of jishuku, chindon-ya, through their soundings at the antinuclear rally, enabled an affective alliance between the economically disenfranchised—including chindon-ya themselves—and those threatened by nuclear radiation.[34] In bringing together those who shared deep insecurity in life in the face of economic recession and nuclear crisis, chindon-ya's sound performed ambivalent negotiations about the nation (demanded in silence) and empire (exposed through silence), which brought to the fore the lives of those living on the edge in postindustrial Tokyo.

At the April 10 rally, then, chindon-ya's resonances impelled an unexpected

FIGURE 5.4 "*Abunē! Genpatsu Osoroshī!*" (Dangerous! Nuclear power is terrifying!). Poster for the first demonstration after the disaster, held on April 10, 2011, in Kōenji, Tokyo.

reconfiguration of what "social precarity" meant in post-disaster Japan. "Precarity" no longer simply evokes the condition of the underemployed, but rather the larger segment of the society whose lives and futures are uncertain under the risk of radiation exposure. The frequent use of the rhythmic chant "protect our children!" at the protest attests to how antinuclear protest has become a kind of politics over life, or survival against the precarity of life caused by economic recession and nuclear disaster. Given this new emphasis on life and survival as the nodal point of political engagement in the post-Fukushima street protests, it seems appropriate that the song "Anpanman March"—celebrating the simple joy of being alive and what Antonio Gramsci calls optimism of the will—has become a popular anthem for the survivors of the disasters as well as for the anti-nuclear-power movement.

Forged through chindon-ya's sounds, what these new affective alliances have produced is a kind of politics of survival against different kinds of insecurity. At this conjuncture in postindustrial, post-3.11 Tokyo, chindon-ya's sound performed what anthropologist Marc Abélès calls the "politics of survival": a political preoccupation symptomatic of the neoliberal moment plagued by global insecurity (2010). While this notion aptly captures the political orientation toward preservation of life in the face of environmental, economic, and biological threats, I distinguish my use of the term from Abélès's by insisting on the social and the conjunctural. I augment this precautionary, insecurity-driven orientation of the politics of survival by highlighting both the potency and the ephemeral nature of such an unexpected alliance built around the politics of survival.[35]

I do not intend to celebrate desperate precarity as the necessary condition for subversive politics of survival, or to reduce and romanticize affective labor as inherently subversive in the neoliberal condition. Rather, the politicization of chindon-ya's sound was made possible precisely through its fleeting, temporary configuration of particular contingencies. While chindon-ya were forced out of work, the resourceful redirection of their labor yielded political traction—but the political affordances were necessarily transient. Over the several months following the first demo in 2011, as chindon-ya started to regain employment, their participation in antinuclear demos gradually declined. As a sense of normalcy has returned to their lives, the momentum and urgency at antinuclear rallies have subsided. The kind of political traction I just described has also dissipated—only to be further challenged by the election win of the pro-nuclear-power Abe cabinet in September 2012.

But it was not simply the building of affective alliances among various constituents invested in the politics of survival that chindon-ya's sound illuminated. Even after the initial formation of politicized chindon-ya dissipated as they regained employment, the imprints and associative connections remained latent in their sounds, in the cultural imaginary of chindon-ya, and in the streets, waiting to be activated to produce multiple resonances in other configurations.

LIVELINESS AND THE ETHICS OF SURVIVAL

On a muggy summer evening in August 2012, Jinta-la-Mvta was invited to collaborate with other local musicians at a local bon-odori festival in Suginami Ward, one of the more vocal Tokyo neighborhoods against nuclear power (figure 5.5).[36] Bon-odori is a popular summertime folk dance festival, held annually during the *obon* season when the living honor ancestral spirits, who are believed to revisit household altars.[37] Usually hosted by local neighborhood associations (*chōnaikai*), bon-odori memorializes ancestral spirits through dancing, socializing, and feasting.[38] Although chindon-ya has not historically been part of bon-odori musical accompaniment, the malleability of the cultural imaginary of chindon-ya as synonymous with the festive and the popular, as well as the familiar sound of kane that is used both in chindon-ya and bon-odori musical accompaniment, made it a seamless fit for the occasion.

The bon-odori festival started in the early afternoon. Incessant cicada sounds and children's excited screams filled the woodsy park, where a *yagura* (wooden tower and raised stage) had been built at its center. Food and drink vendors lined up along the periphery. The tower and a raised stage were colorfully decorated with traditional red-and-white drapes and a huge banner with antinuclear messages and images drawn in vibrant colors—without which the festival would not look any different from an ordinary local bon-odori. The prerecorded bon-odori tracks were playing from the speakers on repeat, accompanied by live taiko drumming at the top of the tower. Occasionally emcees and singers took to the stage to sing along. Festivalgoers, both young and old, were dressed for the occasion in *yukata* (a cotton kimono worn for summertime events), while some wore outlandish costumes including Mexican *lucha libre* masks, feather boas, and sparkly tights. People would join the circle of dancers around the yagura tower/stage whenever they felt like dancing to a tune or two. As the sun began to set, hours of dancing, socializing, and drinking started to loosen the dancers' movements. By the time the chindon-ya performers took to the stage after dark, the crowd was ready for revelry.

FIGURE 5.5 Antinuclear *bon-odori* festival in
Suginami Ward, August 2012. Photo by the author.

Particularly ostentatiously dressed among the crowd, the musicians played
several bon-odori tunes on the chindon drums, the big taiko drum, electric gui-
tar, amplified *sanshin*, trumpets, trombones, saxes—almost twenty musicians
in total, myself included on the accordion. With the boisterous and exuberant
sound of the performance, the crowd went wild; stepping outside of the circular
formation, the dancers broke into improvised movement, as if they were in a
mosh pit. On one particular original composition we prepared for the occasion,
called "Meltdown Blues," the singer sang an original tune satirizing then-prime
minister Yoshihiko Noda, while the dancers swirled, jumped, and tumbled. In
the atmosphere and sounds of nigiyakasa, the politics of festivity—the real matsurigoto—was palpable.

While the lyrical content of the tune explicitly addressed a dissident stance
against the government's nuclear policy, it wasn't simply in the lyrics where
the political potency of chindon-ya was felt. Although neither discursively indexed nor melodically referenced in the performance, the parallel between the
bon-odori custom of honoring the suffering and the sacrifice of ancestors and
memorializing the victims of the disaster was contextually evoked. Moving to
the familiar and typical bon-odori beat (*don-don-ga-don*) while hearing the

out-of-the-ordinary sounds of chindon-ya, dancers and their footsteps not only bridged the dead and the living—as bon-odori customarily is meant to do—but also articulated the social imaginaries of the ancestral spirits, the disaster victims' souls, and anticipated nuclear death. Miwazō told me over drinks at a bar later that night: "That was fun, wasn't it? I was able to play with prayers for the ancestors, disaster victims, and everyone."[39] Prominent folklorist Origuchi Shibuo argues that the Japanese belief system, inflected by Buddhism, does not distinguish between the spirits of the living and the dead. He maintains that "the bon festival is an amalgamation of two festivals: that of the spirit of the living and that of the spirit of the dead" (Origuchi [1947] 1995, 1). Folded into the localized and historically specific context of the bon-odori festival, chindon-ya's professional commitment to imaginatively empathize with, and perform for, listeners who may or may not be physically present was extended to the deceased—ancestors, the victims of the disaster—as well as those whose lives may be lost to radiation exposure in the future.

I suggest that chindon-ya practitioners creatively mobilized the traditional communal dance practice to reconfigure antinuclear politics as more than the preoccupation of the living for their own survival. While a shared concern over insecurity brought together different constituents, from the precariat to mothers and farmers threatened by radiation exposure, chindon-ya's sound resonated with particular, localized sensibilities to move beyond the rhetoric of insecurity. Performed at a politicized folk dance festival, outside chindon-ya's usual commercial context, this particular form of affective labor inculcated what the politics driven by insecurity lacked: a sense of interdependence, a relational understanding of sociality, and an ethical orientation that prioritized not only atomized, precautionary politics that sought to prevent future catastrophe, but also the desire for a better future based on the past/death being integral to the present/life.

The festive and sonorous remembrance of the dead stood in stark contrast with the silence of jishuku that had been mandated to honor the victims of the disaster. Resonances of chindon-ya, heard within the resonances of the silence of jishuku, instilled an embodied and empathetic sociality among the demo participants, shifting the weight away from insecurity and the neoliberal politics of survival toward an ethics of survival—underscored by the local cosmological understanding of life as constitutively defined through its relation to the dead. Chindon-ya's sounds reminded participants, through their dance moves, how their lives were inextricably linked with the lives and deaths of millions of unknown others. And perhaps with that relational awareness comes, for some, a sense of responsibility to partake in political life.

———

Responding to the demonstration in front of his official residence on June 29, 2011, then Prime Minister Noda was quoted as saying: "Oh, there's some big sound out there." This comment unleashed a surge of criticism, accusing him of being indifferent to the citizens' "voices." One older activist decried: "Our voices aren't heard; our voices are just simple 'sound' to him." Yet this loud "sound" does as much work as the voicing of citizens' opinions, if not more. This "big sound" that operates beyond the realm of the discursive, that is felt and that moves bodies, that reactivates latent sociality and political possibilities sedimented in the streets and in the silence of jishuku, is what is behind the growing anti-nuclear-power movement.

A kind of affective labor that has been present throughout the past century, chindon-ya has rather unexpectedly gained traction as a vehicle for a broad-based anti-nuclear-power movement. By insisting on performing in the street despite the silence of jishuku that put them out of work, chindon-ya made a subtly subversive move. When chindon-ya's "sound business" of producing sociality transposes from their usual commercial routine onto the political protest against the social precarity of contemporary Japan, they redirect their musical labor away from the market and toward critique of the silence that hindered their livelihood and foreclosed affective responses to the disaster. Chindon-ya's sociality not only produced the politics of survival, but also moved beyond it; their lively performances activated the latent socialities that do not simply re-act to insecurity and threat, but are also grounded in the local ontology of the social inherently defined through the relations of the living and the dead. What we hear in chindon-ya's sonic presence in the antinuclear movement, then, is a reclamation of labor from capitalist logic to the production of sociality in its own right, among not only the living but also the cultural imaginary of the dead—however provisional, fleeting, or incidental it may be. And it is here—in this temporary reclamation of their own affective labor into the realm of poet-ics—where we hear emergent political possibilities in post-3.11 Japan.

EPILOGUE

Affordances of Resonance

[An atmosphere] is an attunement of the senses, of labors,
and imaginaries to potential ways of living in or living through things.
A living through that shows up in the generative precarity of ordinary
sensibilities of not knowing what compels, not being able to sit still, being
exhausted, being left behind or being ahead of the curve, being in love with
some form or life that comes along, being ready for something—anything—
to happen, or orienting yourself to the sole goal of making sure
that nothing (*more*) *will* happen.

Kathleen Stewart, "Atmospheric Attunements" (2011)

It has been ten years since I first started tracing the resonances of chindon-ya musical advertisement and its offshoot musical practices in Japan. Throughout this book, I have sought to capture moments in which histories of various economic formations, modes of social difference, cultural memories, and their affective attachments became entangled and afforded the allegedly obsolete practice of chindon-ya an economic, social, and political valence.

These moments were often elusive, invisible and yet tangible—like sound, atmosphere, air, or wind, which were recurring metaphors in my conversations with chindon-ya practitioners. The ability to "sense the atmosphere" (*fun-iki o kanjitoru*) or "read the air" (*kūki o yomu*) was valued both generally as an ethics of collective sociality and as a sensibility to cultivate in chindon-ya performance. Several practitioners called chindon-ya "music exposed to the wind" or "music of the wind." The Chinese character "wind" appears repeatedly in the way Kawaguchi describes chindon-ya: it is simply part of the neighborhood's *fūkei* (wind-view, scenery), *fuzei* (wind-affect, affective scenery), or *fūbutsu* (wind-thing, a thing that makes the place or time unique). My fieldwork often felt like my own exercise of attunement to chindon-ya's art of attunement to these palpable, sensorial, and immanent forces that make up Kawaguchi's "wind-affect"—the affective sceneries of the everyday, of which chindon-ya is an integral part.

Chindon-ya, imbued with traces of old itinerant performing arts, redolent of the modern nostalgia for the uncommodified, and operating as an entrepreneurial business made viable again in the contemporary market, continues to entice those who overhear it today. Neither music nor noise, street performance nor street vendor, traditional nor modern, chindon-ya persists amid contradictions inherent in the neoliberal present. Chindon-ya is rooted in capitalist modernity and yet is a critique of it through deviant traces of the precapitalist past. Chindon-ya valorizes the neoliberal abstraction of sociality through its affective labor, while doggedly maintaining a humanistic commitment to creating social encounters irreducible to capital. Chindon-ya sounds out both histories of difference and narratives of social cohesion. Though chindon-ya is considered out of time, its resonances reveal how its presumed obsolescence is part of the temporal heterogeneity that constitutes the present moment. Despite a powerful public perception of chindon-ya as strange and out of place (bachigai), chindon-ya has always had its place as an integral part of the affective scenery of the streetscape precisely through its difference, producing space—as Lefebvre would have it—as it articulates social relations, histories, and imaginaries through its soundings. The relevance and appeal of chindon-ya today, however small and seemingly outdated, emerge from these tensions and dynamics that chindon-ya embraces with a nonchalant smile and a playful skip.

On an unusually warm winter day toward the end of my fieldwork, I got a phone call from Yoshino Shigeru, a Tokyo-based chindon-ya known for his cross-dressing act. He happened to be in my childhood neighborhood in Tokyo for the day, for a gig advertising a new *izakaya* (bar/restaurant), and invited me to tag along. I immediately threw my camera and audio recorder into a small bag and ran out the door. Finding his chindon-ya troupe was not difficult. When I reached the *shōtengai* shopping street on the western side of the train station, I immediately heard the unmistakable sound of kane. Following the sound, I turned a few corners, and there they were—Yoshino in bright pink kimono with heavy makeup and a big wig leading a gorosu drummer and flyer person zigzagging the streets. The street was one that I bike through often to run errands, or to go to eat. Walking toward them, I noticed how animated the street seemed. Places and people I normally pass by without taking note suddenly became a dynamic web of interactions; chindon-ya's presence seemed to galvanize the street by bringing forth connections, conversations, and interactions among the city dwellers in ways I had never witnessed before. I felt a renewed connection to the neighborhood, engaging in more exchanges of words, eye contact, and smiles than ever before. Although I was already familiar with the strategies, techniques, and effects of chindon-ya after two years of observing Chindon Tsūshinsha in Osaka and others elsewhere, I was nonetheless surprised by how my perceptions of my neighborhood were transformed while following Yoshino and his troupe. It was as if I found a whole new layer to the neighborhood that I never knew before. I was engrossed, even tickled. I was humbled into a radically different way of being in, and moving through, my own childhood neighborhood.

This experience distilled how the act of listening, sounding, and walking with chindon-ya has opened my ears and mind to question the preconceived ways of understanding space—as a passive, preexisting, physically delineated enclosure. Chindon-ya's soundings harness sociality through the inseparable process of producing acoustic and affective resonances—space is these very resonances, actively produced through soundings, surroundings, and time. This dynamic conception of space, conceived as hibiki (resounding), fore-sounded several of the themes traced throughout this book: the politics of cultural memory in neoliberal Japanese society; listening, sounding, and walking as spatial practices in Japan's modern cities; affective alliances across social differences that gesture toward multicultural Japan; and the affordances of sound in political interventions against socioeconomic precarity in postindustrial, post-3.11 Japan.

Most broadly speaking, the dynamism of resonance—the articulation of sound, space, and sociality—commands us to listen to how listeners, performers, landscapes, and cultural memories are dynamically, relationally, and asymmetrically produced. Far from being transparent, passive, or neutral, the sounded space of resonance emerges from the particularities of situated practices, moments, forces, soundings, localities, and social relations. In contrast to the autonomy of the liberal subject, resonance implies a relational concept of the subject as constituted through a geographically and historically specific conjuncture of multiple temporalities and spatialized practices. Chindon-ya's aesthetics of sound and movement move away from the understanding of a subject grounded in individuality and self-expression. Rather, chindon-ya hear the inextricable interrelations of not only those who are sharing the physical space where their sounds resound, but also those beyond the concrete walls, across the street, and across temporalities and imagined relations. This emphasis on dynamic relationality necessarily entails an ontology of listening that takes into account the imagined audience and affective sociality therein, as well as the nonhuman: the physical environment and its acoustic properties, the climate, the materiality of musical instruments, and so on.

Because resonance challenges an absolutist conception of space through its focus on dynamic relationality and an emphasis on situated practice, it offers broad implications for understanding how difference is produced in space. While a passive notion of space can evoke a homogeneous identity attached to a place within geographical delineations (e.g., Japan as a monoethnic nation), the dynamism and relationality of resonance denaturalizes the isomorphism between a place and the presumed homogeneity of subjectivity therein. Various forms of difference—gendered, ethnic, racial, classed, caste—thus can be understood as the tangible effects of these processes of both local and translocal encounters and a reworking of historically sedimented meanings. This enables chindon-inspired practitioners to draw on chindon-ya as a way of raising the multicultural question of Japan by articulating historical forms of difference with contemporary difference in the register of ethnicity and socioeconomic precarity.

Lastly, resonance makes terrains of political action tangible and imaginable—as seen in the politicization of chindon-ya in post-disaster Kobe in 1995 or in Tokyo in 2011—in projecting new, potential webs of sociality. Particularly through affective and imaginative registers, resonance highlights not only structural constraints but also conjunctural possibilities, at least in two ways. First, affective resonances can be made as a mode of social critique by reworking historically sedimented meanings. Soundings of resonance can move, lift up, pick out, recall, activate, and amplify historical meanings, practices, and memories in a particular location, or in people's sentiments—including the deviant, the residual, and the subversive. Second, resonance compels us to listen differently, to imagine differently, and to care differently, across geographical confines, social boundaries, and historical differences. Through their soundings, chindon-ya make tangible the historically and socially contingent ways in which we have become socialized to walk, listen, perceive others, and experience the world. In turn, the sensory experiences—of walking, listening, sounding, dressing, and so on—open up possibilities, albeit with no guaranteed outcome, for imagining different perceptions of space, time, and sociality, as well as for assembling previously disconnected sentiments, ideas, persons, and movements. Embodying different ontologies of space, history, and sociality is the first step toward cultivating empathy and the imagining of creative and political possibilities. Resonance enables the politics of imagination as not essentially resistant or instrumental, but rather something emergent, diffractive, and indeterminate in need of constant renewal and improvisation.

———

As with any ethnographic endeavor, this book represents only a selective portion of its subject, the broad world in which chindon-ya operates. There are many more aspects of chindon-ya than what I was able to include that would provide a rich area of inquiry for future studies. When I initially approached contemporary chindon-ya practitioners for my research, they often ardently urged me to turn to the older generation, then reaching their eighties and nineties. The sense of "disappearing history" of chindon-ya is real and urgent among those who are involved in chindon-ya practices. This is one immediate and important concern, although I insist that contemporary and younger practitioners, as much as they may humbly divert researchers to their predecessors and historical research, have much to offer in understanding what social and cultural forces enable chindon-ya to stay relevant and in presenting creative possibilities for many to realize their entrepreneurial, artistic, and political aspirations.

Another area that warrants closer analysis is gendered labor within chindon-ya. While traditional gender roles remain in chindon-ya, there is also significant fluidity in both performance and economic practice. There is much to think through at the intersection of the histories of itinerant performers and gender. The now-defunct all-female family troupe Takada Sendensha in Menuma presents a fascinating case study (plate 11). Having close connections to itinerant taishū theater troupes and all-female sword-fight play, the sisters in this troupe developed a dynamic choreographic and rhythmic style that stood out among other chindon-ya of their generation.

Regional differences also provide a lens through which to understand chindon-ya's relation to discourses of Japaneseness and urban economy. Although my book focused predominantly on Osaka, the Tokyo chindon-ya scene—the largest in the country—has its own histories and dynamics that demand close attention; significantly, there are also a few troupes in more rural areas that would provide a welcome counterpoint to my emphasis on urban examples. Shiogama Chindon CM Sha in the northeast, for example, is the only chindon-ya that has continued over three generations, and the troupe has much to offer in analyzing the nonurban economic realities and social dynamics they have navigated as they sustained their business practice.

Lastly, the transnational circulation of chindon-ya as both cultural imaginary and practice deserves greater attention. Although on a smaller scale, through individual connections, chindon-ya troupes and chindon-inspired bands have been making appearances abroad at various festivals since the 1980s. I myself have become entangled in the increasing international circulation of chindon-ya sounds, representations, and practitioners; I spent the summers of 2015 and 2016 touring on the klezmer circuit with the band Jinta-la-Mvta. The uncanny musical resemblances that listeners recognize in the aesthetic form of chindon-ya and klezmer raise many questions for ethnomusicologists and devotees of Japanese and Jewish musics. There is also one active Asian American chindon-inspired group in the United States, Happy Fun Smile. Investigating how chindon-ya embodies and mobilizes Japaneseness differently outside of Japan, by whom, and for whom would provide another dimension to the discussion of the contemporary perception of chindon-ya.

———

On my most recent visit back to Japan in January 2017, the future of chindon-ya seemed uncertain. I spoke with several chindon-ya practitioners both in Tokyo and Osaka, and the word on the street was that the industry had become somewhat stagnant. There was concern that many amateur groups have popped up and taken some business away. But most troubling, as always, are the shifting modes of the economy. Hayashi feels that the chindon-ya industry has arrived at a divergence point similar to the state of affairs when he joined the business back in the early 1980s. Back then, the previous major employers—local associations of commerce and *shōtengai* shopping arcades—were being dislodged by corporate capitalism and urban development. At that time, Hayashi could not have predicted that chindon-ya would pick up again as new corporate in-dustries came in to employ them, such as nationally franchised convenience stores and cell phone companies. Now having solidly established their presence on the market, these enterprises no longer need chindon-ya's help with pub-licity. Longtime employers like pachinko parlors won't be enough to support chindon-ya's future, as they are no longer developing a new customer base. To-day, with the continued stagnation of the Japanese economy and the lack of new industries that employ chindon-ya, the resilience and malleability of the practice are being put to the test again.

Hayashi remains optimistic, though. He wonders if homes for old people may become the next large-scale employers of chindon-ya, considering the aging population of Japan. In the meantime, he says, he will continue to en-courage his troupe members to join him in cultivating great care, experience, sensibility, and commitment to maintaining the delicate balance required of being chindon-ya on the streets—barely audible when overheard, but resonant when listened to, especially by those whose lives are precarious. Today, in the tightly surveilled sonic environment of the city, where neighbors' stereos or children's squeals from kindergartens can cause social conflicts, the pressure is higher than ever for chindon-ya to sound in ways that do not invite annoyance or complaints yet capture the overhearer's attention and imagination. Hayashi told me his aspiration: "We need to maintain the presence as a chindon-ya that can allow people to forget the profit and loss, or interest . . . [bringing them] beyond the current time-space, where they can be released from their worries about debts, rent, spousal quarrels, gambling addictions. That would be nice. It wouldn't last forever, but maybe just for a moment." The aesthetic and pro-fessional commitments of chindon-ya practitioners, I realized, lead them to ask questions that are not so dissimilar from the ones that keep me at work as an ethnomusicologist. What historical forces have conditioned our precarious present? What sonorous events resonate with people and make them tick, as they navigate their everyday struggles? How might we coexist and coanimate space through sound? How might we care for each other? How might we imag-ine alternatives? And how might we stay attuned to the resonances, of which we are a part?

四丁目 Shichôme

FIGURE E.1 *Shichōme*. Typical chindon-ya tune played at the end of a gig.
Transcription by the author.

Chindon Drums

APPENDIX

This transcription by Kawamura Mitsuji, tuba player of Chindon Tsūshinsha, is taken from the 2001 Second National Chindon Expo program pamphlet. He provided four different ways of playing the chindon drums to rhythmically accompany the same melody of "Takesu" (see figure P.1) to demonstrate the basic principles and complexities of playing chindon drums.

- *A* shows how the same tune is accompanied by three percussionists in yose variety theater, each of whom plays a different instrument of kane, shime daiko, and ōdō.
- *B* is a hypothetical example, showing how it would be to consolidate the same three parts for one chindon drummer, playing kane with the right hand and both shime daiko and ōdō with the left hand.
- *C* is a transcription of a recording in the late 1920s, performed by Suzukan. You can see that one chindon drummer can perform more complex rhythms than three percussionists in a yose band.
- *D* is a transcription of Yamamoto Tōzaburō, a veteran chindon drummer with more than fifty years of experience. It is an excellent example of an elaborate rhythmic improvisation that requires dexterity and skill.

NOTES

Prologue

1. I had to seek temporary housing arrangement at internet cafés not because of financial struggles as other net refugees did, but because of a threat made by an anonymous stalker who came to the apartment I first moved into. Gendered risks and violence are a real concern in fieldwork, and I draw attention to the efforts made by the Fieldwork Mentoring Program sponsored by the Section for the Status of Women and the Gender and Sexualities Taskforce of the Society for Ethnomusicology.

2. David Riesman offers a sociological analysis of this phenomenon (1950).

3. I draw on the conceptualization of sociality by Marilyn Strathern et al. (1990). For in-depth discussion of the challenges and stakes of different theorizations of the term "sociality" see Long and Moore 2013.

4. For an expansive overview of various approaches to the intersection of music, sound, and space within musicology and ethnomusicology see Georgina Born (2015).

5. Speaking about an embodied, meaning-producing everyday practice, Lefebvre accounts for nonverbal "signifying sets" as a possible means of merging the perceived and the conceived, and of challenging abstract space. Nonverbal artistic expressions, including music, are important to the concept of "spatial code." Defined as a means of living in a space, of understanding it, and of producing it, spatial code, according to Lefebvre, brings together verbal signs and nonverbal signs (music, sounds, evocations, architectural constructions) (Lefebvre [1974] 1991, 48). The role of the embodied practice of music as part of the construction of spatial code here is central to Lefebvre's project of advancing a unitary theory of space. Situated vis-à-vis the lived and perceived, spatial code is a "language common to practice and theory, and to inhabitants, architects and scientists," which "recaptures the unity of dissociated elements, breaking down such barriers as that between private and public, and identifying both confluences and oppositions in space that are at present indiscernible" (64). Thus conceived, for Lefebvre's project to bring together the mental and physical fields, the construction of a spatial code is a significant

process toward "the reversal of the dominant tendency" (64). Lefebvre's inclusion of artistic and musical practices in what constitutes a spatial code thus reinforces the necessity of understanding sound in relation to the production of space.

6. This point seems to have been lost on David Harvey, who observed that Lefebvre's inspiration lies in the "animating power of the spectacle, of poetry" (1991, 426).

7. Pointing out that the sonic conception of space—"space as sounding or resound-ing"—has received little attention, Feld draws on music philosopher Victor Zuckerkandl (1956), who "argued vigorously against the notion that music was purely an experience of tone as time" by detailing the ways "space is audibly fused with time in the progression and motion of tones" (Feld 1996, 95).

Introduction

1. Ana Hofman (2015) and Gavin Steingo (2016) offer a productive framework within which to understand musical labor relative to Hardt and Negri's narrative of "immaterial labor"—labor that produces "an immaterial good, such as service, knowledge, or com-munication" (Hardt 1999, 94).

2. Here, I am riffing on Donna Haraway's theorization of diffraction (1997, 273).

3. The definition of what chindon-ya is varies among chindon-ya practitioners and chindon-inspired musicians. I have noted that for many, including chindon-inspired musicians, it is the chindon drum set that visually and aurally signifies chindon. However, I learned from my fieldwork with the Chindon Tsūshinsha troupe that it is not necessarily the instrument itself but the process of sonically communicating and creating relation-ships with customers on the streets that defines a chindon-ya. According to that view, chindon-ya can theoretically be chindon-ya without chindon drum.

4. This is more the case in Tokyo than in Osaka. In Tokyo, married couples often took up chindon-ya as their family business, with wives taking the task of playing the drum. Ōkuma Wataru has highlighted the role of women in chindon-ya business (Ōkuma 2005). Hosokawa Shūhei also provides an explanation for why more women played in chindon-ya in the 1930s: since cross-dressing was banned, women gained more popu-larity, much like dancers and waitresses. Thus, women were encouraged to play melodic instruments in chindon-ya, and often earned more salary than male chindon-ya prac-titioners (Hosokawa, n.d. A, 11). Although the issue of gender in chindon-ya warrants close analysis in developing a historiography of chindon-ya, it is outside the scope of the central questions I ask in this book.

5. Musicologist Hosokawa Shūhei points out that, among the various street perfor-mance groups consisting of percussion and brass instruments, chindon is unique for its absence of a bass melodic instrument (n.d. A, 23).

6. *Chanbara* theatrical performances were suppressed during the U.S. occupation of

Japan (1945–1952), as the Civil Information and Education Section considered them a glorification of feudalism, imperialism, or militarism. Informal street performances of chanbara, by chindon-ya and itinerant theatrical actors, were one way to evade the surveillance. Chanbara's popularity grew again after the occupation, into the 1950s.

7. These unspoken customary codes tend to be followed more closely in Tokyo, where an older generation of chindon-ya still exists and whose members are treated as tradition bearers by younger practitioners. In contrast, in Osaka, where there are not many older generation chindon-ya practicing today, younger chindon-ya members tend to be less concerned about following such customary codes.

8. Yoshino Shigeru, the leader of the chindon-ya troupe Chindon Yoshino in Tokyo, has consistently claimed cross-dressing as his theatrical trademark. He was one of the earliest musicians to apprentice with veteran chindon-ya, and founded his own troupe in 1995.

9. Fritsch is the only scholar who has published on chindon-ya in English to date.

10. The description of the 1900 New Year parade of the Lion Toothpaste company is telling for its magnificent size: fifty to sixty banner holders, a musical band, an Edo-period-style float, another float with a lion statue, another musical band, followed by dozens of beautifully decorated horse carriages loaded with the company's products.

11. While Horie sees the 1923 earthquake as a detriment to chindon-ya business, Asakura Kyōji argues that it led to the later development of chindon-ya in the 1930s. After the earthquake, street performers and vendors lost their jobs as the historical geographies that supported them disintegrated. Thus they sought new opportunities in chindon-ya, as its popularity and demand grew at that time (Asakura 1991, 55–56).

12. Pachinko slot-machine parlors flourished in the early 1950s, and the majority of the business owners are of Korean descent, especially in Osaka.

13. *Taishū* is a highly contested term; it is laced with "nostalgic references to 'folk' and 'traditional' ways of life in addition to less sanguine associations with nationalism, mass consumption, and citizen's movements" (Robertson 1998, 72). Although the word has existed in a Buddhist context since the Middle Ages, it was only in the early twentieth century that taishū began to refer to the masses, the popular, and the public. European and American discourses of mass and popular culture, which are embedded in the discourses of modernization (as in inevitable historical forces of progress emanating from Euro-American powers), industrialization, urbanization, capitalism, and media, have deeply inflected the use of the term *taishū*. I will discuss taishū further in chapter 2.

14. There has also been a considerable lack of attention to chindon music in both academic and popular discourses. Hosokawa remains the only scholar who has published about chindon-ya in Japanese, and Fritsch the only other scholar writing in English. What little attention has been given to chindon-ya in magazines, newspapers, and TV shows has been in response to the recent rise of activities since the late 1980s, with less emphasis falling on chindon-ya's history.

15. Although they are beyond the scope of this book, it also warrants mention that there are amateur and volunteer chindon-ya practitioners throughout Japan. Several chindon-ya clubs have sprung up on university campuses both in Tokyo and Osaka, and there are numerous amateur chindon-ya teams who sometimes perform at retirement homes and kindergartens on a volunteer basis. This population has grown large enough that there is now an amateur section at the annual Toyama Chindon Contest.

16. Regionalism holds great significance in Japan; even within the same region or city, microgeographies inform and inflect the popular discourse and cultural production. Chindon-ya, however, is not considered to be a regional practice belonging to a specific locale.

17. Here I endorse Lisa Lowe's critique that hybridity refers not to a free oscillation between or among chosen assumed entities but to uneven processes and encounters of various historical and social forces (Lowe 2003). I also draw on Robert Young's use of Bhaktin's dialectical model of "intentional hybridity," which refers to a politicized contestatory activity that has interrogative effects of hybridization on contemporary culture (Young 1995, 24).

18. *Nihonjinron* refers to a body of popular discourses beginning in the 1970s that explicate the "ethnic uniqueness" of the Japanese. All too often, the notion of the class, cultural, and ethnic homogeneity of Japan is treated as an axiomatic truth and goes unquestioned in both public and academic discourses. This deep-rooted belief in Japanese homogeneity has been traced among numerous prominent figures, including "National Learning" scholars of the eighteenth century, the popular nihonjinron writers of the twentieth century, and present-day government officials and Japanese and non-Japanese journalists and scholars (Denoon et al., 2001; Komai 1994; Ishii and Yamauchi 1999; Lie 2001; Oguma 1995, 1998; Weiner 1994, 1997).

19. Noh is said to date back to the Muromachi period (1338–1443), and Kabuki is said to have emerged in the early Edo period (around the 1600s). For a useful overview of Japanese cultural identity and musical modernity see Wade (2005, 2013) and Matsue (2016).

20. Pointing out that "Japan is literally unimaginable outside its positioning vis-à-vis the West," anthropologist Marilyn Ivy asserts that the cultural is a domain inextricably linked to the idea of the nation. Furthermore, since the discourse of a unified Japan emerged only in the eighteenth century, Ivy maintains that "the articulation of a unified Japanese ethos with the 'nation' to produce 'Japanese culture' is entirely modern" (1995, 4).

21. Such a narrative of music pitted against noise resembles the analysis of noise by Jacques Attali, who is interested in the ideological work that creates and maintains the boundary between music and noise, which is a political one. For Attali, the boundary always reflects a political reality; the structure of music reveals/conceals/becomes/reflects the order of things. Chindon-ya poses an interesting challenge to Attali's formulation of

"noise," as it is embedded within the capitalist economy but not commodified via mass production. Instead, it is improvised, which Attali equates to the "refusal of the cultural alienation inherent in repetition" typical of capitalist economy ([1977] 1985, 138).

22. See Hankins and Stevens (2014) for more case studies of ethnographic analyses of sound in the anthropology of Japan. As an extension of this volume, Carolyn Stevens has also launched the multimedia digital repository *Sonic Japan*, http://sonicjapan.clab .org.au/about.html.

23. The contested boundary between sound, noise, and music has been critically questioned and surpassed by experimental musicians in Japan whose art was termed *onkyō*—literally, sound and vibration. Hosokawa, in a tongue-and-cheek manner, suggests that chindon-ya perhaps should be called *onkyō* instead of *ongaku* (1991, 13). While the relativistic perspective that considers environmental sounds and humanly organized sounds equal may resemble the "oneness" of chindon-ya sounds and surrounding urban noises, what is decidedly different is that chindon-ya practitioners or listeners have never made a conscious effort to define the practice in relation to sound or music. For comprehensive and critical discussion of onkyō and the transnational circulation of the term itself see Novak 2010b and Plourde 2008.

24. There had been recordings of chindon-ya made previously, but they were meant to be used for publicity purposes primarily and not for the consumer public.

25. Uchino Makoto, personal communication, Osaka, April 13, 2007.

26. During this period, the lifetime employment system eroded, and temporary employment and a part-time labor force called *frītā* became prevalent by the late 1980s, signaling the furthering of postindustrial capitalism and the advance of neoliberal policies.

27. Hayashi Kōjirō, personal communication, September 3, 2007.

28. Several Japanese words that I encountered during fieldwork can be translated as "resonance": *yoin* (reverberations, an aftereffect), *hibiki* (resonating sound), *zankyō* (reverberation, echo), and *kyōkan* (empathy).

29. While my use of the term "resonance" is rooted in the local discourse, the trope of resonance has been mobilized in various scholarships in sound studies and ethno/musicology. For examples of the use of "resonance" with an emphasis on the vibrational materiality, spatiality, embodiment, and social articulation see Nina Sun Eidsheim (2015) and Steve Goodman (2010). Veit Erlmann has provided an extensive treatise on the subject in his analysis of modern aurality in the West (2010). My approach to resonance in part echoes Ellen Lila Gray's elegant theorization of Portuguese *fado* as a musical genre that produces, circulates, and transforms affects and the "social, historical, and corporeal (sensed) dynamics of feelings" (Gray 2013, 9). Ronaldo Radano brings in the discursive in his conceptualization of resonance as a "formulation of sound into text and back again as a social articulation or utterance" (Radano 2003, 23). Likewise, Christine Yano, drawing on Shield, discusses resonance as an interactive communicative exchange

between performers and audience members in her analysis of Japanese *enka* (Shield 1980, 106; Yano 2002, 78).

30. Following Massey (1994), I distinguish "place" from "space." While space is dynamically produced through social relations and histories, place is constantly produced by a mixture of distinct local and wider social relations and histories that intersect at a particular spatial nodal point. Following this definition, identity of place is never singular but multiple. Place, then, highlights the processes of drawing and contesting boundaries that allow place itself to emerge out of dynamic social relations. Donald Moore's rendering of place illuminates the similarities between articulation and dynamically conceived "place": for him, "place emerges as a distinctive mixture, not an enduring essence, a nodal point where these translocal influences intermesh with practices and meanings previously sedimented in the local landscape" (Moore 2005, 20). Like articulation, place is a temporary fixing of meaning, a moment in a complex and contradictory interaction of meanings that are constituted through ongoing practices.

31. While there are numerous works that use the term "sounding," my choice is rooted in Antonio Gramsci's focus on praxis at the center of his theorization (2000, 333–35).

32. Among a relatively small number of authors who take on the subject of listening and imagination, Don Ihde insightfully discusses the role of imagination in listening practices (Ihde 2003).

33. My conception of "field" as interrelations, interconnections, and translocal movement echoes anthropologist Ian Condry's notion of *genba* (sites of performance) in his work on hip-hop in Japan (Condry 2006). As a creative response to the calls for rethinking the notion of "field" and space in anthropology (Gupta and Ferguson 1992, 1997; Marcus 1998), Condry's use of the *genba* concept redefines the "field" of his research by shifting the ethnographic focus from a geographically enclosed unit of analysis toward performative practices that unfold within geographically dispersed but socially interrelated relations. The word *genba* was used among chindon-ya quite often as well. Most often, the term was used in professional occasions when money was made for advertisement business.

ONE Walking Histories

1. Hayashi Kōjirō, personal communication, October 7, 2006.

2. While Certeau is known for his work on walking, I take distance from his approach. Certeau's work treats space primarily as a pre-given field to be read as a text and made meaningful through sensory experience. The phenomenological approach of space as a general construct that can be made concrete through practice goes against Lefebvre's theorization of space as dynamically produced through social practice. I instead take inspiration from the ethnographers who theorize walking as a generative practice productive of space.

3. Watanabe follows popular music scholar Wajima Yūsuke's assertion that the predominantly "Western" phenomenon of world music revealed Japan's ambivalent relation to the dichotomous undercurrent of "West" and "rest" that was operative in the world music industry. Consequently, Japan turned its self-Orientalizing gaze to its own "authentic" roots to counter the supremacy of Western music since the Meiji era (Wajima 2002).

4. France, Holland, and Great Britain were the main European countries to introduce their military systems to Japan at this time (Hosokawa 1989b). Research on the role of brass bands in the modernization process in Japan has drawn attention since the 2000s; for insightful analyses see Hosokawa 1989b and Abe et al. 2001.

5. "Han" refers to a feudal domain. During the Edo period, Japan was divided into regional territories. The Satsuma domain officials ordered musical instruments, including flutes, clarinets, cornets, trumpets, euphoniums, trombones, double basses, bass drums, and snare drums, from the Besson Company in London and hired John William Fenton as an instructor to form their own military band (Hosokawa 1989b, 95–96).

6. Historical musicologist Tanaka Yasuko discusses how European music was a crucial component in public rituals and events where the emperor's authority was to be established and recognized in public in the early Meiji period (Tanaka, quoted in Hosokawa 1989b). Once a feminized figure wearing women's attire, with a shaved face and makeup, the emperor was quickly transformed by the government into a beard-wearing military commander. Military music was a crucial sonic accompaniment in this masculinization and militarization of both the nation and the public imagery of the emperor, who was the symbolic parallel of the nation.

7. For more discussion on the relationship between military bands and Japan's musical modernity see Hosokawa 1989b.

8. This narrative of a rhythm-deficient national body is pervasive in contemporary popular culture in Japan. See Kaneda 2014 for a compelling analysis of this discourse as it manifests in the popular video game "Rhythm Heaven."

9. The navy band officer Kayama Tsutomu was the first to form a civilian brass band in 1886, named Tokyo Shichū Ongakukai (Tokyo City Musical Performance). He saw that there were too many demands for a military band to meet and decided to form a band exclusively to cater to those demands. Based in Tokyo, it performed actively at hotels, horse races, celebratory ceremonies, and garden parties (Hosokawa 1989d, 81).

10. Later, after the Russo-Japanese War, a new wave of civilian brass bands surfaced. Large department stores, such as Nihonbashi Mitsukoshi (Tokyo) and Ito Gofuku Ten (Nagoya), formed children's brass bands (shōnen ongaku tai) to perform for publicity and in concerts (Hosokawa 1989e, 133).

11. In January 1906, the magazine Ongaku Zasshi (Music magazine) described a band called Genkan Gakutai, named after the only song that the members could perform, all of whom had been expelled from a certain military unit. In the same magazine, criticism

was leveled against many civilian brass bands that sacrificed musical quality and work ethic for financial pursuit (quoted in Hosokawa 1989d, 83).

12. Hosokawa notes that, in addition to the difference in repertoire and instrumentation, the place of street musical bands in relation to other musical media is a key difference between chindon-ya and jinta. While jinta was popular during the time when there were rarely any media that disseminated musical sounds otherwise, chindon-ya is a "secondary live media" in an era of mass mediation through records and radio. Thus, Hosokawa speculates that Horiuchi's dissatisfaction with chindon-ya has less to do with the fact that they did not play "light classical" music than with the fact that there were other ample opportunities to listen to high-standard musical performances (1990, 107).

13. This observation I have made, via Hosokawa's notion of accidental heterophony and accent, parallels that of Marcel Mauss (1973) in his discussion of what he calls techniques of the body as an embodied habitus. While Mauss primarily considers various techniques of the body across societies (French vs. English, for example) and one's lifetime (enculturation), I emphasize that Hayashi's approach to walking is a creative exercise of assembling different techniques of the body across historical times, and that it is founded on the principle of cultivating improvisatory flexibility rather than disciplining a uniform style of walking. Therein lies room for slippage and innovation—there are no standard and unified techniques of the chindon-ya body, and each troupe and each region has its own (Takada Sendensha in Menuma in particular are known for their distinct choreographical movements). I thank Jairo Moreno for bringing this point to my attention.

14. Despite its short-lived musical presence on the streets almost a hundred years ago, jinta is evoked and referenced quite frequently among contemporary chindon-inspired musicians and chindon-ya practitioners. For instance, the influential 1994 album by the Okinawan folk singer Daiku Tetsuhiro that subsequently gave rise to the chindon-inspired musical projects is titled *Uchinā Jinta* (Okinawa Jinta). The album includes tunes popular in the early 1900s that must have been played by jinta, arranged for a unique combination of instruments including the traditional Okinawan lute-type instrument called *sanshin*, and chindon drums. Other examples include the clarinet player and writer Ōkuma Wataru's chindon-inspired band Cicala Mvta, which has a musical alter-ego called Jinta-la Mvta; Osaka's Chindon Tsūshinsha has given historical performances of jinta wearing historical military uniforms at a performance series at the Osaka History Museum.

15. Having never interviewed chindon-ya practitioners themselves, Watanabe does not take into account the dilemmas they have faced. In my conversation with Ōkuma, he shared with me the delicate and fraught relationships he has always been aware of. Speaking of the first day he encountered chindon-ya, he said: "I was very excited, but also thought I had to be very careful—I didn't want it to be a postcolonial, Orientalist thing. After releasing the *Tokyo Chin Don* album, our relationship with the veteran chindon-ya changed, albeit subtly . . . kind of like the Heisenberg principle. I thought, you can't ap-

proach this kind of thing lightly. It's class difference—this is their livelihood" (Ōkuma, personal communication, January 12, 2016).

16. Watanabe provides archival evidence to highlight the role of Ōsawa Gakutai as the harbinger of Westernizing and "modernizing" efforts within the rural community, which shows the limitations of urban-centric narratives that cast the rural as a remnant of the past that provides clues to pre-Western sensibilities (Watanabe 2013, 121–24).

17. The production of drums was historically delegated to a group of people designated *buraku*, a labor-based marginalized group that has been historically discriminated against. For an incisive and critical elaboration on the production of buraku difference, particularly through the labor of working with leather, see Hankins 2014.

18. Hayashi Kōjirō, personal communication, January 15, 2015.

19. Hayashi Kōjirō, personal communication, August 12, 2012.

20. Hayashi Kōjirō, personal communication, January 15, 2015.

21. While the embodied heterophony of chindon-ya resembles Charles Keil's notion of participatory discrepancies (1987)—the power of music that arises from textural or temporal idiosyncrasies that elicit social participation—my analysis of their walking, understood as a kind of Lefebvrean rhythmanalysis, broadens the scope beyond the musical moment within a particular performance to larger social rhythms across historical times.

22. Ibid.

23. Kamiya Kazuyoshi, personal communication, January 5, 2008.

24. Wind is a metaphor that recurred throughout my fieldwork. For instance, when asking two clarinet players who both play for chindon-ya why they like to draw connections with and play repertoire from Balkan Roma (or Gypsies, as they call them) and klezmer music, Seto Kazuyuki mentioned that both chindon-ya and Gypsy music were music "exposed to the wind," a reference to the outdoor street spaces in which they are performed, as well as to the often "cold" social receptions faced by itinerant musicians. Ōkuma Wataru also describes the sound of chindon-ya as a "music of wind" (Ōkuma 2001, 7). See the epilogue for a brief commentary on the trope of wind.

25. James Rhys Edwards provides an illuminating case study that shows how such nativist and naturalist discourses of a uniquely Japanese mode of listening have fed into the popular discourse of nihonjinron (Rhys Edwards 2016).

26. The discourses of the uniquely Japanese sense of musical time, *ma*, is a case in point. It has become a cliché trope to identify the distinctly Japanese conception of temporality that focuses on the relationality among sounding events and movements. I do not use this concept here, as the practitioners never invoked the notion of ma in describing their way of listening or embodying the walked rhythm. But I do not dismiss the relevance of ma entirely; while I do find the over-ethnomusicologized trope to be prone to ethno-nationalist essentialism, it nonetheless points to the local perception of temporal relationality as it extends to social relationality.

27. And to be successful in this labor necessitates the ephemeral, fleeting, and relational sense of time—the "rhythm that sways with the wind"—which, paradoxically, Kamiya tries to commodify as a record label owner.

28. While the street observation studies group formed in the 1980s, it was directly tied to members' earlier practices, such as Akasegawa Genpei's Tomassons Project of the 1970s and the Mixer Plan of the 1960s.

29. There has been a resurgence of interest in Kon and his modernology in recent years, leading to the publication of various books dedicated to his materials in Japan. See Koyama 2013, Kon 2011, and Izumi 2011.

30. Nango Yoshikazu offers a similar insight in his analysis of kōgengaku. See Nango 2013, 139.

31. This reading of chindon-ya via Lefebvre also offers a corrective to the limitations of *kōgengaku* that Silverberg points out. She notes that Kon Wajirō was "trapped by his own constructivist belief in the explanatory power of the diagrammatic . . . similarly to [Certeau], he was concerned with an urban 'Text written by walkers in the city.' . . . But he didn't recognize [Certeau's] realization that 'surveys of routes miss what was; the act itself of passing by' and such 'fixations' of 'walking, wandering, or window-shopping' in fact 'constitute procedures for forgetting.' Such rapping has the effect of making invisible the operation that made it possible" (Silverberg 1992, 44; Certeau 1984, 93, 97). By refusing to understand walking as text, or a diagram, or photo but stubbornly insisting on the embodiment, Hayashi's footwork evades the trapping Silverberg critiques—while simultaneously deeply embedded within it by sheer virtue of being an advertisement agent, the epitome of commercialism and consumerist market economy.

32. Lefebvre discusses the importance of dressage as a way to physiologically condition humans through instituting a regulatory sense of time. "Military knowledge" is a prime example Lefebvre uses to illustrate this point. Stuart Elden suggests a similarity between Lefebvre's discussion of time, body, and discipline and Karl Marx's *Capital*, which deals with "the mechanical repetition of the cycles of capitalist production . . . imposed over our circadian rhythms" (Elden 2004, xii). Much like his critique of the prevalent Cartesian understanding of space, Lefebvre also critiques the reductive understanding of time by emphasizing "the lived, the carnal, the body" that keeps multiple rhythms that cannot only be measured against "rational" rhythms (Lefebvre 2004, 9).

TWO Performing Enticement

1. *Zainichi* literally refers to residents of Japan of foreign origin but is usually used to refer to people of Korean descent and their descendants living in Japan as permanent residents.

2. Cho Paggie, *Gārikku Chindon*, Pandora Records, 2000.

3. Cho Paggie, personal communication, March 30, 2007.

4. Civilian brass bands writ large were referred to as *shichū ongaku tai* (inner-city musical bands); jinta was a subcategory of this group.

5. See chapter 1 for another quote by Horiuchi that illustrates this: "The mystery of jinta lies in that self-destructive, tired, nihilistic, decadent manner of playing. There is a rhythm that would make the listener imagine that the all of the players are lacking filial devotion, [are] ex-convicts, outlaws, womanizers, and patients of some sexually transmitted disease" (Horiuchi 1936, 25).

6. Kariyasaki Ikuko, personal communication, March 17, 2007.

7. For detailed analyses of historical materials on the intimate connection between outcastes, discrimination, and performing arts see Ozawa 1989; Morita 1974; Yamamoto 1989; Okiura 2007a, b, c, d, e, 2006a, b, 2006a. *Kinsei no Minsyu to Geino* (Modern people and performing arts) (1989), edited by the History of Kyoto Buraku Research Group, reinforces the close connection between *burakumin* (the underclass) and street performances. Commenting on the strictly enforced social hierarchy and resultant discrimination of the pre-Meiji era, Yamamoto Naotomo historically positions the politically and socially discriminated-against population (1989).

8. Many performance arts in this list are mentioned as one of the main means of livelihood among the underclass population in *Nihon no Kaso Shakai* (Japan's underclass society), written by journalist Yokoyama Gennosuke (1941, 45–47). Yokoyama's book is one of the first journalistic writings on the slums of Tokyo. Drawing on his ethnographic research between 1940 and 1941, Yokoyama describes in detail the everyday lives of textile factory workers in Kiryū, industrial factory workers in the Hanshin area, peasants, and the underclass population living in the big three slum neighborhoods in Tokyo, including street performers.

9. The outcaste group was further categorized into two types, *eta* ("full of filth") and *hinin* ("nonperson"). While *eta* is a hereditary class designated to handle types of labor considered "dirty" (often dealing with human or animal death), *hinin* often refers to people who previously belonged to another social but who later became outcaste (Yamamoto 1989, 7; Yoshida 1969, 16–18). For a thorough overview in English of the structural dynamics within the marginalized outcaste classes during the Edo period see Howell 2005.

10. See Horie 1986, 106–7. Although a comprehensive genealogical study of women street performers warrants close analysis, it is outside the scope of this chapter to examine how gender figures into the genealogical performances of chindon-ya today. I will include the expressions and voices of female chindon-ya members whenever possible. For a journalistic account highlighting the role of women in the Shōwa-era chindon-ya practices see Ōkuma Wataru's "Onna tachi no Chindon" (Women's chindon) (2005).

11. Okiura provided unpublished texts for each lecture. See Okiura 2007a, b, c, d, e.

12. Uchino Makoto, personal communication, April 13, 2007.

13. Jiuta has its roots in Biwa Hōshi, blind monks who were primarily known for narrating the stories of the Genpei War (1180–1185) to *biwa* lute accompaniment.

14. Kawaguchi apprenticed at Taiko Masa in the Taishō Ward of Osaka city for a few years. Partly this was his own ethnographic interest in understanding the history of leatherwork, which has traditionally been associated with the descendants of the outcastes; but he faced difficulty being completely accepted within the somewhat closed community. The relationship has continued, however, and Chindon Tsūshinsha still occasionally holds events at Taiko Masa, such as the walking workshop (chapter 1).

15. For example, Uchino Makoto argued that older kane were made with different proportions of metal material that is not reproducible today.

16. In his astute analysis of ice cream truck jingles, Daniel T. Neely takes on similar questions of timbre, materialities, and characteristics of particular mobile sounding, collective memory, and experience of nostalgia. See Neely 2014.

17. Seigworth and Gregg's notion of affect as "visceral forces beneath, alongside, or generally *other than* conscious knowing, forces insisting beyond emotion—that can serve to drive us toward movement, toward thought and extension, that can likewise suspend us . . . or can even leave us overwhelmed" seems fitting here (2010, 1). The indexical sound of kane as a deeply affective aural trigger echoes Brian Massumi's take on affect as intensity, or resonation of kind, that invites autonomic bodily responses, which points to the visceral response preceding conscious perception (see Massumi 1995).

18. Kawaguchi Masaaki, personal communication, March 15, 2007.

19. Hayashi Kōjirō, personal communication, March 22, 2007.

20. Although Butler's theory is based on her discussion of gender and sex, her conceptualization of the interdependency between the "subjects" and those who are "not yet subjects" provides a useful lens through which to understand the historical resonances that chindon-ya have produced in relation to those who have been historically marginalized.

21. Among many competing notions that refer to the popular in Japanese, *taishū* is the most frequently used term. But it is also highly contested. Robertson (1998) shows how competing notions of "the popular" exist in different terminologies such as *taishū*, *minshū*, and *jōmin*, which are all entangled in notions of class, region, difference, and power relations. *Jōmin*, used by Yanagida, is an essentialized reservoir of Japanese past, customs, and authenticity. *Minshū* is often used in opposition to the aristocrat, and to class- and region-bound categories (e.g., *minyō*). Robertson argues that the notion of taishū is laced with "nostalgic references to 'folk' and 'traditional' ways of life in addition to less sanguine associations with nationalism, mass consumption, and citizen's movements" (1998, 72).

22. Some Japanese writers assert that *taishū* emerged as a translation of the English term "mass" in the 1950s (Sekiguchi 2001; Itō1983), asserting that the idea of "crowd, public, mass" emerged as capitalist modernity increasingly homogenized culture (Sekiguchi 2001,

8–9). Sekiguchi seems to equate the emergence of the "new middle class" or "the working class mass" to the notion of "new mass." The Tokyo earthquake of 1926 was an impetus for various levels of transformation: "from imitating to groping for something new, crafts to industry, individual to mass" (Itō 1983, 203), that turned Tokyo from city to metropolis. For Itō, urbanization and its accompanying contradictory forces of standardization and creativity were instrumental in shaping Japan's taishū culture.

23. Anthropologist Jennifer Robertson shows that the term *taishū* is caught within the tension between a nativist view of Japanese popular culture and the West, and inflected by various nationalist claims, thus creating a wide array of conflicting interpretations and contested meanings (Robertson 1998). A survey of the term among various Japanese scholars shows the two competing ideologies of Japaneseness: the nativist view of Japanese culture as unique and authentic on the one hand, and that of a newly formed culture created through selected Western and Japanese elements and institutions on the other. Sociologist Katō Hidetoshi uses *taishū bunka* (popular culture) as an egalitarian notion of "the national culture" that erases the boundary between hegemonic and popular culture (Katō 1980). Kōgengaku sociologists Gonda Yasunosuke and Kon Wajirō emphasize the gender and class difference among the taishū, although later they conflate the term with *Kokumin* and *Jōmin* to designate the hegemonic national culture as a whole. Continuity with the Edo *tsūzoku bunka* (culture of people without pedigree) has been denied by the sociologist Kurihara Akira, who defines taishū as a whole new formation occasioned by the high-growth industrialization of the postwar period (Kurihara 1997).

24. For further discussion of taishū see Yokoi 1979; Robertson 1998; Sekiguchi 2001.

25. For an overview of sound in the history of advertisement in Japan see Endō 1958.

26. Kawaguchi Masaaki, personal communication, February 17, 2007.

27. Etymologically speaking, *shitamachi* refers to the flat lowland areas closer to the ocean or river in contrast to uplands and hills within the city. *Shitamachi* is most commonly used in Tokyo to refer to the traditional working-class entertainment and commercial district. It is often used in relation to the term *yamanote* (uptown), referring to the upper-middle-class residential areas closer to the mountains. In Osaka, the term is less popularly used and does not have the same connotation, but rather its opposite term *uemachi* (uptown) remains in common use.

28. See Ivy 1993, 239–58.

29. Such an assumption of popular culture permeating through all classes seems to run against Ukai Masaaki's analysis of the fragmentation of the contemporary taishū culture. A practicing public intellectual, Ukai Masaaki is not only a sociologist but also an active taishū engeki actor. He was one of the invited guest performers for the theatrical performances Chindon Tsūshinsha gave in theaters that I described above. Ukai points out that the qualities that were once associated with mass culture before the 1950s—mass in opposition to educated elites, mass as homogenized culture, mass as majority, mass as

passive and subordinate, and so on—are now obsolete. Instead, new forces, such as the rapid economic development of the 1950s through the 1970s, the forces of Americanization, changes in media technology that allow more participatory forms of consumption, higher education levels, and the creation of niche markets, urge for a newly conceptualized postwar mass culture that is "compressed, dense, multi-layered and multi-dimensional" (Ukai, Nagai, and Fujimoto 2000, 6).

30. Anne Allison succinctly describes "Japan, Inc." as follows: "the corporatization of its social economy and the 'marriage' between the social factory at home and the postindustrial factory at work that fueled its off-the-charts productivity" (Allison 2013, 21).

31. Hayashi Kōjirō, personal communication, January 25, 2007.

32. Ibid.

33. A paternalistic gaze toward Asia, including South and Southeast Asia, has long existed. Christine Yano provides an example by offering a cogent analysis of the gendered politics of exoticism within popular songs in imperial Japan during the first decades of the 1900s. See Yano 1998, 257.

34. The choice of the word *esunikku*—transliteration of the English word "ethnic"—also sidesteps the imperial genealogy of the word *minzoku*, which has an entirely different genealogy from the English word "ethnicity" (Doak 2007).

35. Marilyn Ivy notes that between 1970 and 1984 in Japan there was a shift from nostalgia as recuperation of the past to "neo-nostalgia," "nostalgia as style," or "the notion of the (ever)-new as nothing more than the repetitive insistence of the (re)marketed commodity" integral to emergent forms of Japanese modernity and its mass culture (Ivy 1995, 58).

36. For notable ethnographic monographs that cogently theorize nostalgia, sensory experience, and modern state/public see Svetlana Boym's *The Future of Nostalgia* (2001), Nadia Seremetakis's *The Senses Still* (1994), and Esra Özyürek's *Nostalgia for the Modern* (2006).

37. Stewart describes the multiplicity of nostalgia: "Hegemonic and resistant nostalgias, 'middle class' and 'working class' nostalgias, the nostalgia of a 'mass culture' and the nostalgia of and for local, nameable places are a three-ring circus of simultaneous images in the arenas of life-style, spectacle, and loss" (1998, 227).

38. See Kelly 1986, Robertson 1998, Yano 2002, and Sand 2013 for examples of ethnographic analyses of nostalgia consumerism in post-1980s Japan.

39. Robertson argues that paternalistic discourses of nostalgia inherent in the "native place-making" projects of cultural tourism are central to the "containment of multicultural difference" (Robertson 1998, 115) and the formation of "Japanese national cultural identity" (128). Kelly also argues that nostalgia was deployed by mass media and the state alongside the notion of rationalization in rural Japan as part of the cultural construction of Japan as a "New Middle Class" society. Viewing nostalgia as a tool to "deny the past," Kelly warns of the risks and dilemmas nostalgia poses for people who are associated with the imagined past: "nostalgia's dangers are as much that it misrepresents the present as that

it misrepresents the past" (Kelly 1986, 614). Yano has shown how the popular music genre enka is an "active exoticizer" of the past, playing a dual role of creating national and cultural memory and archiving the nation's collective past in the process (Yano 2002, 14–18).

40. Yano notes how the past becomes a kind of "internal exotic" in enka; actions, gestures, and affects associated with socially marginalized characters such as gangsters, sailors, and bar hostesses become the object of fascination, longing, and consumption in enka's nostalgia (2002, 15). In his insightful analysis of the consumerist trends of the 1980s, Sand notes how the object of longing was a particular kind of classed sociality—not the internationalist, "national icons of achievement" in that era but rather "the relics of the era's relative poverty" (2013, 106).

41. Kawaguchi Masaaki, personal communication, March 15, 2007.

42. Here I follow Gavin Steingo's move to draw on Dipesh Chakrabarty and take into account both Western-derived theories of labor and indigenous understandings of value in analyzing musicians' affective labor (2016, 253). By deliberately performing different historical pasts simultaneously, chindon-ya shows how what Chakrabarty call histories 1 and 2 are indelibly entangled (2000). History 1, history with a capital *H*, refers to "modernizing narrative(s) of citizenship, bourgeois public and private . . . the nation state" and especially the operations and perceived inevitability of capitalism. History 2 emerges within the logic of capital as a manifestation of its contradictions, frequently as seemingly archaic material not yet fully vanquished.

THREE Sounding Imaginative Empathy

1. This quote comes from his troupe's performance at Ebisuza, Osaka, on January 25, 2007. Here Hayashi is riffing on the phrase "ludicrous roadside advertisement business with musical instruments," which was coined by an innovative forefather of chindon-ya, Tanba Kurimaru, around the 1890s (Horie 1986, 70).

2. This followed shortly after the closure of the famous popular restaurant Kuidaore just a few feet away on the same main riverside street. The automated doll in the storefront Kuidaore Tarō became a symbol of not only Dōtonbori but also Osaka as a city, and the restaurant's closure elicited various obituaries and media attention that lamented the end of the era/place.

3. See Sugiura and Shimizu 1986, 73; Moroi 1991.

4. Mizuuchi, Katō, and Ōshiro note that while *roji* means "alleyway" or "small side streets" in standard Japanese, in Osaka and Kyoto it refers to the space that includes *nagaya* houses as well as small pathways that connect them to the small plaza space in the back of a house, away from the main street (2008, 167).

5. In many photography books that capture the urban cityscapes (mostly Tokyo) from the 1950s and 1960s, these alleyways are often described as a place of "human emotions"

(*ninjyō*), trivial life happenings, play, and social relations. With this assumption of alley-ways as a site of production of everyday life and affect, Endō Tetsuo advocates a *yokochō gaku* (side-alley-ology) as a way to rethink Japanese urban sociology (1998).

6. In their discussion of youth movements in Japanese public space, Hayashi and McKnight (2005) assert that public space in Japan has shifted in the postwar era from being a heterogeneous space of resistance to a homogeneous space of political and social control. This sense of alienation is evident in the film-based *fūkeiron* (landscape theory) of the late 1960s. Characterized by a propensity for human-less scenes in the everyday urban landscape, this cinematic technique critiqued the increasing control over territorialized space and the consolidation of postwar state capitalism (Furuhata 2007, 353).

7. See Leheny (2006), Roquet (2008), and Allison (2009b, 2013) for more on this social malaise in Japan.

8. *Furītā* is a hybrid loan word, combining the sounds of the English prefix "free-" (as in freelancing) with the German word *Arbeiter*, meaning "worker"; a "freeter" is someone who freelances without fixed and permanent employment.

9. See Jackson 2003; Woodward 1982.

10. Kobayashi Shinnosuke, personal communication, August 26, 2007.

11. Hayashi Kōjirō, personal communication, July 24, 2008.

12. Since 2016 the troupe has consolidated the functions into the same space at the workshop, and it began renting another space in the back for more costumes and wig storage.

13. Seto Nobuyuki, personal communication, July 20, 2007.

14. Such dynamics are quite distinct to Osaka, however; in Tokyo, according to chindon-ya troupe leader Takada Yōsuke, chindon-ya often do submit the required forms (*dōro shiyō kyoka shō*) to the police in advance.

15. This is the price the troupe names at the beginning of the negotiation; often, the settling price is lower. The associated costs will then be deducted from this price, in-cluding transportation fees, per diem, and so on, as well as the operational cost of the business. Thus, the amount that each member takes at the end of the gig is much lower than these figures.

16. For an astute analysis of the monetary exchanges between taishū engeki performers and audiences see Ivy 1995, 192–239.

17. Hayashi Kōjirō writes that "*nigiwai* [another way of describing the state of nigiya-kasa] is good" is a distinctly Osakan philosophy (135).

18. According to Masui Kanenori, the term *nigiwau* (the verb form of nigiyakasa) was allegedly first used sometime around the 600s BCE (2012, 265–66). It appears also in 720 CE referring to harmonious sociality (Maeda 2005, 860), and by the thirteenth century it was used to describe both the dynamic liveliness and the loud sounds that accompany a large gathering (Nihon Kokugo Daijiten Henshū Iinkai 2004, 394).

19. Seto Nobuyuki, personal communication, July 20, 2007.

20. The metaphor of the feedback loop has offered a conceptually and acoustically productive lens for scholars of sound; see Keil and Feld (1994), Keil (1995), Condry (2006), and Novak (2013b) for notable examples.

21. Hayashi Kōjirō, personal communication, March 22, 2007.

22. Many freelance chindon-ya melodic instrumentalists (gakushi) in Tokyo are active in various music scenes. Notable players include Yoshino Shigeru, Takada Yōsuke, Nakao Kanji, Hotta Hiroyuki, Nishiuchi Tetsu, Kizzu-kun, among others. The first two have formed their own full-time chindon-ya troupes, while others remain part-time freelance musicians working with various chindon-ya troupes. As evidence of the number of active musicians who work as chindon melody instrumentalists part time, there are larger ensembles formed by musicians in the chindon-ya freelance circuit, such as Nikoniko Pinpin Shitsunai Gakudan and Nishiuchi Tai. The connection between free jazz and chindon-ya has been briefly discussed in an interview with Yoshino Shigeru and Takada Yōsuke as well (Ōba 2010, 23–24).

23. Shinoda Masami, quoted in Ōkuma 2001, 106–7.

24. Hayashi Kōjirō, personal communication, September 3, 2007.

25. Hayashi Kōjirō, personal communication, March 22, 2007.

26. Kobayashi Shinnosuke, personal communication, August 27, 2007.

27. Hayashi Kōjirō, personal communication, August 24, 2008.

28. In his analysis of the "idol" phenomenon in Japanese popular music industry, Patrick Galbraith offers a similar analysis in which "lack of talent," or "the aesthetic of 'non-ability' [hijitsuryoku], or innocence and inexperience" is a desirable quality as it encourages fan support and empowers them to become involved in the idol's growth, development, and success (2012, 189).

29. Hayashi Kōjirō, personal communication, January 25, 2007.

30. In Japanese, "to see" and "to hear" are the only verbs that have this special conjugation.

31. Henri Lefebvre also writes of the ability of musical resonance to create sociality: "It is in this way, and at this level, in the non-visible, that bodies find each other" ([1974] 1991, 225).

32. For a comprehensive discussion of the phenomenon and the term see Kane 2014.

33. Hayashi Kōjirō, personal communication, March 22, 2007.

34. Lila Ellen Gray's work on fado is an exquisite example of "sonorous ethnography" that traces inquiries in a similar trajectory (2013).

35. Guilbault qualifies that her use of the term "intimacy" does not draw upon Lisa Lowe's conceptualization of intimacies, but rather on Ann Laura Stoler's work. For more see Guilbault 2010.

36. Based on conversations I've had with chindon-ya across Japan, it seems that when

they do hear complaints, they come predominantly from nearby businesses when the chindon-ya are performing itsuki (staying put in one place) for a long period of time. Takada Yōsuke in Tokyo also said that there are often certain characters in some neighborhoods who are known to be "claimers" (serial filers of complaints, who call police daily about every annoyance they find).

37. Hayashi Kōjirō, personal communication, March 22, 2007.

38. With the large influx of migrants from Okinawa and Korea into Osaka since the 1930s, there are numerous pockets of ethnically segregated neighborhoods in the city. Furthermore, compared to Tokyo, which underwent major rebuilding after the 1945 air raids, Osaka has retained some of the historic neighborhoods that segregated people of different historical social strata (Mizuuchi, Katō, and Ōshiro 2008).

39. Chindon Tsūshinsha members, along with many Osakans, referred to this area as "Nishinari." However, technically Nishinari refers to the broader ward and not this particular day laborers' neighborhood—the current official name for this area is "Airin." The older name "Kamagasaki," used to denote the specific area, is still in use among the locals but is discouraged by officials. I use Kamagasaki to follow the local use, but not Nishinari, in order to avoid confusing the day laborers' district with the ward at large.

40. Although contemporary chindon-ya practitioners are not necessarily from socially marginalized groups, the historical association between chindon-ya and the underclass or socially marginalized has often been mobilized by both listeners and practitioners in creating imagined alliances. For more discussion of chindon-ya's social positioning and its relation to the marginalized population today, such as the day laborers, see chapters 1 and 2.

41. Kawaguchi Masaaki, personal communication, March 15, 2007.

FOUR Politicizing Chindon-ya

1. This song was censored from broadcasting systems in the 1970s for allegedly alluding to the discriminated populations. This continued until the 1990s.

2. This was a prevalent narrative after the disaster; for a critical analysis of the post-disaster discourses and the relevance of "urgent ethnography" in response to the disasters in Japan see Gill, Steger, and Slater (2015).

3. Founded in 1993, Soul Flower Union is an amalgamation of two popular groups, Mescaline Drive and Newest Model.

4. Although it was initially supposed to be released by Sony, the album was rejected because the lyrics were considered too antiestablishment and problematic by the record label.

5. Dekansho refers to Dekansho Bushi, a popular folkloric bon-odori tune in the region.

6. There is also a New York City–based group called Happy Fun Smile that is inspired by chindon-ya, founded by Japanese American musician Wynn Kiayama. Although within Japan chindon-ya has not been officially embraced as a signifier of Japaneseness, here

chindon drums and the festival-like atmosphere invoked by them are in the forefront of "Japaneseness" expressed by the group. See http://www.happyfunsmile.com.

7. As I briefly mentioned in the introduction, as part of the resurgence there has been a remarkable increase in the number of *shirōto* chindon (amateur) groups throughout the country. Many university clubs have formed groups, and there is not only an amateur section at Toyama's annual chindon contest (introduced in 1998), but also an independent amateur-only chindon contest in Kawagoe that began in 2004. The majority of these groups' activities are not explicitly political, in contrast to groups I discuss in this chapter; they advertise, or provide entertainment at kindergartens and old people's homes. Although the popular desire to become chindon-ya among these amateur practitioners deserves attention in itself, here I have curtailed the presence of amateur chindon-ya groups, as my research focuses on hybridized and often politicized practices that depart from chindon-ya as an advertising practice.

8. Many such collaborative projects are planned and organized by individuals; the Jadranka–Chindon Tsūshinsha show at a temple was organized by a small publisher called SURE, and the Daiku–Chindon Tsūshinsha project was pitched by the independent record label owner and curator Kamiya Kazuyoshi. Ōsawa Gakutai and Chindon Tsūshinsha's record was also distributed by Kamiya's label Off-note, although Hayashi himself planned this collaboration as part of his genealogical approach to chindon-ya.

9. The earliest of these books, *Bokutachi no chindon-ya nikki* (Our chindon-ya diary), was coauthored by Hayashi Kōjirō and his then-wife Akae Mariko, who penned together another autobiographical book in 1993 (Hayashi and Akae 1986). In addition, Chindon Tsūshinsha has published a monthly newsletter to circulate among families and friends. Buchi Furutani, a chindon-ya fan and aficionado of other popular performing arts, has also published a monthly magazine *Usan Musan*, featuring chindon-ya and chindon-inspired practitioners based in the Osaka area.

10. For scholarly publications on chindon-ya in Japanese see Aihara 1996, 2001, 2002; Hosokawa 1989a, b, c, d, e, 1990, 1991, 1992, 1999; Nishioka 1999; Yoshimi and Kitada 2007.

11. Sharon Hayashi and Anne McKnight have offered an insightful theorization of the shifting notion of "public space" through leftist activism in Japan. Comparatively analyzing the leftist activities in the '60s and '70s and demonstrations today, Hayashi and McKnight show how "city streets" shifted from anonymity to hide within to public space to be reclaimed (Hayashi and McKnight 2005).

12. There are helpful pieces focusing on these issues in the DeMusik Inter book. See Haraguchi 2005 and Yamakawa 2005. For a concise analysis of the acoustic politics of aozora karaoke see Novak 2010a.

13. Hayashi and McKnight 2005 focuses on this incident, examining the role of sound demonstration against the backdrop of shifting spatial politics from the 1970s to today.

14. Quoted in DeMusik Inter 2002, 6.

15. Reclaim the Streets!, http://rts.gn.apc.org/propo1.htm.

16. I follow Henri Lefebvre's use of "abstract space" here to refer to the notion of space as alienated from the social processes of reproduction. Abstract space is a "repressive economic and political space of bourgeoisie, male space . . . formal, homogeneous, and quantitative, [abstract space] erases all differences that originate in the body (like sex and ethnicity) or else reifies them for its own quantitative ends" (Merrifield 2000, 176). While David Harvey's well-known notion of "time-space compression" points to a similar "crisis of space" where capitalist production annihilates social time and space, I suggest that DeMusik Inter's writing is more in line with the notion of "time-space colonization" put forward by Lefebvre. As Derek Gregory points out in his comparative analyses of Harvey and Lefebvre's theorization of space in relation to capitalism, Lefebvre eschews such an attempt to establish a homological relation between representations of space and modes of production. Lefebvre's notion of "time-space colonization" highlights the superimposition and hyperextension of abstract space onto everyday life (concrete space), which often are violent processes of occupation, dispossession, and reterritorialization. While this is an outward movement that acknowledges processes of spreading, invading, and occupying, Harvey's metaphor of time-space compression is an inward movement that implies "a world collapsing in on itself" (Gregory 1995, 414). I suggest that, seen in this light, DeMusik Inter's attempt to critique the expansion of abstract space is more in line with Lefebvre's understanding of space, whereby they seek possible openings through micropractices of musicking on the street. Instead of offering an inward reflection of the homogenizing, undifferentiated space of the West as Harvey does, DeMusik Inter might be looking into the contradictions inherent to abstract space as theorized by Lefebvre, in which lie the seeds of a new kind of space (Lefebvre [1974] 1991, 49).

17. DeMusik Inter 2002, 111.

18. For a detailed description of the emergence of sound demo in Japan see Manabe 2015, 155–75.

19. This poster is also seen on a wall in Gaza, with a stenciled slogan "Our drum beats blast through this Apartheid wall" (featured in a YouTube video of a performance by Hattler, at http://www.youtube.com/watch?v=jrcJI3RxwZA).

20. See Kobe City, Nagata Ward, http://www.city.kobe.lg.jp/ward/kuyakusho/nagata/.

21. See "Hanshin Awaji Daishinsai 18 Nen: Kodokushi 1000nin Kosu" [18 years since Hanshin Awaji Earthquake: More than 1,000 lonely deaths], in *Shimbun Akahata* [Red Flag newspaper] January 17, 2013, http://www.jcp.or.jp/akahata/aik12/2013-01 -17/2013011704_02_1.html. For insightful analysis of the social precarity that such "solitary deaths" of the elderly population epitomize see Allison 2013.

22. Over forty-six thousand units were built to provide housing for the survivors of the earthquake.

23. Itami Hideko, personal communication, August 13, 2015.

24. For more information on sōshi enka in English see Atkins 2000.

25. I must note briefly here that the enka that emerged at this time—an amalgam of "political speech" (*enzetsu*) and song (*uta*)—sounded drastically different from the popular music genre that is known by the same name today. The latter emerged in postwar Japan as a melodramatic popular song, and the connection between the two is contested. Hosokawa notes that enka was screamed rather than sung, and suggests a similarity to punk (Hosokawa 1989a, 91). For more on the postwar popular music genre enka see Yano 2002 and Wajima 2010.

26. See liner notes for *Asyl Chindon* (1995, Sony, Respect Record, RES-6).

27. Wajima Yūsuke maintains that the father-and-son duo were not active at the height of the liberal democracy movement in Japan, and draws on extensive historical research that contests their claim. Instead, Wajima suggests that they successfully created a now widely accepted myth that enka was born of the liberal democracy movement (Wajima 2010, 53–56).

28. There was a marked rise in the "new system of popular performing arts which purely pursued amusement" under feudal oppression (Yoshida 1969, 23). Yoshida reads a strong oppositional power into such street performances, as he claims that the peak of the development of street performance art was met with the fall of the Edo shogunate. He concludes: "The street performances and exhibit shows were challenges against the system of order and rule centered around the samurai class, prompting the collapse of the system" (28).

29. Daiku Tetsuhiro, personal communication, December 9, 2008.

30. Drawing on Edward Said (1978), cultural geographer Derek Gregory (1995) coins the concept "imaginative geographies" to refer to this colonialist representational process of reducing difference into distance as a means of domesticating the Other. I suggest that through the same process, Okinawa's marginality in Japan is naturalized through geography. The process of imaginative geography, whereby physical separation allows for abstracting of the lived realities of a distant place, elucidates how the media depoliticizes Okinawa as a space of faceless "theirs" as opposed to "ours," rendering the place void of lived specificity and multiplicity. This in turn enables and perpetuates the Japanese and U.S. military hegemonic presence in Okinawa. I posit that it is this spatial politics that Daiku's album set out to challenge through musical sounds.

31. Quoted from Nakagawa Takashi's short note for his fans on the album *Asyl Chindon*.

32. Itami Hideko, personal communication, August 13, 2005.

33. Ibid.

34. For a critical analysis of the multicultural question through ethnographic studies on buraku communities see Hankins 2008, 2014.

35. Keeping in mind Talal Asad's critique of Paul Gilroy and Homi Bhabha on the account that cultural hybridity and multiculturalism can undermine certain political

projects and open the back door to Enlightenment reason (Asad 1993), I draw on Hall's notion of the "multicultural question" here to critique the problematic tension between the constitutive outside's particularist claim for recognition of difference on one hand, and the universalist notion of citizenship and liberty upon which the modern liberal state is founded on the other.

36. For an analysis of the shifting matrix of the notions of race and ethnicity in Japan see Doak 2007.

37. Itami Hideko, personal communication, March 2, 2007.

38. See Trisha Rose (1994) and Matt Sakakeeny (2013).

39. For example, anthropologist Christopher Nelson details how comedian Fujiki Hayato critiques the Okinawan complicity in the neocolonial present by drawing on the traditional *nuchi nu suji* (celebration of life) ritual and calling upon the festive and joyful spirit of *karī* (Nelson 2003); or Miyume Tanji chronicles how women Okinawan activists chose to express their concern against the U.S. military bases through the traditional female domain of social gatherings, *kamadu-gwa no tsudoi* (Tanji 2006). I thank James Roberson for bringing this to my attention.

40. Maruyama (1989) 1994.

41. Here I am drawing on Chantal Mouffe's discussion (2008) of art and democracy. Abe Kosuzu (2001) also notes this trend in the 2000s toward festivity as politics and offers an incisive analysis of the limitations of applying the global trend of festive protest to Okinawa.

42. See Wajima 2010, 220–51. I thank Hiromu Nagahara for pointing me to this work to contextualize the chindon-ya resurgence of the 1990s within the larger history of leftist cultural politics.

FIVE Resonances of Silence

1. Noriko Manabe has offered extensive discussions of the various musical presentational styles at antinuclear demonstrations (Manabe 2012, 2013, 2015), and David Novak has also provided insightful analyses of musical responses to the Fukushima disaster (2013a, c).

2. The melody of "When Johnny Comes Marching Home" was adapted by pro-democracy activists, with pro-democracy lyrics, during the democracy struggles in Korea in the 1980s.

3. The National Police Agency counted 18,498 dead or missing as of July 10, 2014 (http://www.npa.go.jp/archive/keibi/biki/higaijokyo.pdf). According to the Reconstruction Agency, as of June 24, 2014, 234,558 were displaced from their homes (http://www.reconstruction.go.jp/topics/main-cat2/sub-cat2–1/20140624_hinansha.pdf).

4. Although the phrase "post-Fukushima" is popularly used in English, I choose "post-

3.11" instead, as the former singles out the nuclear crisis in Fukushima while overlooking other towns affected by the nuclear crisis, as well as the devastating effects of the tsunami and earthquake disasters. In Japan, 3.11 is a more commonly used term to denote the disasters as well. It also presents a parallel to 9/11, underscoring the magnitude the date's impact had on the nation.

5. Here I use the commercial and the political domains as a framework to emphasize the unexpected recontextualization of chindon-ya from advertisement to protest, although the two domains always intersect.

6. ANPO was signed on June 19, 1960, despite opposition from a vibrant peace movement including students, artists, and activists. For an overview on the topic see McCormack (2010) and Bestor (2002).

7. In their ethnographic analysis of the 2003 anti–Iraq War sound demos in Tokyo, Sharon Hayashi and Anne McKnight describe the composition of the demo participants as "baggy," referring to the loose assemblage of irregularly employed youths from diverse backgrounds and subcultural tastes.

8. For a discussion of the efficacy of street demos, and chindon-ya in particular, in appealing to a diverse audience during recent antinuclear protests see Novak 2013c.

9. Masaru Murakami, Twitter post, September 20, 2009, 7:11 a.m., http://twitter.com /damian16002000. Translation by the author.

10. Personal communication, July 28, 2012.

11. "Anpanman March," official translation by Naoki Takao. Permission granted by Masashi Sugimoto at Nihon TV Music.

12. The lyrics were written by the author of the cartoon, Yanase Takashi. It has been alleged that Yanase wrote the lyrics in memory of his younger brother, who perished as a kamikaze pilot during World War II.

13. Another song that Jinta-la-Mvta played often in family bloc was "Ue wo muite arukō" (Let's walk with chin up), a 1961 hit from the popular singer Sakamoto Kyū. Similarly to the "Anpanman March," this song has an appeal both as an instrumental tune—its melody is widely known—and as a song whose lyrics are politically relevant to those who lived through the 1960s. The lyricist Ei Rokusuke wrote the song in despair, lamenting the violent repression of the student movement in the 1960s, of which he was part. Even though the musicians at the demo were playing the melody instrumentally and without lyrics, the chindon-ya's sounds were eliciting the latent memory of the social movements of the 1960s for those who were in the know, inviting them to sing along with the lyrics and to articulate the two historical moments.

14. While many studies in ethnomusicology have addressed silence as lack of voice or agency, some ethnomusicologists have offered analyses that attend to the productive forces and creative potentiality of silence. For insightful overview on theorizations of sound see Ochoa Gautier 2015. For examples of ethnomusicological works examining

involute powers of silence see Dave 2014, Schwartz 2012, Shelemay 2009.

15. Such voices or questions were hardly publicly expressed, with the exception of a newspaper column series in the newspaper *Asahi Shimbun*. See Asahi Shimbun Shakaibu 1989.

16. The public channel NHK had three days of special programming. Other private channels had slightly shorter programming, with no commercials; for example, TBS broadcast for forty-two hours and thirty-five minutes. Complaints from viewers about canceled programs and special programming amounted to twenty-six thousand phone calls (*Asahi Journal* shuzai han 1988, Shūkan Showa 2009).

17. For one of the few documentations of jishuku measures see *Asahi Journal* shuzai han 1988, 16.

18. For a comprehensive analysis of the acoustic politics of the right-wing soundtrucks see Smith 2014.

19. The sonic effects of jishuku order on everyday life are not easy to find in historical records. For journalistic documentations see Shinno 2001, Asahi Shimbun Shakaibu 1989.

20. See Hōgaku Seminā editorial team 1989; Akatsuka 1989; Shinno 2001; Kanai 2013; Nakazato 2013.

21. See Matsudaira 2013; Kanai 2013; Nakazato 2013; Hasebe 1989.

22. The Liberal Democratic Party made sure to put a handwritten, calligraphic letter "kizuna" on every campaign poster along with its nationalist slogans.

23. Especially because the period of jishuku marking the emperor's illness coincided with the end of the year and New Year season of 1989—the most profitable time of the year for street vendors—many rotenshō suffered significant financial damage. The suicide of a rotenshō couple was reported in Yokohama on September 29, 1988 (Nakajima 1990, 248).

24. This was the beginning of the economically tenuous position chindon-ya had to negotiate as Japan went through a long-term recessionary period. For critical analyses of the historical shift in the knowledge production on Japan from the post–cold war period to the neoliberal present see Harootunian and Yoda 2006.

25. As the capital and the place of residence for the imperial family, Tokyo was the epicenter for national mourning. In contrast, Chindon Tsūshinsha in Osaka was affected for only a month, according to its report.

26. Hayashi Kōjirō of Chindon Tsūshinsha also mentioned how this jishuku may have provided an opportunity for small and midsize businesses, particularly pachinko parlors, to enact austerity measures: "Once they cut down the cost, they kind of realized they could do without chindon-ya" (personal communication, January 14, 2014). For employers, hiring chindon-ya was as much of a social investment as a carefully calculated financial strategy; the financial return was not the sole purpose for hiring chindon-ya. Once the social expectations and convention of hiring chindon-ya became disrupted by the 1989 jishuku order, however, businesses instead preferred profit maximization. Eliminating the

social relevance of chindon-ya, the employers tightened their wallets in order to survive the economic crisis that plagued the country for decades to come.

27. To clarify, silence generally is not seen as reparative of sociality in Japan. The silence of jishuku is a particular, nationalizing silence that attempts to repair sociality in the context of collective mourning; silence is not a favored sonic strategy for chindon-ya in their sonic labor that prioritizes the production of sociality. The exception is when the chindon-ya troupe passes by a hospital. Out of respect to those who are struggling with illness and injuries, the unspoken rule is for chindon-ya to stop sounding their instruments on the block where the hospitals are located.

28. A fuller consideration of this alignment requires a careful analysis of chindon-ya as a historically precarious labor within Japan's distinct history of capitalisms. As I showed in chapters 1 and 2, since its inception in the late nineteenth century and throughout the development of Japan's capitalist modernity, chindon-ya was practiced by those who were living on the edge or socially ostracized. The participation of chindon-ya in the rally articulated different constituents of precarious laborers, produced through different capitalisms within Japan's history. I thank Gavin Steingo for pointing me to the necessity to historicize these constituents of precarious laborers.

29. For an overview of the emergence of flexible labor (and freeter or NEET, two terminologies referring to the underemployed or unemployed) and its articulation with political movements since the early 1990s in Japan see Mōri 2005.

30. The total number of underemployed and unemployed between the ages of fifteen and thirty-four was 1.79 million in 2014, a figure that problematically excludes female domestic labor. Statistics Bureau, Ministry of Internal Affairs and Communication, http://www.stat.go.jp/data/roudou/sokuhou/nen/dt/index.htm.

31. In her incisive analysis of social precarity in Japan for the last two decades, Allison weaves together Japanese activist Amamiya Karin's work on *ikizurasa* (difficulty in life) with Judith Butler's discussion of the politics of social life through the notions of precarity and precariousness (Amamiya 2007; Allison 2013, 64–71; Butler 2004).

32. Midori Ishida, personal communication, August 16, 2012.

33. Ibid.

34. In Hardt's words, chindon-ya's affective labor produced "biopower from below"—"collective subjectivities, sociality, and society itself" (Hardt 1999, 98–100)—among those who shared precarity in the aftermath of the nuclear crisis. I am indebted to Anne Allison's work taking on Hardt's formulation of affective labor and its subversive potential to contest neoliberal regulation of labor and life in contemporary Japan (Allison 2009a, 92; 2013).

35. Critiquing the limits of the previous mode of political investment in maintaining harmonious social coexistence, which has led to the very global insecurity we confront today through its production of wealth in pursuit of equality, Abélès puts forward the

politics of survival as a pragmatic alternative that is oriented toward preservation of life in the face of environmental, economic, and biological threats. On the one hand, the politics of survival aptly captures the social and nuclear precarity in Japan as symptomatic of the neoliberal global order. On the other hand, the anti-nuclear-power movement I observed does not neatly fit within Abélès's formulation of the politics of survival: prioritization of preventive measures against potential catastrophe instead of improving the status quo, away from the hope for a better world and toward fear of a worse one. The tension here stems from the fact that Abélès collapses the necessity for the politics of survival with demands for ethics without addressing the contingencies and complexities of the latter. It is this gap that I seek to address in my analysis of the bon-odori in the later section of this chapter.

36. The bon-odori festivals are typically held by local associations in district schoolyards or parks, catering to specific neighborhoods.

37. Obon season is supposed to be around July 15 on the old calendar, but the time of observation varies slightly from region to region. In the central Tokyo area, it is typically during the middle of August.

38. Although the precise historical and religious origins of bon are contested, the consensus is that it emerged as part of the Buddhist *urabon-e* ceremony, which is a period of memorializing spirits based on syncretic amalgamation of ancient indigenous ancestral worship and Buddhism. This calendrical cycle of honoring the dead is believed to have been established by the eighth century.

39. Kogure Miwazō, personal communication, August 18, 2012.

REFERENCES

Abe Kanichi, Hosokawa Shūhei, Tsukahara Yasuko, Tōya Mamoru, and Takazawa To-
momasa, eds. 2001. *Burasu bando no shakai shi* [Social history of brass bands]. Tokyo:
Seikyūsha.

Abe Kin'ya. 1995. *Seken towa nanika* [What is seken?]. Tokyo: Kōdansha.

Abe Kosuzu. 2001. "Repetition and Change: Direct Action in Okinawa." *Seisaikagaku
Kokusaikankeironshū* 13:61–90.

Abe, Marié. 2010. "Resonances of Chindon-ya: Sound, Space, and Social Difference in
Contemporary Japan." PhD diss., University of California, Berkeley.

———. 2016. "Resonances of Silence: Sounding against Nuclear Power in Post-3.11 Japan." *Ethnomusicology* 60 (2): 233–62.

Abélès, Marc. 2010. *The Politics of Survival*. Translated by Julie Kleinman. Durham, NC:
Duke University Press.

Adachi Hideya. 2005. *Warau kado niwa chindon-ya* [Around the corner where there is
laughter, there is chindon-ya]. Fukuoka: Sekihūsha.

Aihara Susumu. 1996. "Chindon-ya wo tsūjite kangaeru rojō ni okeru 'ba' no sōshutsu"
[Creation of "place" on the streets, observed through chindon-ya]. Graduation thesis.

———. 2001. "Kamigata chindon-ya shōshi" [Small notes on chindon-ya in Kansai re-
gion]. *Osaka Shinjū* 105:80–86.

———. 2002. "Gendai Chindon-ya Jijō" [Contemporary situation of chindon-ya]. *Kamigata Geinō* 146.

Akatsuka Yukio. 1989. "Jishuku ikō no sesō wo kangaeru" [Considering the society after
jishuku]. In special series *Tennōsei mondai, Gekkan shakaitō*, 145–56.

Allison, Anne. 2009a. "The Cool Brand and Affective Activism of Japanese Youth." *Theory Culture and Society* 26 (2–3): 89–111.

———. 2009b. "Ordinary Refugees: Social Precarity and Soul in Twenty-First Century
Japan." *Anthropological Quarterly* 85 (2): 345–70.

———. 2013. *Precarious Japan*. Durham, NC: Duke University Press.

Althusser, Louis. 1971. *On the Reproduction of Capitalism: Ideology and Ideological State Apparatuses.* London: Verso.

Amamiya Karin. 2007. *Ikisasero! Nanminkasuru wakamonotachi* [Survive! the refugee-ization of young people]. Tokyo: Ōta Shuppan.

Amano Yūkichi. 1997. "Kakeashi kōkoku gosen nen shi" [Quick five-thousand-year history of advertisement]. In *Kōkoku Dainyūmon*, edited by Kōkoku Hihyō, 26–39. Tokyo: Madora Shuppan.

Asad, Talal. 1993. "Multiculturalism and British Identity in the Wake of the Rushdie Affair." In *Genealogies of Religion: Discipline and Reasons of Power in Christianity and Islam*, 239–68. Baltimore: Johns Hopkins University Press.

Asahi Journal shuzai han. 1988. "Yomigaeru 'shinkakuka' no kairo: ichioku jishuku wo 'kyōsei' shita no wa dareka" [Resurgence of the deifying circuit: Who "forced" jishuku on the hundred million?]. *Asahi Journal* 30 (42): 14–21.

Asahi Shimbun Shakaibu. 1989. *Rupo jishuku: Tokyo no 150 nichi* [Report jishuku: 150 days in Tokyo]. Tokyo: Asahi Shimbunsha.

Asakura Kyōji. 1986. *Geinō no shigen ni mukatte* [Toward the source of performing arts]. Tokyo: Myūjikku Magajin.

———. 1991. "Tōzaiya kara chindon-ya e" [From Tōzaiya to chindon-ya]. *Music Magazine Special Issue Noise* (11). Tokyo: New Music Magazine, 50–56.

Atkins, E. Taylor. 2000. "Can Japanese Sing the Blues? 'Japanese Jazz' and the Problem of Authenticity." In *Japan Pop! Inside the World of Japanese Popular Culture*, edited by T. Craig, 27–59. New York: M. E. Sharpe.

Attali, Jacques. (1977) 1985. *Noise: The Political Economy of Music.* Manchester, UK: Manchester University Press.

Barad, Karen. 2007. *Meeting the Universe Halfway: Quantum Physics and the Entanglement of Matter and Meaning.* Durham, NC: Duke University Press.

———. 2014. "Diffracting Diffraction: Cutting Together-Apart." *Parallax* 20 (3): 168–87.

Berlant, Lauren. 1998. "Intimacy: A Special Issue." *Critical Inquiry* 24 (2): 281–88.

Bestor, Theodore. 1989. *Neighborhood Tokyo.* Stanford, CA: Stanford University Press.

Bestor, Victoria. 2002. "Toward a Cultural Biography of Civil Society in Japan." In *Family and Social Policy in Japan: Anthropological Approaches*, edited by Roger Goodman, 29–53. Cambridge: Cambridge University Press.

Bhabha, Homi. 1984. "Of Mimicry and Man: The Ambivalence of Colonial Discourse." *October* 28:125–33.

Born, Georgina, ed. 2013. *Music, Sound and Space: Transformations of Public and Private Experience.* Cambridge: Cambridge University Press.

Boym, Svetlana. 2001. *The Future of Nostalgia.* New York: Basic Books.

Brinkema, Eugenie. 2011. "Critique of Silence." *difference* 22 (2): 211–34.

Bull, Michael. 2003. "Soundscapes of the Car: A Critical Study of Automobile Habitation." In *The Auditory Culture Reader*, edited by Michael Bull and Les Back, 357–80. New York: Berg.

———. 2004. "Thinking about Sound, Proximity, and Distance in Western Experience: The Case of Odysseus's Walkman." In *Hearing Cultures*, edited by Veit Erlmann, 173–90. New York: Berg.

Butler, Judith. 2004. *Precarious Life*. New York: Verso.

Casey, Edward. 1996. "How to Get from Space to Place in a Fairly Short Stretch of Time: Phenomenological Prolegomena." In *Senses of Place*, edited by Steven Feld and Keith Basso, 13–52. Santa Fe, NM: School of American Research Advanced Seminar Series.

Certeau, Michel de. 1984. *The Practice of Everyday Life*. Berkeley: University of California Press.

Chakrabarty, Dipesh. 2000. *Provincializing Europe: Postcolonial Thought and Historical Difference*. Princeton, NJ: Princeton University Press.

Chion, Michel. 1994. *Audio-Vision: Sound on Screen*. Edited and translated by Claudia Gorbman. New York: Columbia University Press.

———. 1999. *Voice in Cinema*. Edited and translated by Claudia Gorbman. New York: Columbia University Press.

Cho Paggie. 2003. *Boku wa zainichi kansai jin* [I am a zainichi Osaka-ite]. Osaka: Kaihō Shuppan sha.

Condry, Ian. 2006. *Hip Hop Japan: Rap and the Paths of Cultural Globalization*. Durham, NC: Duke University Press.

Daughtry, Martin. 2015. *Listening to War: Sound, Music, Trauma, and Survival in Wartime Iraq*. New York: Oxford University Press.

Dave, Nomi. 2014. "The Politics of Silence: Music, Violence and Protest in Guinea." *Ethnomusicology* 58 (1): 1–29.

Davidson, Ronald A. 2013. "'Friendly Authoritarianism' and the *Bedtaun*: Public Space in a Japanese Suburb." *Journal of Cultural Geography* 30 (2): 187–214.

DeMusik Inter, ed. 1996. *Oto no chikara: Cultural Studies*. Tokyo: Impact Shuppankai.

———. 2002. *Oto no chikara: Sutorīto o torimodose* [Power of Sound: Let's reclaim the street]. Tokyo: Impact Shuppankai.

———. 2004. *Oto no chikara: Sutorīto fukkō hen* [Power of Sound: Reconstruction of the street]. Tokyo: Impact Shuppankai.

———. 2005. *Oto no chikara: Sutorīto senkyo hen* [Power of Sound: Occupation of the street]. Tokyo: Impact Shuppankai.

Denoon, Donald Mark Hudson, Gavan McCormack, and Tessa Morris-Suzuki, eds. 2001. *Multicultural Japan: Palaeolithic to Postmodern*. Cambridge: Cambridge University Press.

Doak, Kevin. 2007. "The Concept of Ethnic Nationality and Its Role in Pan-Asianism in Imperial Japan." In *Pan-Asianism in Modern Japanese History: Colonialism, Regional-*

ism and Borders, edited by Sven Saaler and J. Victor Koschmann, 168–82. New York: Routledge.

Eidsheim, Nina Sun. 2015. *Sensing Sound: Singing and Listening as Vibrational Practice*. Durham, NC: Duke University Press.

Eisenberg, Andrew. 2013. "Islam, Sound and Space: Acoustemology and Muslim Citizenship on the Kenyan Coast." In *Music, Sound and Space: Transformations of Public and Private Experience*, edited by Georgina Born, 186–202, Cambridge: Cambridge University Press.

Elden, Stuart. 2004. "Rhythmanalysis: An Introduction." In *Rhythmanalysis: Space, Time and Everyday Life*, by Henri Lefebvre, vii–xv. New York: Continuum.

Endō Takeshi. 1958. "Koe to oto no kōkokushi" [History of advertisement of voice and sound]. Dentsū Kōkoku Nenkan. Tokyo: Dentsū, 78–92.

Endō Tetsuo. 1998. "Yokochō gaku omoitsuki" [Wonderings on alleyways philosophy]. In *Kindai shomin seikatsu shi geppō*, 20. Tokyo: San ichi Shobō.

Erlmann, Veit. 2010. *Reason and Resonance: A History of Modern Aurality*. New York: Zone.

———. 2015. "Resonance." In *Keywords in Sound*, edited by David Novak and Matt Sakakeeny, 175–82. Durham, NC: Duke University Press.

Fabian, Johannes. (1983) 2002. *Time and the Other: How Anthropology Makes Its Object*. New York: Columbia University Press.

Feld, Steven. 1996. "Waterfalls of Song: An Acoustemology of Place Resounding in Bosavi, Papua New Guinea." In *Senses of Place*, edited by Steven Feld and Keith Basso, 911–36. Santa Fe, NM: School of American Research Press.

———. 2003. "A Rainforest Acoustemology." In *The Auditory Culture Reader*, edited by Michael Bull and Les Back, 223–40. New York: Berg.

Foucault, Michel. 2003. *"Society Must Be Defended": Lectures at the Collège de France, 1975–1976*. New York: Picador.

Freeman, Elizabeth. 2010. *Time Binds: Queer Temporalities, Queer Histories*. Durham, NC: Duke University Press.

Fritsch, Ingrid. 2001. "Chindonya Today: Japanese Street Performers in Commercial Advertising." *Asian Folklore Studies* 60:49–79.

Fujii Sōtetsu. 1977. "Chindon-ya: Sono horobi no bigaku" [Chindon-ya: Its aesthetics of extinction]. *Gekkann Pen*, May 1: 172–80.

Fujimori Terunobu. 1986. *"Rojō kansatsu no hata no moto ni"* [Under the banner of street observation studies]. In *Rojō kansatsugaku nyūmon*, edited by Akasegawa, Fujimori, and Minami, 15–33. Tokyo: Chikuma Shobō.

Funakoshi Koichi. 1990. "Tennōsei konfōmizumu to J. S. Miru jiyūron" [Imperial conformism and J. S. Mill's liberalism]. *Nagasaki Daigaku Kyōikugakubu Shakaikagaku Ronsō* 41:1–18.

Furuhata, Yuriko. 2007. "Returning to Actuality: Fūkeiron and the Landscape Film." *Screen* 48 (3): 345–62.

Galbraith, Patrick. 2012. "Idols: The Image of Desire in Japanese Consumer Capitalism." In *Idols and Celebrity in Japanese Media Culture*, edited by Patrick W. Galbraith and Jason G. Karlin, 185–208. New York: Palgrave Macmillan.

Gershon, Ilana, and Allison Alexy. 2011. Introduction to "The Ethics of Disconnection in a Neoliberal Age." Special collection. *Anthropological Quarterly* 84 (4): 799–808.

Gill, Tom, Brigitte Steger, and David H. Slater, eds. 2015. *Japan Copes with Calamity*. Oxford: Peter Lang.

Goodman, Steve. 2010. *Sonic Warfare: Sound, Affect, and the Ecology of Fear*. Cambridge, MA: MIT Press.

Gupta, Akhil, and James Ferguson. 1992. "Beyond 'Culture': Space, Identity, and the Politics of Difference." *Cultural Anthropology* 7 (1): 6–23.

———. 1997. "Beyond 'Culture': Space, Identity, and the Politics of Difference," and "Culture, Power, Place: Ethnography at the End of an Era." In *Culture, Power, Place: Explorations in Critical Anthropology*, edited by Akhil Gupta and James Ferguson, 1–51. Durham, NC: Duke University Press.

Gray, Ellen Lila. 2013. *Fado Resounding: Affective Politics and Urban Life*. Durham, NC: Duke University Press.

Gregory, Derek. 1995. "Imaginative Geographies." *Progress in Human Geography* 19 (4): 447–85.

Gramsci, Antonio. 2000. *The Gramsci Reader: Selected Writings, 1916–1935*. Edited by D. Forgacs. New York: NYU Press.

Grossberg, Lawrence. 1984. "Another Boring Day in Paradise: Rock and Roll and the Empowerment of Everyday Life." *Popular Music* 4:225–58.

Guilbault, Jocelyne. 2005. "Audible Entanglements: Nation and Diasporas in Trinidad's Calypso Music Scene." *Small Axe* 17 (1): 40–63.

———. 2010. "Music, Pleasure, and Politics: Live Soca in Trinidad." *Small Axe* 31 (1): 16–29.

Hall, Stuart. 1980. "Race, Articulation, and Societies Structured in Dominance." In *Sociological Theories: Race and Colonialism*, 305–45. Paris: UNESCO.

———. 1985. "Signification, Representation, Ideology: Althusser and the Post-Structuralist Debates." *Critical Studies in Mass Communication* 2 (2): 91–114.

———. 2000. "Conclusion: The Multi-Cultural Question." In *Un/Settled Multiculturalisms: Diasporas, Entanglements, "Transruptions,"* edited by Barnor Hesse, 209–41. New York: Zed.

———. 2002a. "Créolité and the Process of Creolization." In *Créolité and Creolization: Documenta 11 Platform 3*, edited by Okwui Enwezor et al., 27–42. New York: Hatje Cantz.

Hananoya Kei. 2007. *Bonjūru chindon* [Bonjour, chindon]. Tokyo: Shinpūsha.

Hankins, Joseph. 2008. "The Stakes of Japanese Multiculturalism." *Journal of Buraku Liberation*. November.

———. 2014. *Working Skin: Making Leather, Making a Multicultural Japan*. Berkeley: University of California Press.

Hankins, Joseph, and Carolyn S. Stevens, eds. 2014. *Sound, Space and Sociality in Modern Japan*. London: Routledge.

Haraguchi Tsuyoshi. 2005. "Toshikukan no dakkan" [Reclaiming urban space: Reconsidering open-air karaoke in Tennōji Park]. In *Oto no chikara: Sutorīto senkyo hen* [Power of Sound: Occupation of the street]. DeMusik Inter, 62–65. Tokyo: Impact Shuppankai.

Haraway, Donna. 1997. *Modest_Witness@Second_Millenium.FemaleMan©_Meets_OncoMouseTM*. London: Routledge.

Hardt, Michael. 1999. "Affective Labor." *boundary 2* 26 (2): 89–100.

Hardt, Michael, and Antonio Negri. 2001. *Empire*. Cambridge, MA: Harvard University Press.

Harootunian, Harry, and Tomiko Yoda, eds. 2006. *Japan after Japan: Social and Cultural Life from the Recessionary 1990s to the Present*. Durham, NC: Duke University Press.

Hart, Gillian. 2002. *Disabling Globalization: Places of Power in Post-Apartheid South Africa*. Berkeley: University of California Press.

———. 2004. "Denaturalizing Dispossession: Critical Ethnography in the Time of Resurgent Imperialism." Paper prepared for the conference on Creative Destruction: Area Knowledges and the New Geographies of Empire. April.

Harvey, David. 1991. Afterword in *The Production of Space*, by Henri Lefebvre, 425–34. Oxford: Oxford University Press.

Hasebe, Yasuo. 1989. "Jishuku to jijitun o kihanryoku" [Jishuku and standardization of facts]. *Jurisuto* 933:160–63.

Hayashi Kōjirō. 2002. "Waga Hyōryū no chindon seikatsu zakkan" [My numerous thoughts on drifting chindon life]. In *Oto no chikara: Street o torimodose*, edited by DeMusik Inter, 110–33. Tokyo: Impact Shuppankai.

———. 2004. "Chindon-ya." In *Ōsaka ryoku jiten* [Osaka's power dictionary], edited by Hashizume Shinya, 132–35. Osaka: Sōgensha.

———. 2006. *Chindon-ya! Kōjirō* [Chindon-ya! Kōjirō]. Tokyo: Shinjuku Shobō.

Hayashi Kōjirō and Mariko Akae. 1986. *Bokutachi no chindon-ya nikki* [Our chindon-ya diary]. Tokyo: Shinjuku Shobō.

———. 1993. *Chindon-ya desu* [We are chindon-ya]. Tokyo: Shisōno Kagaku Sha.

Hayashi, Sharon, and Anne McKnight. 2005. "Goodbye Kitty, Hello War: The Tactics of Spectacle and New Youth Movements in Urban Japan." *Positions* 13 (1): 87–113.

Henriques, Julian. 2011. *Sonic Bodies: Reggae Sound Systems, Performance Techniques, and Ways of Knowing.* New York: Continuum.

Hesse, Barnor. 1993. "Black to Front and Black Again: Racialization through Contest Times and Spaces." In *Place and the Politics of Identity*, edited by Michael Keith and Steve Pile, 162–82. New York: Routledge.

Hofman, Ana. 2015. "Music (as) Labour: Professional Musicianship, Affective Labour and Gender in Socialist Yugoslavia." *Ethnomusicology Forum* 24 (2): 29–50.

Hōgaku seminā editorial team. 1989. "Naishin no jiyū to jishuku būmu" [Interior freedom and jishuku boom]. *Hōgaku seminā zōkan sōgōtokushū shirīzu* 44:158–77.

Horie Seiji. 1986. *Chindon-ya chimatsu ki: Gaitō no piero tachi ni miru kokoku senden no pafōmansu* [Chronicle of chindon-ya: Performance of advertisement as seen through clowns on the street corner]. Tokyo: PFP Kenkyu Sho.

Horiuchi Keizō. 1936. *Jinta konokata* [Since jinta]. Tokyo: Aoi Shoten.

Hosokawa, Shūhei. 1989a. "Enka: Seiyō ongaku no nihonka, taishūka 6" [Enka: Japanization and popularization of Western music 6]. *Music Magazine*, September, 90–95.

———. 1989b. "Gungakutai 2: Seiyō ongaku no nihonka, taishūka 2" [Military bands: Japanization and popularization of Western music 2]. *Music Magazine*, May, 92–97.

———. 1989c. "Jinta: Seiyō ongaku no nihonka, taishūka 10" [Jinta: Japanization and popularization of Western music 10]. *Music Magazine*, January, 102–7.

———. 1989d. "Shichū ongakutai: Seiyō ongaku no nihonka, taishūka 9" [City civilian music bands: Japanization and popularization of Western music 9]. *Music Magazine*, December, 80–85.

———. 1989e. "Shōnen ongakutai: Seiyō ongaku no nihonka, taishūka 11" [Youth music bands: Japanization and popularization of Western music 11]. *Music Magazine*, April, 130–35.

———. 1991. "Chindon-ya Rhythm Machine." *Noise Magazine*, November, 57–64.

———. 1992. "Chindon-ya: Japanese Street Music." Translated by Kevin and Hiroko Quigley. In liner notes to *Tokyo Chin Don Vol. 1*, 73–88.

———. 1999. "Blacking Japanese: Experiencing Otherness from Afar." In *Popular Music Studies*, edited by David Hesmondalgh and Keith Negus, 223–37. London: Arnold.

———. n.d. A. "Chindon-ya." Unpublished manuscript.

———. n.d. B. "Jinta." Unpublished manuscript.

Howell, David. 2005. *Geographies of Identity in Nineteenth-Century Japan.* Berkeley: University of California Press.

Ihde, Don. 2003. "Auditory Imagination." In *The Auditory Culture Reader*, edited by Michael Bull and Les Back, 62–66. New York: Berg.

Ingold, Tim, and Jo Lee Vergunst, eds. 2008. *Ways of Walking: Ethnography and Practice on Foot.* Burlington, VT: Ashgate.

Ishida Masataka. 2014. *Soul Flower Union: Tokihanatsu uta no wadachi* [Rut of released songs]. Tokyo: Kawaide Shobō.

Ishii Yoneo and Yamauchi Masayuki. 1999. *Nihonjin to tabunka shugi* [The Japanese and multiculturalism]. Tokyo: Kokusai bunka Koryu shuisin Kyokai: Hatsubai Yamakawa Shuppansha.

Itō Toshiharu. 1983. "Japan's 1920s: Urban Popular/Mass Culture Development Centered around Tokyo." In *Establishment of Urban Mass Culture*, 175–204. Tokyo: Yūhikaku.

Ivy, Marilyn. 1993. "Formations of Mass Culture." In *Postwar Japan as History*, edited by Andrew Gordon, 239–58. Berkeley: University of California Press.

———. 1995. *Discourses of the Vanishing: Modernity, Phantasm, Japan*. Chicago: University of Chicago Press.

Izumi Asato. 2011. *Tokyo Gōgengaku zukan* [Tokyo kōgengaku illustrated book]. Tokyo: Gakken.

Jackson, Daniel. 2003. *Sonic Branding*. New York: Palgrave Macmillan.

Kaiser, Birgit Mara, and Kathrin Thiele. 2014. "Diffraction: Onto-Epistemology, Quantum Physics and the Critical Humanities." *Parallax* 20 (3): 165–67.

Kanai Mieko. 2013. "Jishuku to kotobano kaigenrei" [Jishuku and restrictions of words]. *Issatsu no hon* 18 (3): 60–65. Tokyo: Asahi Shimbun Shuppan.

Kane, Brian. 2014. *Sound Unseen: Acousmatic Sound in Theory and Practice*. Oxford: Oxford University Press.

Kaneda, Miki. 2014. "Rhythm Heaven: Video Games, Idols, and Other Experiences of Play." In *The Oxford Handbook of Mobile Music Studies*, edited by Sumanth Gopinath and Jason Stanyek, 2:427–52. Oxford: Oxford University Press.

Kanetsune Kiyosa. (1935) 1992. *Ongaku to seikatsu* [Music and life]. Edited by Sugimoto Shūtaro. Tokyo: Iwanami Bunko.

Kata Koji. 1969. *Machi no geijutsuron* [Art theory of the city]. Tokyo: Shakai Shiso Sha.

Katō Hidetoshi. 1980. *Taishū bunka ron* [Theory of taishū culture]. Tokyo: Chūō Kōronsha.

Kawachi Ryūtarō. 2016. *Chindon daibōken: Boku ga chindon-ya ni natta wake* [Great adventure of chindon: The reason why I became a chindon-ya]. Nagasaki: Nagasaki Bunken sha.

Kaye, Nick. 2000. *Site Specific Art: Performance, Place and Documentation*. London: Routledge.

Keil, Charles. 1987. "Participatory Discrepancies and the Power of Music." *Cultural Anthropology* 2 (3): 275–83.

———. 1995. "The Theory of Participatory Discrepancies: A Progress Report." *Ethnomusicology* 39 (19): 1–19.

Keil, Charles, and Steven Feld. 1994. *Music Grooves*. Chicago: University of Chicago Press.

Kelly, William. 1986. "Rationalization and Nostalgia: Cultural Dynamics of New Middle-Class Japan." *American Ethnologist* 13 (4): 603–18.

———. 2002. "At the Limits of New Middle Class Japan: Beyond 'Mainstream Consciousness.'" In *Social Contract under Stress: The Middle Classes of America, Europe, and Japan at the Turn of the Century*, edited by Olivier Zunz, Leonard Schoppa, and Nobuhiro Hiwatari, 232–54. New York: Russell Sage Foundation.

Kōsō, Sabu. 2006. "Angelus Novus in Millennial Japan." In *Japan after Japan: Social and Cultural Life from the Recessionary 1990s to the Present*, edited by Harry Harootunian and Tomiko Yoda, 415–38. Durham, NC: Duke University Press.

Kikunoya Shimemaru. 2002. *Chindon hitosuji 70nen* [Only chindon for 70 years]. Tokyo: Iwanami Shoten.

Kimura Seiya. 1987. *Soeda Azembō, Tomomichi: Enka nidai hūkyoden* [Soeda Azembō, Tomomichi: Crazy stories of the two enka generations]. Tokyo: Riburopoto.

Kōkami Shōji. 2009. *Kūki to seken* [Kūki and seken]. Tokyo: Kōdansha.

Kōkoku Hihyō. 1996. "Tanbaya Kurimaru." In *Kōkoku hihyō*, December, p. 17. Tokyo: Madora Shuppan.

Komai Hiroshi. 1994. *Imin shakai Nihon no kōso* [Structure of Japan as an immigrant society]. Tokyo: Kokusai Shoin.

Kon Wajirō. 1987. *Kōgengaku nyūmon* [Introduction to modernology]. Tokyo: Chikuma Shobō.

———. 2011. *Kon Wajirō saishū kōgi* [Kon Wajirō lecture collection]. Tokyo: Seigensha.

Koyama Shigeki, ed. 2013. *Kon Wajirō to kōgengaku* [Kon Wajirō and kōgengaku]. Tokyo: Kawade Shobō.

Kurihara Akira. 1997. *Kyōsei no hō e* [Toward symbiosis]. Tokyo: Kōbundō.

Lefebvre, Henri. (1974) 1991. *Production of Space*. Oxford: Blackwell.

———. 2004. *Rhythmanalysis: Space, Time and Everyday Life*. New York: Continuum.

Leheny, David Richard. 2006. *Think Global, Fear Local: Sex, Violence, and Anxiety in Contemporary Japan*. Ithaca, NY: Cornell University Press, 27–48.

Lie, John. 2001. *Multiethnic Japan*. Cambridge, MA: Harvard University Press.

Long, Nicholas, and Henrietta L. Moore. 2013. *Sociality: New Directions*. New York: Berghahn.

Lowe, Lisa. 2003. "Heterogeneity, Hybridity, Multiplicity: Marking Asian-American Differences." In *Theorizing Diaspora: A Reader*, edited by Jana Evans Braziel and Anita Mannur, 132–55. Oxford: Blackwell.

Maeda Tomiyoshi. 2005. *Nihon gogen daijiten* [Great dictionary of Japanese etymology]. Tokyo: Shōgakkan.

Manabe, Noriko. 2012. "The No Nukes 2012 Concert and the Role of Musicians in the Anti-Nuclear Movement." *Asia-Pacific Journal* 10 (29).

———. 2013. "Music in Japanese Antinuclear Demonstrations: The Evolution of a Contentious Performance Model." *Asia-Pacific Journal* 11 (42).

———. 2015. *The Revolution Will Not Be Televised: Protest Music after Fukushima*. Oxford: Oxford University Press.

Marcus, George. 1998. *Ethnography through Thick and Thin*. Princeton, NJ: Princeton University Press.

Maruyama Masao. (1989) 1994. "Matsurigoto no kōzō: Seiji teki ishiki no shitsuyō teion" [The structure of matsurigoto: The *basso ostinato* of Japanese political consciousness]. *Gendai Shisō* 22:56–75.

Massey, Doreen. 1993. "Politics and Space/Time." In *Place and the Politics of Identity*, edited by Michael Keith and Steve Pile, 141–61. New York: Routledge.

———. 1994. *Space, Place and Gender*. Minneapolis: University of Minnesota Press.

Massumi, Brian. 1995. "The Autonomy of Affect." *Cultural Critique* 31:83–109.

Masui Kanenori. 2012. *Nihon gogen kōjiten* [Japan encyclopedia of etymology]. Tokyo: Mineruva Shobō.

Matsudaira Tokujin. 2013. "Jishuku to narēshon to shiteno Nihon gata kyōdōtaishugi" [Japanese collectivism as jishuku and narration]. *Kenpōmondai* 24. Tokyo: Sanseidō.

Matsue, Jennifer Milioto. 2016. "Japanese Cultural Identity and Musical Modernity." In *Focus: Music in Contemporary Japan*, 36–64. New York: Routledge.

Matsumiya Saburo. 1968. *Edo no monouri* [Street merchants of Edo]. Tokyo: Toho Shobo.

Mauss, Marcel. 1973. "Techniques of the Body." *Economy and Society* (2) 1: 70–88.

McCormack, Gavan. 2010. "Ampo's Troubled 50th: Hatoyama's Abortive Rebellion, Okinawa's Mounting Resistance and the US-Japan Relationship (Part 1)." *Asia-Pacific Journal* 22 (3).

Merrifield, Andy. 2000. "Henri Lefebvre: A Socialist in Space." In *Thinking Space*, edited by Mike Crang and Nigel Thrift, 167–92. London: Routledge.

Mizuuchi Toshio, Katō Masahiro, and Ōshiro Naoki, eds. 2008. *Modan toshi no keifu: Chizu kara yomitoku shakai to kūkan* [Geneaology of modern cities: Social space read from maps]. Kyoto: Nakanishiya Shuppan.

Monbiot, George. 2014. "The Age of Loneliness Is Killing Us." *Guardian*, October 14. https://www.theguardian.com/commentisfree/2014/oct/14/age-of-loneliness-killing-us.

Moore, Donald S. 2005. "Introduction: Situated Struggles." In *Suffering for Territory*. Durham, NC: Duke University Press.

Mōri, Yoshitaka. 2005. "Culture = Politics: The Emergence of New Cultural Forms of Protest in the Age of *Freeter*." *Inter-Asia Cultural Studies* 6 (1): 17–29.

———. 2009. *Sutorōto no shisō: Tenkanki to shiteno 1990 nendai* [Philosophy of the streets: The 1990s as a turning point]. Tokyo: NHK.

Morita Yoshinori. 1974. *Chūsei senmin to zatsugeinō no kenkyū* [Studies of middle age outcasts and popular performance arts]. Tokyo: Yūzankaku Shuppan.

Moroi Kaoru, ed. 1991. *Shōwa seikatsu bunka nendaiki* 3: 30 nen dai [Chronicles of Shōwa social life 3: The Shōwa '30s]. Tokyo: Toto Shuppan.

Mouffe, Chantal. 2008. "Art as an Agnostic Intervention in Public Space." *Open* 14:6– 15.

Murch, Walter. 2004. "Womb Tone." *Transom Review* 5 (1): 1. http://transom.org/?p=6992.

Nakajima Michio. 1990. *Tennō no daigawari to kokumin* [Change of the emperors and the national citizens]. Tokyo: Aoki Shoten.

Nakazato Ryōhei. 2013. "Sairei no jishuku, chūshi ni kansuru kenkyū: Hisaichi igai no chiiki kara mita higashi nihon daishinsai" [Research concerning jishuku and cancellation of festivals: East Japan Earthquake seen through regions outside the disaster-affected areas]. *Minzokugaku ronsō* (28): 33–45.

Nango Yoshikazu. 2013. "Warau rojō kansatsugakkai no manāshi: Toshi no rizumu bunseki e mukete" [The gaze of the laughing street observation association: Toward a rhythmanalysis of an urban city]. In *Rojō to kansatsu o meguru hyōgenshi: Kōgengaku no genzai* [Expressive history of street and observation: Kōgengaku's present], edited by Hiroshima City Modern Museum. Tokyo: Filmart.

Neely, Daniel T. 2014. "Ding, Ding! The Commodity Aesthetics of Ice Cream Truck Music." In *Oxford Handbook of Mobile Music*, vol. 2, edited by Sumanth Gopinath and Jason Stanyek, 146–71. Oxford: Oxford University Press.

Nelson, Christopher. 2003. "Nuchi Nu Suji: Comedy and Everyday Life in Postwar Okinawa." In *Japan and Okinawa: Identity and Subjectivity*, edited by Glenn D. Hook and Richard Siddle, 208–24. London: Routledge.

Nihon Kokugo Daijiten Henshū Iinkai. 2004. *Nihongo kokugo daijiten* [Encyclopedia of Japanese language]. 2nd ed., vol. 10. Tokyo: Shōgakkan.

Nishioka Nobuo. 1999. "Chindon to Gorosu" [Chindon and gorosu]. In *Jiisan no Hue*, 175–82. Tokyo: Ongaku no tomo sha.

Novak, David. 2010a. "Listening to Kamagasaki." *Anthropology News* 51 (9): 5.

———. 2010b. "Playing off Site: The Untranslation of Onkyo." *Asian Music* 41 (1): 36–59.

———. 2013a. "Disturbance." In *To See Once More the Stars: Living in a Post-Fukushima World*, edited by Daisuke Naito, Ryan Sayre, Heather Swanson, and Satsuki Takahashi, 99–102. Santa Cruz, CA: New Pacific.

———. 2013b. *Japanoise: Music at the Edge of Circulation*. Durham, NC: Duke University Press.

———. 2013c. "The Sounds of Japan's Antinuclear Movement." Museum of Modern Art (MoMA), New York. http://post.at.moma.org/content_items/251-the-performance-of-protest-the-sounds-of-japan-s-anti-nuclear-movement-in-fukushima-tokyo-and-osaka.

Novak, David, and Matt Sakakeeny. 2015. Introduction to *Keywords in Sound*, edited by David Novak and Matt Sakakeeny, 1–11. Durham, NC: Duke University Press.

Ōba Hiromi and Yada Hitoshi. 2009. *Chindon kikigaki chindon-ya monogatari* [Chindon: Oral histories of chindon-ya stories]. Tokyo: Bajiriko.

Ochoa Gautier, Ana María. 2015. "Silence." In *Keywords in Sound*, edited by David Novak and Matt Sakakeeny, 183–92. Durham, NC: Duke University Press.

Oguma Eiji. 1995. *Tan'itsu minzoku shinwa no kigen: "Nihyonjin" no jigzaō no keifu* [The origin of mono-ethnic myth: A genealogy of "Japanese" self-images]. Tokyo: Shin'yō sha.

———. 1998. *"Nihonjin" no kyōkai: Okinawa, Ainu, Taiwan, Chōsen, shokuminchi shihai kara fukki undō made* [Borders of the "Japanese": Okinawa, Ainu, Taiwan, Korea, from colonization to decolonization]. Tokyo: Shin'yō sha.

Okiura Kazuteru. 2006a. "Akusho'no minzokushi" [Ethnography of "akusho"]. Tokyo: Bungei Shinjū.

———. 2006b. *Nihon minshū bunka no genkyō* [Source of the Japanese popular culture]. Tokyo: Bungei Shunjū.

———. 2007a. "Akusho wo henrekishita yūjo tachi" [Courtesans who wandered through "bad places"]. Printed supplement to lecture. July 7.

———. 2007b. "Dosa mawari de ikita 'yūgeimin'" [Itinerant performers who survived by circulating on the streets]. Printed supplement to lecture. July 21.

———. 2007c. "Igei no marebito 'kadotsuke geinin'" [Street performers "kadotsuke": Rare people of unusual talents]. Printed supplement to lecture. July 28.

———. 2007d. "Minatomachi, yadobamachi" [Port towns and hostel towns]. Printed supplement to lecture.

———. 2007e. "Rekishi no yami ni umerareta 'sanka' zanzō" [Residues of "sanka" who were buried in the dark corners of the history]. Printed supplement to lecture. July 14.

Ōkuma Wataru. 1991. "Tokyo chindon: Hasegawa Sendensha to Takada Sendensha ni tsuite" [Tokyo Chindon: On Hasegawa Sendensha and Takada Sendensha]. In liner notes to Shinoda Masami, *Tokyo Chin Don Vol. 1*. Puff Up, 1992. Puf-7, 25–40.

———. 2001. *Rafu Myūjikku Sengen: Chindon, Punk, Jazz* [Declaration of rough music: Chindon, punk, jazz]. Tokyo: Impact Shuppankai.

———. 2005. "Onna tachi no chindon" [Women's chindon]. *Tōkyōjin*, July, 96–203.

———. 2007. "Biruma no Gunkan Māchi" ["Warship March of Burma"]. In *plan B Tsūshin*, October. http://www.cicala-mvta.com/__diary/wataru/?mode=next&date=200702&id=35.

Ōkuma Wataru, Mizuno Keiko, and Ikeuchi Bunpei, eds. 2008. *Konposutera: Hoshi no hiroba de* [Compostela: At the star plaza]. Tokyo: Seisakushitu Kurāro.

Oliveros, Pauline. 1974. *Sonic Meditations*. Baltimore: Smith.

Origuchi Shinobu. (1947) 1995. *Bon odori no hanashi* [Story of *bon-odori*]. Tokyo: Aozora Bunko.

Ōyama Makoto. 1995. *Chindon Kikunoya no hitobito* [People of Chindon Kikunoya troupe]. Tokyo: Kawaide Shobo Shinsha.

Ozawa Shōichi. 1989. *Geinō to shakai* [Performing arts and society]. Tokyo: Hōsō-daigaku Kyōiku Shinkō Kai.

Özyürek, Esra. 2006. *Nostalgia for the Modern: State Secularism and Everyday Politics in Turkey*. Durham, NC: Duke University Press.

Peterson, Marina. 2010. *Sound, Space, and the City: Civic Performance in Downtown Los Angeles*. Philadelphia: University of Pennsylvania Press.

Plourde, Lorraine. 2008. "Disciplined Listening in Tokyo: Onkyo and Non-Intentional Sounds." *Ethnomusicology* 52 (2): 270–95.

Radano, Ronald. 2003. *Lying Up a Nation: Race and Black Music*. Chicago: University of Chicago Press.

Rhys Edwards, James. 2016. "Critical Theory and Ecomusicology." In *Current Directions in Ecomusicology*, edited by Aaron Allen and Kevin Dawe, 153–64. London: Routledge.

Riesman, David. 1950. *The Lonely Crowd: A Study of the Changing American Character*. New Haven, CT: Yale University Press.

Robertson, Jennifer. 1998. *Takarazuka: Sexual Politics and Popular Culture in Modern Japan*. Berkeley: University of California Press.

Rōdō Bunka. 1968. "Sono sugata wa machi kara kieteyuku: Zenkoku de tatta 500nin no chindon-ya" [They are disappearing: Only 500 chindon-ya left in the country]. *Rōdō Bunka*. Tokyo: Rōdō Bunkasha, 6–7.

Roquet, Paul. 2008. "Ambient Literature and the Aesthetics of Calm: Mood Regulation in Contemporary Japanese Fiction." *Journal of Japanese Studies* 35 (1): 87–111.

Rose, Trisha. 1994. *Black Noise: Rap Music and Black Culture in Contemporary America*. Middletown, CT: Wesleyan University Press.

Said, Edward. 1978. "Imaginative Geography and Its Representations: Orientalizing the Oriental." In *Orientalism*, 49–72. New York: Vintage.

Sakakeeny, Matt. 2010. "Under the Bridge: An Orientation to Soundscapes in New Orleans." *Ethnomusicology* 54 (1): 1–27.

———. 2013. *Roll with It: Brass Bands in the Streets of New Orleans*. Durham, NC: Duke University Press.

———. 2015. "Playing for Work: Music as a Form of Labor in New Orleans." Oxford Handbooks Online.

Sand, Jordan. 2013. *Tokyo Vernacular: Common Spaces, Local Histories, Found Objects*. Berkeley: University of California Press.

Schafer, R. Murray. 1977. *The Tuning of the World*. New York: Knopf.

———. 2003. "Open Ears." In *The Auditory Culture Reader*, edited by Michael Bull and Les Back, 25–33. New York: Berg.

Schwartz, Jessica. 2012. "A 'Voice to Sing': Rongelapese Musical Activism and the Production of Nuclear Knowledge." *Music and Politics* 6 (1). http://quod.lib.umich.edu/m/mp/9460447.0006.101/-voice-to-sing-rongelapese-musical-activism?rgn=main;view=fulltext.

Seigworth, Gregory, and Melissa Gregg. 2010. "An Inventory of Shimmers." In *The Affect Theory Reader*, edited by Gregory Seigworth and Melissa Gregg, 1–28. Durham, NC: Duke University Press.

Sekiguchi Susumu. 2001. *Taishū goraku to bunka* [Taishū entertainment and culture]. Tokyo: Gakubunsha.

Seremetakis, Nadia. 1994. *The Senses Still: Perception and Memory as Material Culture in Modernity*. Boulder, CO: Westview.

Shelemay, Kay Kaufman. 2009. "The Power of Silent Voices: Women in the Syrian Jewish Musical Tradition." In *Music and the Play of Power in the Middle East, North Africa, and Central Asia*, edited by Laudan Nooshin, 269–88. Farnham, UK: Ashgate.

Shibusawa Tatsuhiko. 1982. "Chindon-ya no koto" [On chindon-ya]. *Ushio*, March, 240–43.

Shield, Renee Rose. 1980. "Country Corn: Performance in Context." In *The Ethnography of Musical Performance*, edited by Norma McLeod and Marcia Herndon, 105–22. Norwood, PA: Norwood Editions.

Shimizu Tatsuya. 1997. *Hibike, chindon* [Resonate, chindon]. Tokyo: Kyōiku Gageki.

Shinno Toshikazu. 2001. "Ō no shi to saisei—1998 nen 1 gatsu 7nichi" [Death and resurrection of the king: January 7, 1998]. In *Nihon no matsuri wo yomitoku* [Reading Japanese festivals], 53–83. Tokyo: Yoshikawa Kōbun kan.

Shinoda Masami. *Tokyo Chin Don Vol. 1*. Puff Up, 1992. Puf-7.

Shirahara Kenichirō. 1972. "Manzoku shiteru: Chindon jinsei" [I am content: Life of a chindon-ya]. *Gekkan Pen*, April, 131–34.

Shūkan Shōwa editorial team. 2009. "Shōwa ga owatta hi" [The day Shōwa ended]. *Shūkan Shōwa* 4063-63: 8–9.

Silverberg, Miriam. 1992. "Constructing the Japanese Ethnography of Modernity." *Journal of Asian Studies* 51 (1): 30–54.

Slater, David. 2009. "Social Class and Identity in Postwar Japan." In *Routledge Handbook of Japanese Culture and Society*, edited by Victoria Lyon Bestor and Theodore C. Bestor, 103–15. New York: Routledge.

Smith, Nathaniel. 2014. "Facing the Nation: Sound, Fury, and Public Oratory among Japanese Right-Wing Groups." In *Sound, Space, and Sociality in Modern Japan*, edited by Joseph Hankins and Carolyn Stevens, 37–56.

Smith, Neil, and Cindi Katz. 1993. "Grounding Metaphor: Towards a Spatialized Politics." In *Place and the Politics of Identity*, edited by Michael Keith and Steve Pile, 66–81. New York: Routledge.

Sneath, David, Martin Holbraad, and Morten Axel Pedersen. 2009. "Technologies of the Imagination: An Introduction." *Ethnos* 74 (1): 5–30.

Soeda, Tomomichi. 1963. *Enka no Meiji Taishō shi* [History of enka in the Taishō and Meiji eras]. Tokyo: Iwanami Shoten.

Stadler, Gus. 2015. "On Whiteness and Sound Studies." *Sounding Out! The Sound Studies Blog*, July 6.

Steingo, Gavin. 2016. "Musical Economies of the Elusive Metropolis." In *Audible Empire: Music, Global Politics, Critique*, edited by Ronald Radano and Tejumola Olaniyan, 246–66. Durham, NC: Duke University Press.

Steingo, Gavin, and James Sykes, eds. Forthcoming. *Remapping Sound Studies*. Durham, NC: Duke University Press.

Stewart, Kathleen. 1998. "Nostalgia—a Polemic." *Cultural Anthropology* 3 (3): 227–41.

———. 2007. *Ordinary Affects*. Durham NC: Duke University Press.

———. 2011. "Atmospheric Attunements." *Environment and Planning D: Society and Space* (29): 445–53.

Stokes, Martin. 2002. "Marx, Money, and Musicians." In *Music and Marx*, edited by Regula Burckhardt Qureshi, 139–66. New York: Routledge.

Strathern, Marilyn, J. Peel, C. J. Spencer, and T. Ingold. 1990. *The Concept of Society Is Theoretically Obsolete*. Manchester, UK: GDAT.

Sugiura Yukio and Shimizu Isao. 1986. *Showa manga fūzoku shi: Sugiura Yukio manga de tadoru 50 nen* [Popular culture history of Showa cartoons: 50 years followed through Sugiura Yukio's cartoons]. Tokyo: Bungei Shunjū.

Takahashi Atsuko, ed. 1996. *No Guru* [No guru]. Vol. 5. Tokyo: Soul Flower Office.

Takeda Rintarō. 1935. "Hirome-ya no michi" [The Street of Hirome-ya]. In *Takeda Rintarō zenshū* [Takeda Rintarō anthology]. Tokyo: Rokkō Shuppan bu.

Tamura Koji. 1970. "Nenmatsu shōsen no 'kishu' chindon-ya seikatsu no butaiura" [Flag-bearer of the year-end business battle: The backstage of the life of chindon-ya]. *Asahi Geinō*, December 17, 40–43.

Tanji, Miyume. 2006. *Myth, Protest and Struggle in Okinawa*. London: Routledge.

Tanuma Takeyoshi. 1996. *Tanuma Takeyoshi shashinshū: Shitamachi konjaku monogatari* [Tanuma Takeyoshi photographic collection: Shitamachi stories of then and now]. Tokyo: Shinchōsha.

Terada Kōji. 1984. "Chindon-ya." *Recreation*. Tokyo: Recreation Kyōkai, 5.

Ukai Masaaki, Nagai Yoshikazu, and Fujimoto Keinichi, eds. 2000. *Sengo Nihon no taishū bunka* [Popular culture of postwar Japan]. Kyoto: Showado.

Vergunst, Jo. 2010. "Rhythms of Walking: History and Presence in a City Street." *Space and Culture* 13 (4): 376–88.

Von Gunden, Heidi. 1983. *The Music of Pauline Oliveros*. Metuchen, NJ: Scarecrow.

Wade, Bonnie. 2005. *Music in Japan: Experiencing Music, Expressing Culture*. Oxford: Oxford University Press.

——. 2013. *Composing Japanese Musical Modernity*. Chicago: Chicago University Press.

Wajima Yūsuke. 2002. "Nihon no wārudo myūjikku gensetsu ni okeru bunka nashonarizumu keikō" [World music as cultural nationalism: An analysis of Japanese discourses]. *Bigaku* 52 (4): 70–83.

——. 2010. *Tsukurareta Nihon no kokoro shinwa: Enka wo meguru sengo taishū ongaku shi* [The invented myth of the "Japanese heart": Postwar history of popular music around enka]. Tokyo: Kōbunsha

Watanabe Hiroshi. 2013. "'Dochakuka' no mou hitotsu no kao" [The other face of "indigenization"]. In *Saundo to media no bunka shigen gaku* [Cultural resource of sound and media], 114–54. Tokyo: Shunjūsha.

Weiner, Michael. 1994. *Race and Migration in Imperial Japan*. New York: Routledge.

——. 1997. *Japan's Minorities: The Illusion of Homogeneity*. New York: Routledge.

Woodward, Walt. 1982. *An Insider's Guide to Advertising Music*. New York: Art Direction Book Co.

Yamakawa Munenori. 2005. "Kōenki" [park documentary]. In *Oto no chikara: Sutorīto senkyo hen* [Power of Sound: Occupation of the street], edited by DeMusik Inter, 26–41. Tokyo: Impact Shuppankai.

Yamamoto Naotomo. 1989. *Kinsei no minsyu to geinō* [Near-modern people and arts], edited by History of Kyoto Buraku Research Group. Kyoto: Aun sha.

Yamamoto, Shichihei. 1977. "Kūki no kenkyū" [Research of kūki]. Tokyo: Bungei Shunjyū.

Yano, Christine Reiko. 1998. "Defining the Modern Nation in Japanese Popular Song, 1914–32." In *Japan's Competing Modernities: Issues in Culture and Democracy*, edited by Sharon A. Minichiello, 247–66. Honolulu: University of Hawai'i Press.

——. 2002. *Tears of Longing: Nostalgia and the Nation in Japanese Popular Song*. Cambridge, MA: Harvard University Press.

Yokoi Kiyoshi. 1979. "Shinkō kara goraku e: Chūsei ni okeru taishū bunka no keifu" [From faith to entertainment: Genealogy of popular culture in the Middle Ages]. *Jurisuto Sōgō Tokushu* 20:7–18.

Yokoyama Gennosuke. 1941. *Nihon no kasō shakai* [Lower societies of Japan]. Tokyo: Iwanami Shoten.

Yoshida Mitsukuni. 1969. "Autorō no Geinō: Misemono, Daidōgei" [Performing arts of the outlawed: Show tents and street performance]. In *Dentō to gendai*, vol. 8, *Taishu Geino*. Tokyo: Gakugei Shorin.

Young, J. C. Robert. 1995. "Hybridity and Diaspora." In *Colonial Desire: Hybridity in Theory, Culture and Race*, 1–28. London: Routledge.

Yoshimi Shunya and Akihiro Kitada. 2007. *Rojō no esunogurafi: Chindon-ya kara gurafiti made* [Ethnography of the streets: From chindon-ya to graffiti]. Tokyo: Serika Shobō.

Zuckerkandl, Victor. 1956. *Sound and Symbol*. 2 vols. Princeton, NJ: Princeton University Press.

INDEX

Page numbers in italics indicate illustrations; color plates can be found following page 118.

equality in, 13, 192, 200n4, 209n10; as genealogical performance (*see* genealogical performance); goals of, 102; hiring of, 110–12, *112*; historical marginalization of, 72–74, 209n7, 209n8, 209n9, 216n40; and history of street walking, 57–63, *59*; and imaginative empathy (*see* imaginative empathy); and improvisation, 113–18, *117*; influence of temperature and weather on, 108; and innocence, 34, 65–68, 91–93, 215n28; instruments of, 6–7; as Japanized brass bands, 43–45, *44*; lack of media attention to, 15, 201n14; and listening while walking, 55–57; and liveliness, 184–87, *185*; marketing and payment of, 32–33, 75; musical labor of, 170–73, *172*; as music of wind, 207n24; and *nigiyakasa* (see *nigiyakasa* [noisiness/ liveliness]); in non-advertisement contexts, 138–42; non-regionalism of, 202n16; and nostalgia (*see* nostalgia); as oppositional forces, 152, 219n28; origin of name, 6; overview, xvii–xxv, 1–3, 188–89; payment of musicians, 1, 110–12, 214n15; as philosophers and ethnographers, 3–6, 78, 104, 116; photos of, *7, 100, 132, plates 1 and 2*; politicization of (*see* politicization of chindon-ya); and politics of survival, 179–84, *182*, 222n24, 223–24n35; and precarious listening publics, 125–31, 216n38; and public intimacies, 122–25; regional differences among, 17, 193; regulation of, 106–7, 214n14; and resonance (see *hibiki* [resonance]); restrictions on, 11; roots in military brass bands, 40–43; and sociality (*see* sociality); socialized listening to

kane, 77–81; sonic presence of, 22–24, 202n21, 203n23; as sound business, 102–3; sounds and histories of, 6–15, *9*; tip income, 95, 110, 130; transnational circulation of, 193; transnational roots of, 19–22; as "unproductive quaternary industry," 25; and walking as art, 50–57; as walking history, 36–63; wartime influences on, 13–14; wind as metaphor for, 13, 56, 188–89, 207n24, 208n27; women street performers, xviii, 13, 200n4, 209n10
Chindon-ya Mannen Sha, 9
Chindon Yoshino, 104–5, 201n8, *plate 7*
Chion, Michel, 123, 125
Cho Paggie, 64–67, 73, 77, 139, 157–60, *157*
chronically underemployed, 180–81
chrononormativity, 69, 92
Cicala Mvta, xviii, 71, 139, 141, 151–53, 206n14
complaints, 11, 23, 126, 195, 216n36
Compostela, 15
corporate capitalism, 35, 60–62, 81–83, 85–86, 94–96, 101, 193
costumes, 8–9
cross-dressing, 189–90, *plate 7*
cultivated imperfection, 118–20
cultural pluralization, 159

Daiku Tetsuhiro, xviii, 139–40, 153–56, *155*, 159, 206n14, 217n8, 219n30
Daughtry, Martin, xxiii
demonstrations. *See* anti-nuclear protests
DeMusik Inter, 141–44, 148, 218n16
Dentsū, 82
diffraction, 6, 29–30, 33
"discourses of the vanishing," 21, 39
Dōtonbori, 97–98, *98*, 213n2
drums: *gorosu* (bass drum), *7*, 75, 78, 105, 109, 136, 154, 190; *ōdaiko* (big drum),

Lefebvre, Henri, xxiv, 29–30, 39, 54–55, 61–62, 96, 107, 189, 199–200n5, 200n6, 204n2, 208n31, 208n32, 215n31, 218n16

Liberty and Civil Rights Movement, 149–51

lingering resonance (*zankyō*), 28, 55, 109

Lion Toothpaste company, 201n9

listening: Don Ihde on, 204n32; and imaginative empathy, 102; importance and significance of, 32; by listening public, xx, 27, 34, 69, 81, 93–96, 125–31, 216n38; as methodology, 32, 68, 166–67; and *nihonjinron*, 207n25; and overhearing, 120–22; reflexive, 108–10, 114–15; to resonance, 28, 31, 115, 190–91; and rhythmanalysis, 39, 54; socialized, 22, 38, 77–81, 210n20; Western conceptions of, xxiii; while walking, 55–57. See also *kikinagaseru* (let-flow-listening); *kikoeru* (overhearing)

liveliness. See *nigiyakasa* (noisiness/liveliness)

loneliness, xix–xx, 5, 128

Lowe, Lisa, 202n17

ma (musical time), 207n26

machimawari (going around the town), *xxiv*, 50, 103–7, *107*, 124

makeup, 8–9

Mametomo, 11

Maruyama Masao, 161–62

mass intimacy, 123–24

Massumi, Brian, 201n17

Matsudaira Tokujin, 174, 178

matsurigoto (politics / festival), 137, 139, 160–64, 185, 220n41

Mauss, Marcel, 206n13

McKnight, Anne, 214n6, 217n11, 217n13, 221n7

michi (street), 14

Midoriya Susumu, *plate 8*

military bands. *See* brass bands

modernology (*kōgengaku*), 57–60, *59*, 208n29, 208n31, 211n23

Monbiot, George, xix

Moore, Donald, 204n30

Mōri Yoshitaka, 160, 162

muen shakai (relationless society), 5

Murch, Walter, 123–25

nagashi (flowing), 104

Nakagawa Takashi, 137, 145–46, 148–49, 156

namari (accent), 44–45

National Chindon Contest, 83

Neeley, Daniel T., 201n16

Negri, Antonio, 90–91, 180, 200n1

Nelson, Christopher, 220n39

nigiyakasa (noisiness/liveliness), 4, 79–80, 110–12, *112*, 128, 132, 137, 139, 162, 184–87, *185*, 214n17, 214n18

nihonjinron (theories of Japaneseness), 21, 39, 80, 177, 202n18, 207n25

Nishinari, 109, 128, 216n39

noh, 21, 72, 202n19

noisiness. See *nigiyakasa* (noisiness/liveliness)

nostalgia, 5, 21–23, 34, 65–69, 76, 86, 88–93, 101, 189, 210n16, 212n35, 212n36, 212n37, 212n39, 213n40

Novak, David, xxiii, 19, 203n23, 215n20, 217n12, 220n1, 221n8

Ōba, Hiromi, 179

Obon season. *See* bon-odori

ōdaiko (big drum), 11

Oda Masanori, 144

ōdō (two-sided drum), 6, *7*, 78

Okinawa, xviii, 100, 135–36, 140, 146–47, 153–56, 159–61, 220n39. *See also* Daiku Tetsuhiro

Barry Shank
Dissonant Identities: The Rock 'n' Roll Scene in Austin, Texas

Jonathan Holt Shannon
Among the Jasmine Trees: Music and Modernity in Contemporary Syria

Daniel B. Sharp
Between Nostalgia and Apocalypse: Popular Music and the Staging of Brazil

Helena Simonett
Banda: Mexican Musical Life across Borders

Mark Slobin
Subcultural Sounds: Micromusics of the West

Mark Slobin, editor
Global Soundtracks: Worlds of Film Music

Christopher Small
The Christopher Small Reader

Christopher Small
Music of the Common Tongue: Survival and Celebration in African American Music

Christopher Small
Music, Society, Education

Christopher Small
Musicking: The Meanings of Performing and Listening

Regina M. Sweeney
Singing Our Way to Victory: French Cultural Politics and Music during the Great War

Colin Symes
Setting the Record Straight: A Material History of Classical Recording

Steven Taylor
False Prophet: Fieldnotes from the Punk Underground

Paul Théberge
Any Sound You Can Imagine: Making Music/Consuming Technology

Sarah Thornton
Club Cultures: Music, Media and Subcultural Capital

Michael E. Veal
Dub: Songscape and Shattered Songs in Jamaican Reggae

Michael E. Veal and E. Tammy Kim, editors
Punk Ethnography: Artists and Scholars Listen to Sublime Frequencies

Robert Walser
Running with the Devil: Power, Gender, and Madness in Heavy Metal Music

Dennis Waring
Manufacturing the Muse: Estey Organs and Consumer Culture in Victorian America

Lise A. Waxer
The City of Musical Memory: Salsa, Record Grooves, and Popular Culture in Cali, Colombia

Mina Yang
Planet Beethoven: Classical Music at the Turn of the Millennium

ERIC WOLFINGER

ABOUT THE AUTHOR

Marié Abe is an assistant professor of music at Boston University. She holds a PhD in ethnomusicology from the University of California, Berkeley.